The Shakespeare Handbooks

THE SHAKESPEARE HANDBOOKS

Series Editor: John Russell Brown

PUBLISHED

John Russell Brown	*Hamlet*
John Russell Brown	*Macbeth*
Paul Edmondson	*Twelfth Night*
Bridget Escolme	*Antony and Cleopatra*
Kevin Ewert	*Henry V*
Trevor R. Griffiths	*The Tempest*
Stuart Hampton-Reeves	*Measure for Measure*
Margaret Jane Kidnie	*The Taming of the Shrew*
James N. Loehlin	*Henry IV: Parts I and II*
Christopher McCullough	*The Merchant of Venice*
Paul Prescott	*Richard III*
Lesley Wade Soule	*As You Like It*

FORTHCOMING

John Russell Brown	*King Lear*
David Carnegie	*Julius Caesar*
Stuart Hampton-Reeves	*Othello*
Ros King	*The Winter's Tale*
Edward L. Rocklin	*Romeo and Juliet*
Martin White	*A Midsummer Night's Dream*

The Shakespeare Handbooks

Henry IV:
Parts I and II

James N. Loehlin

palgrave
macmillan

First published in 2008 by
PALGRAVE MACMILLAN
Houndmills, Basingstoke, Hampshire RG21 6XS and
175 Fifth Avenue, New York, N.Y. 10010
Companies and representatives throughout the world.

PALGRAVE MACMILLAN is the global academic imprint of the Palgrave Macmillan division of St. Martin's Press, LLC and of Palgrave Macmillan Ltd. Macmillan® is a registered trademark in the United States, United Kingdom and other countries. Palgrave is a registered trademark in the European Union and other countries.

ISBN-13: 978–0–230–01910–2   hardback
ISBN-10: 0–230–01910–2   hardback
ISBN-13: 978–0–230–01911–9   paperback
ISBN-10: 0–230–01911–0   paperback

This book is printed on paper suitable for recycling and made from fully managed and sustained forest sources. Logging, pulping and manufacturing processes are expected to conform to the environmental regulations of the country of origin.

A catalogue record for this book is available from the British Library.

A catalog record for this book is available from the Library of Congress.

10 9 8 7 6 5 4 3 2 1
17 16 15 14 13 12 11 10 09 08

Printed and bound in China

Contents

General Editor's Preface

The Shakespeare Handbooks provide an innovative way of studying the theatrical life of the plays. The commentaries, which are their core feature, enable a reader to envisage the words of a text unfurling in performance, involving actions and meanings not readily perceived except in rehearsal or performance. The aim is to present the plays in the environment for which they were written and to offer an experience as close as possible to an audience's progressive experience of a production.

While each book has the same range of contents, their authors have been encouraged to shape them according to their own critical and scholarly understanding and their first-hand experience of theatre practice. The various chapters are designed to complement the commentaries: the cultural context of each play is presented together with quotations from original sources; the authority of its text or texts is considered with what is known of the earliest performances; key performances and productions of its subsequent stage history are both described and compared. The aim in all this has been to help readers to develop their own informed and imaginative view of a play in ways that supplement the provision of standard editions and are more user-friendly than detailed stage histories or collections of criticism from diverse sources.

Further volumes are in preparation so that, within a few years, the Shakespeare Handbooks will be available for all the plays that are frequently performed and studied.

John Russell Brown

Preface

Taken together, the two parts of *Henry IV* – whether or not they were conceived as a unified structure – represent one of Shakespeare's most ambitious and sustained artistic achievements. Entering these plays as a reader, one has the sense of entering a varied and populous world, thick with material realities, bristling with political conflict, and crowded with representatives of many sectors of society. On the stage, the plays' plenitude makes great demands on both actors and audience, but offers great rewards. The number and variety of characters, the range of verbal registers, the interweaving of multiple storylines and dramatic worlds: all add up to make performances of the *Henry IV* plays challenging but potentially thrilling experiences.

It is my goal in this handbook to help the reader imaginatively engage with these plays onstage: to enter into the experience of Shakespearean performance, with its moment-to-moment excitement, its myriad interpretive possibilities, and its continually changing verbal, physical and emotional dynamics. The *Henry IV* plays are particularly suited to such an exercise, because of their great breadth and scope. A company performing these plays must create the worlds of court and tavern, battlefield and highway, autumnal Gloucestershire orchard and boisterous London street. The actors must master the rhetoric of aristocratic politicians and the slang of tapsters, must respond to the subtle linguistic signals by which Shakespeare differentiates some sixty characters over six hours of playing time. Prominent figures like the King, Hotspur, Worcester, Glendower, Shallow, Mistress Quickly and the Lord Chief Justice offer a gallery of human types animated by a range of human passions. In Prince Hal, Shakespeare gives the actor an enigmatic hero whose motives may encompass the noblest chivalry and the meanest calculation, the warmest good-fellowship and the most ruthless ambition. In Falstaff, Shakespeare sketches a titan of misrule, whom make flesh with only an arsenal of words, a padded ⌐ unbridled comic gusto. The outsize energies that drive ⌐naracters, and the richly textured worlds they inhabit, make ⌐ese plays capable of incomparable theatrical life. I try in the pages that follow to trace some of the forms that life can take as the plays unfold on the stage, whether the stage of an Elizabethan playhouse, a modern theatre, or the reader's imagination.

As the text for line references and quotations, both from the two parts of *Henry IV* and other Shakespeare plays, I have used David Bevington's *The Complete Works of Shakespeare*, updated fourth edition, (New York: Addison-Wesley, 1997). Line and scene numbering should correspond fairly closely to that in individual editions of the plays, so these can easily be used as well. For consistency, I have used British spelling throughout ('Rumour' rather than 'Rumor', for instance). I have also modernized spelling in the excerpts from the source texts of Chapter 3.

In pursuing this project I have incurred many debts. One of the greatest is to John Russell Brown, for inviting me to contribute to the series, giving many helpful suggestions, and providing a source of inspiration through his work in the field of Shakespeare performance studies. I am grateful to Felicity Noble, Kate Wallis, Sonya Barker, and everyone at Palgrave Macmillan for their kind and patient assistance. I want to thank my colleagues at the University of Texas for providing a cordial and supportive environment in which to work. I owe a special debt to my students in the Shakespeare at Winedale program, who studied and performed these plays with me in the summer of 2002 and the spring of 2007; those experiences taught me more about the *Henry IV* plays than anything else could have. My last and greatest debt is to my wife Laurel.

1 The Texts and Early Performances

Texts

One of the immediate questions raised by a consideration of *Henry IV: Parts I and II* is the relationship between the two plays, in terms of their conception, composition, performance, and publication. Did Shakespeare conceive of them as two halves of a single work, or, indeed, as part of a larger design encompassing four, or eight, or ten historical dramas? Did he begin *Part I* intending a single play on the reign of Henry IV and then find he had materials sufficient to produce a second part? Or did he write *Part I* as a single, self-contained work, and only afterwards decide to add a sequel?

No definitive answers exist to any of these questions, though scholars have argued persuasively on many sides of the issue. Critics from Dr. Johnson to Tillyard and Dover Wilson have argued that *Henry IV* was conceived as a single ten-act drama, culminating in the coronation of Henry V. Others, from Malone to R. A. Law to Kittredge, have argued just as vehemently that the two parts are separate and contrasting plays. In 'The Structural Problem in Shakespeare's *Henry IV*', Harold Jenkins sums up and synthesizes the arguments:

> *Henry IV*, then, is both one play and two. Part I begins an action which it finds it has not scope for but which Part II rounds off. But with one half of the action already concluded in Part I, there is danger of a gap in Part II. To stop the gap Part II expands the unfinished story of Falstaff and reduplicates what is already finished in the story of the Prince. The two parts are complementary, they are also independent and even incompatible.   (Hunter, p. 171)

Whatever the origins of the plays, the fact that they are now performed together so frequently – and that *Part II* is almost never performed without *Part I* – justifies treating them, in this series, in a single volume. Because the present study considers both parts of *Henry IV*, it will frequently address the relations between them, allowing at least for the possibility that they comprise a single artistic design. This initial discussion of the text and first performances will treat the two plays separately since it seems that they were performed and printed independently, whether or not the playwright conceived of them as part of a unified whole.

The first mention of a play by Shakespeare on the reign of Henry IV is an entry in the Stationer's Register, an official record of books to be printed. An entry for 25 February 1598 refers to 'a booke intituled The historye of Henry the iiijth with his battaile of Shrewsburye against Henry Hottspurre of the Northe with the conceipted mirthe of Sr Iohn Falstoffe.' This evidently is the play we have come to know as *Henry IV: Part I*. The first printed edition, dating from 1598, survives only in a fragment consisting of four leaves, which scholars have designated Q0. A further printing, the First Quarto or Q1, also from 1598, survives in three copies. It is the basis for all modern texts of *I Henry IV*. Its title page, like the entry in the Stationer's register, declares it to be 'THE HISTORY OF HENRIE THE FOVRTH', with no suggestion that there are any other parts, and directs the reader's attention to the 'battell at Shrewsburie, *betweene the King and Lord Henry Percy*' and '*the humorous conceits of Sir* Iohn Falstaffe'.

Q1 provides a clear and reliable text, though it has one notable variant from Q0, where the earlier text seems to have the superior reading. When the Prince and Poins are celebrating their rout of Falstaff at Gad's Hill, Poins closes the scene in Q0 with the line, 'How the fat rogue roared.' In Q1, the line is merely 'How the rogue roared'; most editors follow Q0. Neither early quarto includes act or scene divisions; these first appear in the First Folio (F), the collected edition of Shakespeare's works published by his fellow actors in 1623, some seven years after the playwright's death. Modern editions follow these divisions, though what F presents as Act V, scene ii is now generally presented as two separate scenes, with subsequent scenes renumbered accordingly.

Scholars disagree about whether Q1 was printed from the author's own manuscript or from a later transcription. However, in at least one important respect, the copy text for Q1 was altered from the version Shakespeare and his company originally performed. It is virtually certain that in the earliest performances of both parts of *Henry IV*, the fat knight who accompanies Prince Hal was named, not Sir John Falstaff, but Sir John Oldcastle. Two of his followers were originally known as Harvey and Russell; those names appear once in Q1 of *I Henry IV*. For reasons that will be discussed below, the names were changed before either play was entered for publication.

Henry IV: Part II is first listed in the Stationer's Register for 23 August 1600 as '*the second parte of the history of kinge HENRY the iiiith with the humours of Sir IOHN FFALLSTAFF: Wrytten by master Shakespere.*' The first, and only, quarto edition of the play was published shortly thereafter. Its title page gives considerable information as to the action, characters, and provenance of the play:

THE
Second part of Henrie
the fourth, continuing to his death,

and coronation of Henrie
the fift.
With the humours of Sir Iohn Fal-
staffe, and swaggering
Pistoll.

As it hath been sundrie times publikely
acted by the right honourable, the Lord
Chamberlaine his servants.
Written by William Shakespeare.

The title page establishes the play's relation to an earlier part of the history, and its crucial endpoint with the coronation of Henry V. It also emphasizes the comic characters Falstaff and Pistol. Finally, it stresses the several performances by Shakespeare's company through which the play had become known to the general public.

In comparison with the first part, the Quarto of *II Henry IV* is problematic and unreliable. The first texts issued are missing an entire scene – III.i, the memorable scene of the sleepless King's reflections – that is present only in the later copies. Also, eight passages are absent from the Quarto but appear in the Folio of 1623. As all of these deal with the politically dangerous subject of rebellion, they may have been omitted for fear of the censor, though it is also possible that they were cut for purely theatrical reasons, or even that they were added subsequently. The relation between the Quarto and Folio texts of *II Henry IV* is a notorious editorial puzzle; the Quarto is generally the more authoritative except for the missing passages, but it contains some clear errors that are corrected in the Folio. Editors rely on both versions in preparing modern texts of the play.

It is notable that *Part II* exists only in the single Quarto, whereas *Part I* went through six quarto editions before the Folio of 1623. This may indicate that the first play enjoyed a greater popularity on the stage, but this is far from certain. The text of *Part II*, like *Part I*, seems to reflect a change in the name of Sir John from Oldcastle to Falstaff. The Quarto retains a single speech prefix for 'Old' in Act I, scene ii, and the entrance stage direction for II.ii includes 'Sir Iohn Russel', the character elsewhere renamed Bardolph.

The exact reasons and timetables for these changes remain uncertain, but it is likely that Shakespeare's original characterization gave offense to highly-placed persons connected to the historical Sir John Oldcastle. Oldcastle was a prominent knight in the reigns of Henry IV and Henry V who served both kings but was eventually imprisoned, and finally executed, for his religious beliefs. He was a Lollard, a sort of proto-Protestant, and his death had been celebrated in John Foxe's *Book of Martyrs* (1583) as a heroic defiance of the Catholic Church. As England was now a Protestant country, and as Oldcastle's title, Lord Cobham, was now held by William Brooke, the Lord Chamberlain (whose office controlled the licensing of plays), Shakespeare and his company presumably felt some pressure to alter the name. Shakespeare was not the first to link Oldcastle with Prince Hal's misspent youth. *The Famous Victories of Henry the Fifth*, a probable source for Shakespeare's plays, features a 'Jockey Oldcastle' among Hal's disreputable companions. Nonetheless, Shakespeare expanded and enriched the role so that it not only dominated the two plays, with more lines in either than any other character, but became one of the immortal figures of theatrical history. The character bore little resemblance to his historical namesake, so it probably wasn't difficult for Shakespeare to rechristen him. He adapted the name of a cowardly knight from the *Henry VI* plays, Sir John Fastolfe, and assigned it to his great comic creation. (Fastolfe also had his posthumous defenders, but they proved less influential than Oldcatle's.) As Russell and Harvey were also names belonging to influential families, Shakespeare (or someone) renamed those characters Bardolph and Peto. The Epilogue to *II Henry IV* includes an addendum that seems to apologize for the use of the Oldcastle name, and to distance the fat knight from the Lollard martyr:

> If you be not too much cloyed with fat meat, our humble author will continue the story, with Sir John in it, and make you merry with fair Katharine of France: where, for any thing I know, Falstaff shall die of a sweat, unless already a' be killed with your hard opinions; for Oldcastle died a martyr, and this is not the man.   (Epilogue, 27–30)

In the end, Shakespeare chose not to include Falstaff in *Henry V*, except in the report of his death; but this epilogue reveals not only the theatrical vitality of Shakespeare's creation, but the attempt of the company to distance themselves from the Oldcastle controversy. In 1599 and 1600, a rival theatre company, the Lord Admiral's men, performed two plays on the historical Oldcastle that presented the martyred knight in a more favourable way. Needless to say, *Sir John Oldcastle, Parts I and II*, never supplanted *King Henry IV: Parts I and II*, in the theatrical repertory, but *Oldcastle, Part I* was later spuriously attributed to Shakespeare and included in the third and fourth folios of his works. It seems that having once invoked Oldcastle, Shakespeare had a hard time getting away from him. Indeed, when Stanley Wells and Gary Taylor published *William Shakespeare: The Complete Works* for Oxford University Press in 1986, they reverted to the name Oldcastle for the fat knight – the 'old lad of the castle', as Prince Hal calls him (*I Henry IV*, I.i). From the time the plays were printed, however, Oldcastle was Falstaff, and under that name he immediately became one of Shakespeare's most popular characters. In 1598, the year of the play's publication, the Earl of Essex joked about Sir Henry Brooke (the Lord Chamberlain's son) being Sir John Falstaff; the joke indicates both that the Oldcastle connection was not forgotten and that Shakespeare's character, under his new name, was an instantly recognizable figure of popular culture. A letter from the same year, discussing the leaders of a military campaign, borrows Falstaff's language in remarking that 'Honour pricks them on, and the world thinks that honour will quickly prick them off again' (quoted in Bevington, *Part I*, p. 3). Falstaff surfaces repeatedly in jokes and allusions from a very early date, achieving a ubiquity in English culture he shared with few other Shakespearean characters.

Early performances

Henry IV: Part I was probably first performed in the season of 1596–7 by Shakespeare's company, who at that time were known as Lord Hunsdon's Men (they were previously, and then subsequently, the Lord Chamberlain's Men, and they eventually became the King's Men under James I). *Part II* may have been performed as early as 1597, but certainly no later than 1599, when Ben Jonson alluded to Justice Silence in *Every Man Out of His Humour*. In September 1598, Francis Meres mentioned 'Henry the 4' as evidence for Shakespeare's excellence in tragedy, suggesting perhaps that only a single play of that name was known; but, on the other hand, the reference may point to either or both parts. Some scholars have speculated that Shakespeare may have first written a single *Henry IV* play that was withdrawn, altered and expanded into two plays after the Oldcastle fracas. At any rate, by 1600 there clearly were two plays. Another Falstaff play, the comedy *The Merry Wives of Windsor*, was in existence by the beginning of 1602 and probably before. It seems to have been written after *II Henry IV* and bears little relation to the history plays; it lies outside the scope of this book.

The same company of actors performed the two plays, not necessarily together; though both plays seem to have been performed at Court in the season of 1612–3 with *Part I* going under the title *The Hotspur* and *Part II* played as *Falstaff*. In the original performances, Richard Burbage, Shakespeare's leading actor, probably played Hal, though he might also have played Falstaff or Hotspur. Will Kemp, the famous clown of the company, has been a popular candidate for the first Falstaff, although the company continued to perform the plays after Kemp left in 1599. Other possible Falstaffs were John Lowin, John Heminges and Thomas Pope, but evidence for these matters is slight. The first performance of *Part I* was probably at the Theatre, the original home of the Burbage/Shakespeare company. It was closed owing to a contract dispute in 1597, so *Part II* may have opened at the Curtain Theatre in Shoreditch, where Lord Hunsdon's Men performed until the opening of the Globe in Southwark in 1599.

All three theatres shared the same basic features. An Elizabethan playhouse was a wooden building, probably polygonal in shape, with tiered galleries and a large central yard open to the sky. Into this yard projected a large platform stage, on which the actors performed in daylight to two or three thousand spectators: some seated in the galleries, some standing as 'groundlings' in the yard, some perhaps seated on the stage. Behind the actors was an elaborate façade or *frons scenae* that contained two doors for entrances and exits, a central curtained 'discovery space' and an upper level, which could be used for characters at the windows of houses or on the walls of a city. The relationship between actors and audiences was presumably more direct than in many theatres of more recent times, where audiences sit in darkness and actors are contained behind a proscenium arch. Elizabethan actors engaged the audience directly through soliloquies and asides, and necessarily used a bold, open performance style to meet the physical and vocal demands of reaching a large crowd that surrounded them on many sides and at multiple levels.

The performance conditions of an Elizabethan playhouse would have had interesting implications for the *Henry IV* plays. One of the chief features of these theatres was the relative absence of realistic scenery; the stage remained basically the same whatever the setting. While this prevented the visual verisimilitude of later theatres, it allowed fast and fluid changes of scene. The two parts of *Henry IV* are structured, in part, by the alternation of different worlds: court and tavern, city and country, bedroom and battlefield. On an Elizabethan stage, these worlds would all have been represented in the same space, with few physical changes. Key pieces of furniture, such as a throne or a table, might be brought in to define the palace at Westminster or the Boar's Head Tavern; but for the most part the scenes were defined by the actors themselves, their costumes, properties, and most importantly, their words. At the beginning of *Part I*, the costumes of the King and his lords, together with their stately entrance, would establish the scene as a royal court before any lines were spoken. In the following scene, the very different attitudes of the Prince and Falstaff, together, no doubt, with paraphernalia like tankards and disordered clothes, would reveal the 'riot and dishonour' of Hal's milieu. But Shakespeare was often even more explicit in establishing place and time through his language. In *Part II*, Act IV, scene i begins with the Archbishop asking, 'What is this forest called?' and Hastings replying, ''Tis Gaultree Forest, an't shall please your Grace' (lines 1–2). In *Part I*, II.i, two carriers, holding lanterns in their hands, create – through their sleepy manner, distinctive speech, and road-stained garments – a very precise image of an inn-yard in the early morning:

Enter a Carrier with a lantern in his hand

FIRST CARRIER   Heigh-ho! an it be not four by the day, I'll be hanged. Charles' Wain is over the new chimney, and yet our horse not packed. What, ostler!

OSTLER   [*Within*] Anon, anon.

FIRST CARRIER   I prithee, Tom, beat Cut's saddle, put a few flocks in the point; poor jade is wrung in the withers out of all cess.

Enter another Carrier

SECOND CARRIER   Peas and beans are as dank here as a dog, and that is the next way to give poor jades the bots. This house is turned upside down since Robin Ostler died.

FIRST CARRIER   Poor fellow never joyed since the price of oats rose; it was the death of him.

SECOND CARRIER   I think this be the most villainous house in all London road for fleas: I am stung like a tench.   (1–16)

Neither the characters nor the location has been seen before, and they will never appear again after this brief scene; but Shakespeare here sketches in a remarkably rich and detailed picture of life. Apart from the precise time reference, backed up by a flash of astronomical poetry – 'Charles' Wain' is the constellation we know as the Big Dipper, glimpsed here setting over the 'new chimney' of the country inn – the language of the scene establishes an atmosphere of weariness, discomfort, and labour. The earthy images and simple, monosyllabic words create the smell of the stables. It is scenes like this, capitalizing on the flexible nature of the Elizabethan stage and the vitality of Shakespeare's language, that help the *Henry IV* plays give the impression of a vivid panorama of English life.

The architecture of the stage and playhouse itself may have created systems of meaning for Elizabethan audiences. Robert Weimann, in *Shakespeare and the Popular Tradition in the Theatre*, has suggested that the stage was divided into two symbolic playing areas, the upstage *locus* near the *frons scenae* and the downstage *platea* nearer the audience. According to this view, the *locus* was associated with power and authority, and linked strongly to the historical world of the play; the *platea* was a freer, more unruly space, where clowns could interact with the audience in the here-and-now of Elizabethan London. Such a reading would establish King Henry in the seat of power of the *locus*, while Falstaff and his cronies would engage the groundlings from the *platea*; one of the overall dynamics of the plays would be the movement of Prince Hal between these stage spaces, and his eventual establishment in the centre of the *locus*, the throne. One of the interesting things about the *Henry IV* plays is how openly they appear to play with these systems of signification, these symbolic creations of royal authority. The tavern scene of *Part I*, II.iv, features an extended play-within-the-play in which Falstaff and Hal, by turns, enact performances of royal authority using the very sign-systems of the Elizabethan stage. 'What, shall we be merry? Shall we have a play extempore?' Falstaff asks, and they eventually decide to improvise on Hal's relationship to his father the King:

PRINCE HENRY: Do thou stand for my father, and examine me upon the particulars of my life.
FALSTAFF: Shall I? Content. This chair shall be my state, this dagger my sceptre, and this cushion my crown.
PRINCE HENRY: Thy state is taken for a joined-stool, thy golden sceptre for a leaden dagger, and thy precious rich crown for a pitiful bald crown!   (372–8)

Though Hal mocks the materials of this theatrical illusion, they are essentially the same as those used by Lord Hunsdon's men: and the little tavern-performance takes on a kind of powerful reality as Hal and Falstaff are forced to confront Hal's impending assumption of royal authority.

The performance of the role of King must have had powerful impact in Elizabethan England, where royal authority itself was maintained by theatrical means. As Stephen Greenblatt has pointed out in *Shakespearean Negotiations*, Queen Elizabeth was 'a ruler without a standing army, without a highly developed bureaucracy, without an extensive police force, a ruler whose power [was] constituted in theatrical celebrations of royal glory and theatrical violence visited upon the enemies of that glory' (p. 54). The monarch used royal progresses, public appearances, triumphs and shows – together with public executions – to maintain power. Shakespeare's theatre dramatized, commented upon, and in some cases replicated those very processes. The fact that Elizabethan actors wore, not period costumes, but rich contemporary clothes handed down from the nobility – clothes they would not legally have been permitted to wear in the street – made the connections between theatricality and power even more evident. When King Henry chides Hal for neglecting his princely role in *Part I*, III.ii, he compares him to Richard II, whose poor performance of kingship allowed Henry to win the people's hearts from him:

> Thus did I keep my person fresh and new,
> My presence, like a robe pontifical,
> Ne'er seen but wondered at; and so my state,
> Seldom but sumptuous, showed like a feast
> And won by rareness such solemnity.
> The skipping king, he ambled up and down
> With shallow jesters and rash bavin wits,
> Soon kindled and soon burnt; carded his state,
> Mingled his royalty with cap'ring fools,
> Had his great name profanèd with their scorns ....
>
> (55–64)

According to Henry, Richard lost his kingliness by straying too often into the *platea*, mingling too much with 'shallow jesters' rather than maintaining a proper distance and marshalling carefully quantified manifestations of royal glory. In thus commenting on the performative nature of kingship, the actor of Henry glances both inward at the methods of Elizabethan theatre and outward at the methods of Elizabethan statecraft; such moments may well have created a *frisson* of danger for audiences well schooled in the expressions of power. A few years after *I Henry IV*, supporters of the Earl of Essex hired Shakespeare's company to perform their play about Richard II's deposition on the eve of Essex's attempted rebellion, perhaps hoping to gather public support for the rising. Political theatre and theatrical politics came alarmingly close together, as Shakespeare's fellow actors were called in for questioning and Essex lost his head.

While it quoted and examined the mechanisms of royal power, the Elizabethan stage also invoked performance traditions associated with medieval religion. With the Protestant Reformation and the development of permanent, professional theatres, Tudor drama was largely secularized by Elizabeth's reign. Nonetheless, the inheritances of medieval religious drama were still present, and Shakespeare made full use of them in the *Henry IV* plays. The *locus/platea* dynamic may have derived from medieval mystery cycles, where Biblical figures stood on pageant wagons while disruptive comic devils interacted with the crowd in the street. Morality plays often featured a transgressive 'Vice' character, both attractive and evil, who delighted the audience while tempting the protagonist off the straight and narrow path. Prince Hal calls Falstaff a 'reverend Vice' and this allusion to the morality-play convention hints at a structural device running right through both *Henry IV* plays. Many moralities dramatized a *psychomachia*, an allegorical battle between good and evil forces over the soul of the Everyman hero. This pattern crops up repeatedly in *Henry IV*, with Hal pulled in opposite directions by figures poised on either side of him: usually Falstaff opposed by the King, or Hotspur, or an overtly allegorical figure like the Lord Chief Justice in *Part II*, whose speech prefix, on his first appearance in the Quarto, is merely 'Justice'. The end of *Part I* presents a morality tableau as Prince Hal stands in the middle of the stage, flanked by the bodies of Hotspur on the one hand, embodiment of pride and ambition, and Falstaff on the other, embodiment of gluttony and sloth. Falstaff soon 'riseth up', of course; he understands the conventions too well to be held down by them, at least through *Part I*. Indeed, it is Falstaff who most frequently voices the medieval, emblematic religious language of the play, though invariably with tongue in cheek: 'I never see thy face', he tells the carbuncular Bardolph, 'but I think on hellfire and Dives that lived in purple' (*Part I*, III.iii.31–2).

The polarizing structure of the morality *psychomachia* was reflected in the architecture of the Elizabethan playhouse. The canopy that protected the stage from the elements was called the heavens, and was appropriately painted on its underside. From here angels and deities descended in plays that required them. The 'cellarage' under the stage was similarly associated with hell; demons emerged from a trap door to claim Marlowe's Doctor Faustus. These spaces were probably not used directly in the *Henry IV* plays, but their presence and symbolic value is a part of Shakespeare's universe even in plays that deal with the earthly world of English history. In the tavern scene of *Part II*, Falstaff repeatedly associates his 'wicked' companions with devils and notes of his prostitute companion Doll Tearsheet that 'she's in hell already, and burns poor souls.' When Pistol – whose extravagant language invokes 'Pluto's damned lake', 'th'infernal deep', and 'Erebus' – creates a disturbance, Falstaff repeatedly calls for him to be driven 'downstairs'. It is just possible that the stage trap was used for the entrance and exit from the chamber. On the other end of the scale, when Henry IV is dying, he asks to be carried to a chamber called 'Jerusalem'. While Henry is too worldly a figure to ascend to the heavens, he wishes for a symbolic transfer to a spiritual space to help atone for his sins in compassing the crown. His dying wish reminds the audience of the extent to which the Elizabethan theatre invests space with meaning.

One convention of the Elizabethan theatre that is not much used by the *Henry IV* plays is the playing of female roles by boys. Unlike Shakespeare's earlier history plays, which contained powerful female figures like Joan of Arc and Queen Margaret, the *Henry IV* plays are almost exclusively populated by men. There are over sixty distinct male characters with speaking roles in the two plays, many of which appear in both; there are only five women, and one of them, Lady Mortimer, is given no lines beyond stage directions asserting that '*The lady speaks in Welsh.*' Nonetheless, the boy who played Lady Percy had a challenging and important role with a memorable scene in each play and had to be able to command humour, charm, pathos and authority. Mistress Quickly and Doll Tearsheet are basically comic characters whose performance of gender could have been burlesqued; but each role provides opportunities to show the impact of war, rebellion, poverty and political change on the ordinary women of England, and to turn the audience's attention away, if only temporarily, from the aggressively masculinist world of the plays. Modern actors have certainly seized these opportunities with the roles; we can only speculate as to what Elizabethan boy-players would have done with them.

The final dimension of an Elizabethan performance for which we must account is the audience. Who came to see *Henry IV: Parts I and II* and how did the plays address themselves to them? It seems likely that the broad cross-section of society that is depicted on the stage in the two plays was reflected, to a large extent, in the audience. To be sure, the Elizabethan theatre was not a democratic institution. As in most modern theatres, audiences members were segregated by admission price, and thus effectively by class, into different parts of the house. The wealthiest members sat in upper galleries, or in 'lords' rooms' over the stage, or on the stage itself, where they could be seen by the public as well, or better, than they could see the play. Less affluent audience members sat in the lower galleries, and the poorest stood in the yard, where for a penny they could stand with the groundlings, subject to crowding, weather, and abuse, but with a good view of the stage. Of course, factors besides the relatively low admission price affected who could attend the theatre. A trades-man or apprentice would need to have a whole afternoon off from work, and would need to make his way to the 'liberties', outside the city walls, where the theatres were located. But internal evidence from plays, as well as contemporary documents, suggests that the audience included a diverse collection of people: gentlefolk, law students, grocers, apprentices, clergymen, citizens' wives, orange-sellers, pickpockets and prostitutes.

Plays like *Henry IV: Parts I and II* would have appealed to a broad audience through their very diversity and plurality. According to Thomas Heywood's *Apology for Actors* (1612), historical plays were valued in part for the way they 'instructed such as cannot read in the discovery of all our English chronicles'; some audience members may have come purely to learn more about England's past. Battle scenes were always crowd pleasers, and there would have been many in the audience who could note the finer points of swordplay in the duel between Hal and Hotspur. The comedy of Falstaff and his friends plainly made an impression on audiences to the extent that Shakespeare promised in the added Epilogue to Part II 'to continue the story, with Sir John in it'. One can only speculate about whether particular scenes were played to particular parts of the house, or heard differently by different audience members. At the end of Prince Hal's first scene (*Part I*, I.ii), he has a soliloquy in which he apostrophizes his tavern companions, and then promises to reject them for a life of kingly virtue. Falstaff and Poins have recently left the stage, and Hal begins his speech:

> I know you all, and will awhile uphold
> The unyoked humour of your idleness.

If the actor, perhaps Richard Burbage, were following the convention of addressing his soliloquy directly to the audience, the groundlings in the yard could be forgiven for wondering whether Prince Hal were not directly insulting them. In declaring himself to be one who permits his beauty to be smothered by the 'base contagious clouds' only so he may shine more brightly when he ascends to his true social role, Burbage/Hal could have been playing on the identities of different parts of his audience: perhaps with a knowing, conspiratorial wink, but perhaps in a way that invoked genuine feelings of social unease. If the 'I know you all' speech was indeed a kind of promise to abandon the groundlings for the lords' rooms, it would have set up an audience dynamic that would have resonated throughout the plays to Henry's final ascension to kingship. At the end of *Part II*, some in the pit may have felt that the new King Henry V, in speaking to Falstaff, was speaking to them:

> Presume not that I am the thing I was,
> For God doth know, so shall the world perceive,
> That I have turn'd away my former self;
> So will I those that kept me company.
>
> (V.v.56–9)

2 *Commentary*

Introduction to the commentary

Shakespeare's *Henry IV* plays are about many things: rule and misrule, rebellion in the family and the state, fathers and sons, the contrasting worlds of court, tavern, and countryside. They are about the state of England, at all levels of society, about duty and dereliction, pleasure and strife, holiday and everyday. Perhaps, above all, they are plays about playing, written with a theatrical self-consciousness rivaled in few among Shakespeare's works. They are filled with performances, literal and metaphorical, and their governing action is Prince Hal's preparation for his role as King. Hal is constantly switching characters, from the 'nimble-footed madcap' to the hope of England, from the tavern 'lad of mettle' to the bloody-faced warrior. In extemporaneous performances, he takes on the roles of his rival Hotspur, his father the King, and various versions of himself; all are in some way preparations for the moment in *Part II* when he must play the King in earnest. Such playing is not unique to Hal, but is endemic through both plays. The King attained his title through his enactment of majesty; Hotspur burlesques a perfumed courtier, a cowardly rebel, and Glendower; Falstaff's roles range from prince to penitent, from military hero to surrogate father.

The fact of all of these performances *within* the plays calls our attention to the performance dimensions *of* the plays. Shakespeare's words give us an enormously rich poetic and imaginative experience, but they are only a part of the experience of *Henry IV*. Shakespeare's theatre is a theatre of words and imagination, but it is also a theatre of physical presence. The meanings these texts can generate have to do not only with rhetoric and imagery, but with gesture and action, with the forming and breaking of physical groupings, with the volume or inflection of lines, with the direction of a glance or the angle of a hat. Just as, within the tavern of *Part I*, II.iv, a joint-stool can become a throne, so a performance of the play invites us to take three actors for a rebel army, or an empty stage for a battlefield. Any performance will set up a system of theatrical codes and cues that give vitality, presence and meaning to the world Shakespeare has sketched out in words. The theatrical language of the plays is, to a degree, inscribed in the text: partly in the scant stage directions that have survived into the earliest published editions, but to a larger extent in the action implied in the speeches themselves: as when Hotspur, in his battle oration, declares, 'here draw I / A sword' (*Part I*, V.ii.92–3). On the other hand, much of what constitutes a Shakespeare play in performance is available for interpretation, for discovery in the rehearsal room or invention in the presence of a responsive audience. We know from Shakespeare's text that Hotspur draws a sword, but does he do so exuberantly or gravely, to inspire his followers or to fulfill some private compact with himself? And does his gesture suspend the action onstage for a moment of tension, or propel it forward into the sweeping energy of battle? Such questions have to be asked of virtually every moment of the text, from Falstaff's jokes and the King's musings to the senile prattle of Justice Shallow.

This commentary will attempt to tease out some of the performance possibilities for *Henry IV: Parts I and II*, and their implications for the myriad meanings these two extraordinarily fertile texts can generate. I will consider both the conventions of the Elizabethan theatre and the possibilities available to contemporary performance. The commentary will direct attention to such elements of performance as movement, gesture, costume, and *mise en scène*, to sound effects, music, and the various theatrical means – from symbolic properties to modern lighting – for establishing location, atmosphere and time of day. I will comment on interpretive cruxes within the plays' action, suggesting different possible acting choices, and exploring the way a scene's meaning can hinge on the intention or emotional shading of a given speech or line. The goal of the commentary is to help the reader envision the plays in performance, to perceive the theatrical design Shakespeare creates and the innumerable interpretive possibilities it yields, moment to moment. My purpose is not to define some ideal production; rather, it is to help the reader understand how the plays unfold in performance, and how the text suggests certain theatrical possibilities and demands certain interpretive decisions. I will try to identify the possibilities the text supports, and the implications of different choices as they accrete into whole performances: any of the thousands of potential productions these great plays can yield.

Henry IV: Part I

ACT I

Act I, scene i

Appropriately, the play begins with its title character. In the opening scene, King Henry IV is newly in possession of the crown of England, but threats to his reign are already manifest. The scene hints at the bloody background of Henry's usurpation, and introduces the dangers of the Scots and Welsh, as well as the discontent of Henry's allies, the powerful Percy family of the North. The King's comparison of Harry Percy and Prince Hal sets up a rivalry that will be a major structural feature of the play.

The scene ostensibly takes place within the royal court – King Henry refers to 'this seat of ours' at line 65 – but there is little in the text to define the setting precisely. There could be a throne, though none is required. A throne would have obvious symbolic value as an emblem of the monarchy Henry is defending; it could provide the actor a physical opportunity to express the King's weariness; and it would serve, in Robert Weimann's terms discussed in Chapter 1, to establish the *locus* of the upstage area as a specific historical and geographical space: the court of Henry IV.

When *1 Henry IV* was first played at the Theatre, the scene would likely have opened with a fanfare and some ceremonial entrance for the King and his lords, though the exhaustion expressed in the opening lines might undercut any regal pomp. The stage could be crowded with supernumerary courtiers, but none are required beyond Westmorland and, presumably, the travel-stained Blunt. Prince John is mentioned in the stage direction but never speaks, though the King may address him at points, or even lean on him for support. In any event, the scene plays differently if imagined in a crowded court setting than it does in a quiet antechamber.

Lines 1–33 'So shaken as we are, so wan with care,' the King begins, and his physical appearance likely reflects that enervation. Henry opens the play exhausted by civil conflict, and with his mind on a penitential crusade. Modern productions often begin with the King kneeling at prayer, or some other visual suggestion that he is racked by guilt or illness. If the play is staged in conjunction with *Richard II*, there may be a notable difference in the King's appearance. Henry's opening speech, nevertheless, is measured, rich, and sonorous. It moves from vivid images of civil war to a vision of redemptive religious struggle, presumably raising the King's energy level, as well as his spirits, as it does so. Shakespeare draws on a remarkable range of imagery: the soil of England 'daub[ing] her lips with her own children's blood', the fields trenched with war, the flowers bruised 'with the armèd hoofs/ Of hostile paces'. Although they make no specific mention of the deposition and murder of Richard II, Henry's words can easily convey his guilt over the 'civil butchery' his usurpation has occasioned. There is a marked change at line 18 ('Therefore friends') as Henry turns his focus to his crusade; a yearning for spiritual cleansing comes out in the language of the second half of the speech: 'mother's womb', 'holy fields', 'blessed feet', 'bitter cross'. After the King has worked his way from exhausted guilt to religious hope, however, the speech takes a surprising turn, as Henry acknowledges the domestic crises that impede his crusade. Lines 28–9 could revert to the weary despair that opened the play; but they might also allow the King a moment of self-mocking irony, an acknowledgement that he has more pressing tasks at hand than his 'bootless' pipe-dream of a holy war.

34–75 The Earl of Westmorland brings news of the massacre of a thousand English troops by Owen Glendower, and of the capture of Mortimer, whose ambiguous status as a captive will soon become significant. Westmorland's mention of the 'beastly shameless transformation' done by the Welshwomen on the English corpses will probably cause a shocked reaction among his hearers: its implications of emasculating female violence are deeply disturbing in the primarily male world of the history plays. Henry, perhaps with deliberately ironic understatement, observes that 'this business' will postpone the crusade. Westmorland also brings troubling but inconclusive reports about events on the Scottish front: his short line (56) may indicate uncertainty about how to proceed. Henry is able to reassure him – Walter Blunt has brought 'smooth and welcome news' of the Percies' victory over the Scots, and may step forward with a confident demeanour. But the two conflicting reports highlight the communication problems that will remain important through both parts of *Henry IV*. *Part II* begins with a similar scene, introduced by the deceptive figure of Rumour.

76–107 Westmorland's comment at line 76 may be pointed or unconscious, but its implications about the Prince's shortcomings are clear; it may draw a laugh from knowing audience members. The success of Henry Percy, or Hotspur, in putting down the Scottish rebellion suggests a comparison with the King's own son that is unflattering to the Prince. This invidious comparison will dog Prince Hal throughout *Part I*, right up to the mortal climax at Shrewsbury. The King's feelings here could be portrayed in a number of different ways: he could express an anguished personal concern for his son's welfare, or be coldly dismissive of the wayward prince. His language is harsh: 'riot', 'dishonour', 'stain'. His wish that it could be proved 'that some night-tripping fairy had exchanged/ In cradle clothes our children where they lay' could be simply an exasperated father's joke, or could express real bitterness and rancor. Likewise, his praise of Hotspur could be half-admiring amusement, real envy, or ironic adulation of one he already deems a dangerous enemy. Westmorland, asserting that 'this is his uncle's teaching,' establishes the significance of Worcester as a master plotter, 'malevolent' to the King 'in all aspects.' By the end of the scene, Shakespeare has directed the audience's attention to an upcoming showdown between the King and the Percies. He has also shattered the atmosphere of weary resignation and religious yearning with which the play began, replacing it with one of domestic conflict and political urgency.

Act I, scene ii

In the previous scene, as in the final act of *Richard II*, Shakespeare had teasingly anticipated the appearance of one of the most important characters in English history: the King's 'unthrifty son', the future Henry V. The play's second scene gives Prince Hal a noteworthy introduction, but Shakespeare surprises the audience with an even more important debut: that of Sir John Falstaff, who constantly threatens to dominate the two parts of *Henry IV* on his way to becoming one of the immortal figures in world literature. Prince Hal and Falstaff share the scene more or less equally, displaying their verbal adroitness in a playful battle of wits that allows glimpses, beneath the surface, of the uncertain future that will ensue when Hal becomes King. An exchange between Hal and another of his companions, Poins, gives a promise of madcap comedy to come: but a final verse soliloquy reveals Hal to be a subtler, more enigmatic character than his tavern mates, or the audience, have reckoned on.

1–56 Nothing about the setting is specified in the text, other than that the characters are *not* in Eastcheap, where they plan to rendezvous the following night. Editors often place the scene in 'an apartment of the Prince,' or some such location. At the Theatre, Hal and Falstaff probably just walked out onto the stage, conveying the informal atmosphere of the scene through costume and body language. In any event, the first appearance of the slender young prince and the absurdly fat knight will invariably prompt laughter from its very incongruity. (Shakespeare one-ups this effect in *Part II*, pairing Falstaff with a young page for his first entrance.) Falstaff was clearly represented as fat on the early modern stage – his girth is alluded to in every scene in which he appears – but how fat remains open to question. The first visual representation of Falstaff, the frontispiece to *The Wits* from 1662, shows a portly but by no means obese figure, well-dressed and rather dashing. In modern productions Falstaff and Hal are often discovered onstage, sleeping off a hangover or engaging in some form of tavern dissipation.

The second scene of the play contrasts strongly with the first: it is in prose instead of verse, and an atmosphere of lassitude replaces one of urgency. Falstaff's opening question introduces the theme of time – wasted, suspended or seized – that will be important throughout the play, and will close the scene in Hal's project of 'Redeeming time when men think least I will'. The conversation continues to ring changes on clocks and dials, sun and moon, night and day, and, perhaps most importantly, the present of Hal's 'loose behavior' and the future of his kingship. How seriously either Hal or Falstaff takes these matters is up to the actors, but the scene certainly allows for plenty of foreshadowing of the future relationship of the two men, right up to the rejection that concludes *Henry IV: Part II*.

Falstaff seems in a merry humour through the first part of the scene, though his refrain of 'when thou art king,' repeated four times, could betray a gnawing anxiety. Hal's attitude could range from playful indulgence to nettled exasperation to cold contempt. Yet the two men address each other on what seem to be terms of familiar affection: 'Hal', 'Jack', 'sweet wag', and, glancing at Falstaff's original name, 'my old lad of the castle'. On the whole, the linguistic exuberance of the scene suggests that Hal and Falstaff are enjoying sparring with each other. Hal's long opening speech uses one of the hallmarks of the play's best prose, the bountiful piling up of images, here of time and tavern dissipation. Falstaff's rejoinder introduces the device of mock-heroic hyperbole, as he praises thieves as 'Diana's foresters, gentlemen of the shade, minions of the moon'. Both men freely engage in punning, playing on the double senses of words like grace, government, countenance, steal, reckoning, and credit, with the series culminating in Falstaff's egregious pun on 'heir apparent' at line 56.

57–96 After the gamesmanship of this opening conversation, Falstaff introduces, at line 57, the potentially more serious topic of justice in England when Hal becomes King. The mention of thieves and hangmen could be meant seriously by Hal and laughed off by Falstaff, or the reverse. It is notable that the conversation sends Falstaff into a (real or feigned) melancholy for much of the rest of the scene. The discussion of melancholy in turn leads to another wit-contest, as Hal and Falstaff play one of their most characteristic games, inventing outlandish comparisons, in which Falstaff eventually concedes the field at lines 79–80. Falstaff's melancholy takes the form of mock-pious repentance, a familiar posture for him. As he does various times throughout the two plays, Falstaff gravely laments the sorry state to which Hal's corrupting influence has brought him. In this mode Falstaff makes free use of the language of scripture. Here he invites Hal to recognize an allusion to Proverbs, when he mentions disregarding an old lord who wisely berated him in the street. The allusion is a throwaway here, but it very

precisely anticipates an actual scene in *Part II*, where Falstaff ignores
the remonstrances of the Lord Chief Justice.

97–103   At Hal's abrupt inquiry about where to take a purse, line
97, Falstaff instantly drops the pose: 'Zounds, where thou wilt, lad,
I'll make one.' How the actors play this moment is important in
terms of defining a basic interpretive question in the Hal/Falstaff
relationship: to what extent is Falstaff the butt of others' jokes,
and to what extent does he actually control the scenes in which he
appears to be bested? Critics have debated this issue since Maurice
Morgann's 1777 defense of Sir John, which took him at his word
(*Part II*, I.ii.9–10) that he was not only witty in himself, but the cause
of wit in others. The question is crucial in determining audience
responses to both Hal and Falstaff. In the present instance, does
Falstaff blindly snap at the possibility of a robbery like a Pavlovian
dog, or does he relish the irony of moving seamlessly 'from praying to purse-taking'? His ready response that "Tis no sin for a man
to labor in his vocation', suggests the latter, but the scene works
either way.

104–55   As soon as robbery is introduced as a topic, Shakespeare
brings on Poins to lay out the specifics of the Gadshill plot. Poins
immediately sides with Hal in a series of clever riffs on Falstaff's
gluttony and mock-religiosity. The two young men gang up against
their older companion, giving each other feed-lines and one-upping
each other's witticisms. Falstaff is silent, and Poins himself brings
the conversation back to the plot. The robbing of travelers was one
of the chief features of the 'wild Prince Hal' legend, and a prominent
episode in the source play *The Famous Victories of Henry V*; it is also
one of the misbehaviours associated with Hal at his first mention
in *Richard II*, V.iii. Shakespeare needed to have Hal involved in a robbery, but also needed to distance him from it. How reluctant Hal
appears is up to the actor: he could be very tempted by the exploit,
and only back off with effort; or he could be set against it from the
beginning. He is perhaps deliberately obscure about his intentions
in line 139. Falstaff's frustration with Hal's diffidence leads to a
potentially telling exchange, as he declares (line 142) that he will be
a traitor when Hal is King. Hal's 'I care not' could be a childish rebuff
or a stony anticipation of the rejection. Falstaff manages a bit of

grandiosity for his exit speech, but his true prince/false thief comments put pressure on the question of Hal's future actions.

156–88   In any event, Poins's true plan (lines 157–62) gets Hal, and Shakespeare, off the hook: the Prince will not participate in the robbery of the travelers, but only of the thieves themselves, in what promises to be a classic comic come-uppance. Hal's only responses to the plan are logistical enquiries, and his level of enthusiasm is debatable, but he agrees to go along with the plot. This short exchange allows the actor of Hal to begin to develop his relationship with Poins, who will serve as a crucial foil throughout the two parts of *Henry IV*. As a figure of Hal's own age and inclinations (as Falstaff informs us in *Part II*, II.iv 243–54), Poins is in some ways more of a friend to Hal than Falstaff is. They are certainly oftener in accord, though their relationship begins to show signs of strain by the beginning of *Part II*. For the purposes of *Part I*, Poins seems to be Hal's loyal friend and ally within the tavern world; he exits here with a respectful 'Farewell, my lord.'

189–211   It is all the more striking, then, that it is upon Poins's exit, not Falstaff's, that Hal begins his 'I know you all' soliloquy. The measured monosyllabic verse that starts the speech contrasts sharply with the informal dialogue that preceded it. The change of tone will necessarily be arresting, as Hal apostrophizes the friends he is already planning to renounce. This speech is one of the most important moments an actor has to develop the character of Hal, and it is almost impossible not to extend that conception beyond the bounds of this play, to Hal's coronation and career as Henry V. Whether or not Shakespeare had future plays in mind, he and his audiences knew the story of Hal's reformation, and this soliloquy clearly anticipates it as part of a methodical plan: a plan that includes the rejection of Hal's companions, Poins and Falstaff among them.

The actor is free, of course, to play this speech as a kind of rationalization: Hal is half-heartedly justifying his present life, which he is thoroughly enjoying, and putting off to the future the responsibilities that await him. It may be that he begins the speech with a whimsical notion that develops into a concrete strategy as he responds to the imagery he creates. The 'foul and ugly mists' of line 196 may release some pent-up resentment against his tavern colleagues. On the other hand, the talk of holidays, sport and loose behaviour in the middle of the speech could suggest that Hal is merely reflecting on the happy adolescence he must eventually forego. But there seems to be a shift at line 202, from theoretical contemplation to more determined action, perhaps indicating Hal's commitment to his plan. There is an aggressive energy in the language as he nears the end of the speech, beginning at line 206: 'And like bright metal on a sullen ground, / My reformation, glittering o'er my fault ... .' For the first time in the play, an actor speaks in soliloquy, directly addressing the audience with his innermost secrets and plans. After a long scene of prose, the Prince of Wales drops his slumming posture and speaks in blank verse, in the language of far-reaching political purpose with which the play began. In assuming for himself the regal metaphor of the sun, Hal steps away from the shadowy world of Diana's foresters, and into the bright, hard arena of kingship.

Act I, scene iii

The showdown between the King and the Percies, which occupies the first half of this scene, introduces the formidable character of Hotspur, as well as the two issues in contention. The first is Hotspur's refusal to yield the Scottish prisoners he took at Holmedon, which Hotspur more or less excuses in a testy account of the effeminate lord who allegedly brought him the King's request. The second is the Percies' demand that the King ransom Mortimer, Hotspur's brother-in-law, who is being held by Owen Glendower. The high tempers on both sides over this issue suggest that there is something more at stake, and as soon as the King leaves the stage, Worcester reveals what it is: Mortimer was proclaimed heir to the throne by Richard II. Hotspur plays on the guilt and resentment of his kinsmen, who helped depose Richard and feel inadequately rewarded by Henry, and Worcester unveils a plot to unseat the King. The key interpretive issues in the scene have to do with the balance of power in the impending conflict. Is Henry a forceful king or a haunted usurper? Do the Percies come across as passionate rebel leaders, or as a squabbling dysfunctional family centered on a tantrum-throwing child?

1–28 The scene begins *in medias res*, in the middle of a dispute that has already escalated into a heated argument. Henry seems more commanding than the shaken and wan figure who opened the play, though of course his assertiveness could be played as panicked desperation. The real issue in dispute emerges in Worcester's first speech, when he alludes to the role the Percies played in helping Henry to the crown. The King dismisses Worcester abruptly in lines 15–21, then coldly turns to Northumberland in an effective power play: 'You were about to speak.' Northumberland attempts to excuse his son, but Hotspur quickly speaks up for himself.

29–76 Hotspur's opening speech is the first significant development of a character who made a minor appearance in *Richard II*. Much of his impact will depend on the actor's appearance and bearing. Shakespeare altered history to make Hotspur a young man, and therefore a rival to Hal; but he is regularly played by actors of any age from twenty to forty. He may be large-framed warrior or a wiry youth; physically restless or controlled and still. Hotspurs are frequently bearded, and a disproportionate number have had red hair, presumably based on enduring stereotypes about choleric temperaments. In *Part II*, Lady Percy refers to Hotspur's 'speaking thick', probably meaning fast. Many actors have followed this lead, though a few, notably Olivier, have affected a speech impediment in response to Lady Percy's description.

Hotspur's speech is entirely Shakespeare's invention, though the rest of the scene follows events recorded by Holinshed. The speech, a colourful account of a fastidious courtier demanding Hotspur's prisoners on the battlefield of Holmedon, presents a few interpretive questions. How much does the speech reflect an actual event, and how much is Hotspur inventing or embellishing to excuse himself? Is Hotspur self-consciously telling a funny story about a perfumed lord, or is he himself the object of humour because of his over-the-top exasperation? Does the speech get away from him, or is it a well-crafted strategic ploy? In any event, the speech provides the actor of Hotspur with one of his richest opportunities for characterization. The long sentences, piling up clauses without regard to syntax, reveal the pace and energy of Hotspur's mind, as well as his explosive temper: at line 56 he impatiently interrupts himself midsentence with, 'God save the mark!'. His language is animated and descriptive, full of telling details like 'his chin new reaped / Showed like a stubble land at harvest home' and plosive alliterations like 'to be so pestered with a popinjay'. His personification of the courtier extends to imitating his speech in free indirect discourse, as in his endorsement for 'parmacety' at line 58. His own forceful assertions make a clear contrast, and give a compelling picture of Hotspur as a man of strong passions and unminced words. Sir Walter Blunt, at any rate, is convinced, and steps in on Hotspur's behalf, taking the role as mediator that he will repeatedly adopt throughout the play, until he finally dies at Shrewsbury as a stand-in for the King. His excuse of Hotspur ends with a rather pointed warning to the young lord that he can be forgiven for what he said, 'so he unsay it now.'

77–124 King Henry will have none of it; he recognizes that the prisoners are not really the issue. Taking up the demand that he ransom Hotspur's brother-in-law, Henry escalates the conflict by accusing Mortimer of treason, on the evidence that Mortimer has married Glendower's daughter. His angry rhetorical questions at line 85–8 are forceful, even if self-serving, and lead to the decisive determination to 'on the barren mountains let him starve!' Hotspur leaps to Mortimer's defense, recounting an epic battle between Mortimer and Glendower. Where this account comes from is unclear, as is how far Hotspur actually believes it. The speech has elements of myth and romance, with the combatants pausing three times, by agreement, to drink 'of swift Severn's flood'. The fancifully lyrical language of lines 102–7 comes as something as a surprise from Hotspur, but can be taken as evidence of his romantic spirit. One of the challenges of the scene for the actor of Hotspur is to make all of his speeches come convincingly from the same man. The King refuses to hear further of Mortimer, again demands the prisoners, and dismisses the Percies. As at the scene's opening, the King asserts his authority through a posture of cold formality, disdaining to speak directly to Hotspur. His final line is terse and forceful; Colley Cibber remembered the power Ned Kynaston gave it in Restoration performances, speaking in a whisper more menacing than any shout (Bevington 1987, p. 70).

125–46 Upon the King's exit, Hotspur's rage breaks out – he is 'drunk with choler'. He probably moves restlessly about the stage throughout the scene, as he 'apprehends a world of figures' that set off his imagination and his temper. When Northumberland observes Worcester's approach at line 130, Hotspur completes the verse line with an interrupting outburst: 'Speak of Mortimer?' This is a characteristic device for Hotspur: at least sixteen times in the play, and four times in this scene, he completes verse lines begun by others, suggesting his excited eagerness to make himself heard. With Worcester's return, the conversation turns to its hidden subject: Mortimer's claim to the crown. Historically, the Mortimer they have been discussing was *not* the Mortimer who was heir presumptive to the throne: the latter, the fifth Earl of March, was nephew of the former. The conflation results in greater dramatic clarity. It is interesting that Shakespeare makes Hotspur, to this point, unaware of Mortimer's claim, and that the King himself betrays no knowledge of it in the preceding scene. This allows Henry to hold the high moral ground while he is onstage. In refusing to ransom Mortimer, Henry seems to be defending the interests of the kingdom rather than his own weak claim to it. Hotspur, for his part, is governed more by his impetuous temper than by political considerations; it is only Worcester who has the secret and traitorous agenda.

147–93 In the conversation that ensues, Worcester and Northumberland regret their roles in Henry's usurpation, and Hotspur, forgetting his own part therein, takes them to task. Expressing himself, for the first time, in high political rhetoric, Hotspur invokes fame, justice, and especially honour to shame his father and uncle for having dared 'To put down Richard, that sweet lovely rose, / and plant this thorn, this canker, Bolingbroke.' It is notable that throughout the *Henry IV* plays, when characters recall the events of *Richard II*, they often do so in the language of that play, whether through direct or indirect quotation or, as here, by borrowing its imagery. The metaphor of Richard as a rose recalls the earlier play's extended image of England as a garden, and its overall atmosphere of Book-of-Hours medievalism. While this image is surprising in the mouth of the manly Hotspur, it helps lead him into the flights of chivalric fantasy that distract him later in the scene.

The excitement of the clandestine plot to supplant Bolingbroke leads even the pragmatic Worcester to poetic intensity: he will 'unclasp a secret book' that promises an enterprise as dangerous 'as to o'erwalk a current roaring loud/ On the unsteadfast footing of a spear.' The charged language of such passages is what sustains Shakespeare through long scenes of political plotting and posturing; productions that fail to bring life to this language will have a difficult time maintaining audience interest through the rebels' scenes.

194–256   Hotspur's inability to attend to Worcester's plotting has considerable comic potential. His extravagant paean to honour in lines 201–8 evidently became enough of a set-piece in Shakespeare's lifetime for the apprentice Ralph to burlesque it in the Induction to Beaumont and Fletcher's *The Knight of the Burning Pestle* (1607). It gets a more immediate counterpoint in Falstaff's catechism on honour in V.i of the present play. Hotspur's sudden outbursts of anger over the prisoners and Mortimer are more overtly comic. He may himself be a conscious agent of the humour – when he says he will train a starling to speak nothing but 'Mortimer', he will likely adopt a bird-like voice and get audience laughter. Likewise, in recalling Bolingbroke's fawning behaviour at Berkeley Castle, Hotspur will probably parody his voice and manner. It is notable that King Henry is imitated by all of the other major characters in the play: Hotspur, Hal and Falstaff all take turns at playing him, and Sir Walter Blunt portrays the King at the cost of his life. Role-playing is a prominent feature of 1*Henry IV*, certainly, but Henry seems to be the most popular object of imitation. It is therefore especially helpful if the actor of Henry has a distinctive voice and presence, as, for instance, is the case with John Gielgud in the film *Chimes at Midnight*.

At other points in the scene, the joke seems to be on Hotspur, as his explosions of rage derail the attempts of his uncle and father to develop their plot. When he finally protests that he has finished, Worcester dryly replies, 'Nay, if you have not, to it again; / We will stay your leisure.' (Hal adopts a similar stance of weary tolerance with Falstaff's 'base comparisons' in II.iv. 247–9.) Hotspur must not become as tiresome to the audience as he is to his family; these outbursts give the actor an opportunity to reveal Hotspur's impulsive nature, but they should also get the audience on his side as an amusing firebrand, rather than alienating them from a spoilt child.

257–300   When Hotspur finally settles down, Worcester briefly sketches in the details of the rebellion, setting up lines of historical connection that run throughout the Lancastrian tetralogy. In mentioning the Archbishop of York, Worcester makes reference back to his brother the Earl of Wiltshire (actually his cousin), reported killed in *Richard II*, III.ii, and introduces a character, Richard Scroop, who will only become prominent in *Part II*. (Later, the nephew of the executed Scroop will become one of the traitors who attempts to assassinate Henry V in II.ii of that play.) Douglas, Mortimer and Glendower are again named as the other major players in the planned revolt. A potentially bewildering number of people, places and events are mentioned in this scene, but the main fault-lines of the impending conflict can be established clearly enough. Hotspur makes one throwaway reference, which the actor can point up for the audience, to the man who will prove his rival and nemesis, 'that sword-and-buckler Prince of Wales'. By the end of the scene, the rebellion is in urgent preparation, and the King's tenuous claim to the throne has been exposed.

ACT II

Act II, scene i

One of the characteristic devices of both parts of *Henry IV* is the alteration of scenes involving different characters and different orders of life – scenes that nonetheless bear some thematic or structural relation to each other. After a scene of lords plotting a rebellion, Shakespeare answers it with a scene of low-life crooks plotting a robbery. One of the primary virtues of this brief episode, however, is its vivid and earthy depiction of the life of the inn-yard. In language of unparalleled, and sometimes incomprehensible, colloquialism, the carriers and thieves embody a side of life far from the usual concerns of chronicle history, and help give the play its impression of incomparable richness and felt life.

1–47   The opening stage direction, 'enter a Carrier with a lantern in his hand,' demonstrates Shakespeare's method for swiftly delineating time and place. On the Elizabethan stage, the lantern signifies night; the Carrier's yawning entry and disheveled appearance reinforce the identification. His first lines complete the picture, as he guesses at the time ('four by the day') and picks out the Big Dipper in the sky 'over the new chimney', thus localizing the stage as outdoors in the courtyard of an inn.

Nowhere in the play does Shakespeare employ language as dense or distinctive as that he gives to his lowly Carriers. The grunting, monosyllabic utterances, with their associations of meager food, discomfort, and disease, create a memorable impression even for audiences who don't fully understand them. The Carriers' very words have an aural and emotive impact: 'dank', 'jades', 'bots', 'fleas', 'tench', 'leak', 'loach.' The impression is not wholly negative, as the Carriers' rough camaraderie, concern for their horses, and crude manners – 'we leak in your chimney' – give them a coarse appeal, and their cargo of turkeys, bacon and ginger calls up associations of festive plenty.

The characters will be physically occupied with their work, hauling baskets and bags, perhaps pausing to yawn, stretch, and scratch – the constant talk of fleas seems to demand this action. When Gadshill enters, the Carriers quickly adopt a posture of defensive mistrust, thinking he means to steal their lanterns. They may be merely suspicious people, by trade or nature, but it is equally possible that Gadshill communicates a shifty malevolence by his very presence. In any event, his sights are set higher than lanterns, and he quickly gains information about their route and schedule. Up to this point, the audience will have very little idea what is going on, but Gadshill's sneaky inquiries will probably make it clear that this scene has something to do with the planned robbery discussed in I.ii.

48–98 For the second half of the scene, the honest Carriers exit and leave the stage to the thieves. The Chamberlain provides information about the true mark of the robbery: 'a franklin in the Weald of Kent' with 300 marks in gold. More importantly, the dialogue finally begins to connect to characters we have heard of. The Chamberlain greets Gadshill by name – Poins had mentioned him in the earlier scene – and Gadshill brags that 'if I hang, old Sir John hangs with me.' The plot is beginning to emerge. In a long and lively prose speech, Gadshill hints that he has even higher connections who could 'for their own credit's sake make all whole' if they ran afoul of the law – what Prince Hal eventually does, in repaying the money. Gadshill is a small role, but his linguistic vivacity is a gift to the actor, with his extravagant talk of 'mad mustachio purple-hued malt-worms'. It is a style of speech Shakespeare will revive for Pistol in *Part II*. Gadshill is capable of sudden poetry, as in his line on fernseed and invisibility, but his final exchange with the Chamberlain reveals his essential nature. There is no honour among these thieves, and the line 'Farewell, you muddy knave,' especially if spoken aside, can end the scene with hostility, confirming the gritty nature of this low-life milieu.

Act II, scene ii

The Gadshill robbery is one of the play's best opportunities for broad knockabout farce. The spectacle of Falstaff, who initially complains of having to make the least physical effort, first bestirring himself to rob the travelers and then beating a comic retreat, is inherently funny. But as Poins has pointed out, the chief virtue of the jest is yet to come, in the version of events Falstaff will relate in the tavern. Shakespeare's use of anticipation and retrospection is one of the chief structural ways he holds the play together as he alternates among the different locations and groups of characters.

The sense of a nighttime outdoor location is created in several ways. The characters shout and whistle for each other, hide from each other, lie on the ground, and chase each other about the stage. The large open platform of the Elizabethan stage would serve this scene well, and the pillars could stand in for trees, hiding places, and obstacles in the chase. This is the largest and most active scene in the play so far, with a total of ten people on the stage.

1–29   The chief humour of the first part of the scene comes from the vexation of Falstaff at the physical effort required of him in the robbery. Poins has hidden Falstaff's horse, and in his first soliloquy, he laments the sorry state of the world 'when thieves cannot be true to one another!' Such paradoxical aphorisms provide much of the humour of the speech, and reveal something about Falstaff's topsy-turvy view of the world. Falstaff also adopts his repentant persona, lamenting his inability to get away from the malign influence of Prince Hal – or possibly Poins, lines 17–19 could refer to either. Falstaff has numerous prose soliloquies throughout the two plays. The actor will almost certainly address the audience directly, seizing the opportunity to get on intimate terms with the spectators, to bring us into his confidence and ensure our complicity. In Robert Weimann's terms, Falstaff occupies the *platea*, the space on the platform contiguous with the auditorium (see Chapter 1). Falstaff holds this territory right to the end of *Part II*, and A. C. Bradley suggested that Falstaff's skill in delighting the audience defeats Shakespeare's plans for his eventual dismissal.

29–77 Falstaff's lack of physical fitness occasions a good deal of humour when the Prince and Poins return; though Falstaff arguably makes the best jokes against himself. When the Prince asks Falstaff to lie down and listen for the tread of travelers, he is basically giving a feed line for Falstaff's splendid reply: 'Have you any levers to lift me up again, being down?' The rest of the thieves assemble and put on their masks. When Gadshill reports that there are eight or ten travelers, Falstaff is taken aback – 'Zounds, will they not rob us?' – thus beginning the discussion of his cowardice that will occupy much of II.iv.

78–110 The Travelers enter – only four in total, according to Hal's later report. As with Falstaff at the beginning of the scene, Shakespeare throws in an explanation, lines 78–80, as to why they are not on horseback. They evidently have at least some of their goods with them, though not so much that the Prince and Poins can't carry it offstage at the end of the scene. The thieves – perhaps hiding behind the stage pillars – ambush the Travelers. Falstaff takes a leading role in the robbery, and in his swaggering highwayman pose he projects onto the Travelers his own qualities of age and corpulence. The robbery is certainly a comic opportunity, especially if the violence of the thieves and the terror of the victims are presented cartoonishly. However, the second robbery must trump the first, as the Prince and Poins, masked and dressed in buckram cloth, put the thieves to flight. The stage business can be more or less reconstructed from the Prince's account in II.iv but the Quarto text provides an unusually detailed stage direction:

> As they are sharing, the Prince and Poins set upon them. They all run away, and Falstaff, after a blow or two, runs away too, leaving the booty behind them.

Exactly how much of a stand Falstaff makes is up to the actor; as is what, and how much, he 'roars'. While the episode will certainly be funny, it should probably not be too protracted or elaborate, since the value of Falstaff's account in II.iv is its expansion of a brief panicked flight into an epic battle with a multiplying army of men in buckram.

Act II, scene iii

The scene of Hotspur at home gives an update on the progress of the rebellion and a foretaste of its outcome, as Hotspur responds to a serious setback with pugnacious, foolhardy confidence. More importantly, the scene fleshes out the character of Hotspur by showing him in relation to his wife. The first female character we see in the play, Lady Percy brings a different perspective to the masculine world of war and politics, and though she fails to get full knowledge of her husband's plans, she undermines some of his bravado with her wit and spirit. The scene can be interpreted in a number of different ways. There is much opportunity for comedy, but also for pathos, or for contentious gender politics. However it is handled, the scene does much to establish the audience's attitude to Hotspur for the remainder of the play.

This scene introduces yet another of the play's multiple worlds: in this case, some notion of domesticity and family life. No changes to the setting are required, though modern productions often use warmer lighting or some interior touches for the scene. Hotspur and his wife may wear dressing gowns or some other garments suggestive of homey informality, especially if the scene is played, as the text suggests, at night or in the early morning. Lady Percy's references to Hotspur's sleeplessness support this reading, as does his declaration, 'I will set forward tonight.' There is a closely analogous nighttime scene between Brutus and Portia in *Julius Caesar*, written a couple of years later. On the Elizabethan stage, Hotspur or his servant might carry a candle or other light to define the time clearly.

1–34 Hotspur's long prose soliloquy is not so much a self-reflexive address to the audience as a one-sided argument with the author of the letter. Hotspur enters reading aloud the hesitant excuses of a frightened would-be rebel, and quickly explodes into vociferous denunciation of the 'shallow, cowardly hind'. Sometimes his frustration is expressed with wit and humour, as when Hotspur angrily declares that the rebel 'loves his own barn' better than the house of the Percies. He later compares his correspondent to 'a dish of skim milk' and says he could 'brain him with his lady's fan'. These lines will get laughs, and will probably get the audience on Hotspur's side. But the letter contains serious warnings that Hotspur ought to heed, and represents, as he recognizes, the potential exposure of their plot to the King. Hotspur's rash determination to press ahead, and his confident affirmation of their enterprise even while it is unraveling, expose traits of his character that will have disastrous consequences later in the play. The letter does serve to remind the audience of the names of the major players in the rebellion; it also gives one glimpse of Hotspur's poetic/romantic side in the image of the nettle and the flower.

35–64   Lady Percy's name was actually Elizabeth, and Holinshed calls her Elianor; Shakespeare changes her name to Kate. She is one of a long line of feisty Kates in his plays, ranging from the spirited young women of *The Taming of the Shrew* and *Love's Labour's Lost*, to the French Princess wooed by Henry V, to Katherine of Aragon in *Henry VIII* and the shrewish woman mentioned in Stephano's sea-shanty in *The Tempest*. Though she appears only briefly in each part of *Henry IV*, Kate Percy is given memorable scenes each time, and she is the most impressive female figure in the two plays. On Shakespeare's stage, of course, she would have been played by a boy or young man. In the modern theatre, this relatively small role is often taken by a leading actress, and it has enough variety to yield considerable rewards.

Lady Percy's opening monologue is a beautiful set-piece in rich and measured verse. It combines tender affection, psychological nuance, and a vivid account of the mental stress of combat. Like Portia in *Julius Caesar*, Kate chides her husband for his solitary musings, though she is, perhaps, more openly sensual. She laments her banishment from his bed, his loss of interest in pleasure, and what she calls 'my treasures and my rights of thee'. She conjures up the emotional disorder of her soldier husband in some of the most moving and powerful lines in the play: 'In thy faint slumbers I by thee have watched/ And heard thee murmur tales of iron wars ....' Shakespeare's device of piling up a series of related images, often used in prose speeches in this play, is given added weight here by

the metrical and rhetorical structure of Lady Percy's verse, as she
gives an evocative list of military terms at lines 51–5. The frequent
alliteration, the distinctive vocabulary, the anaphoric repetition of
'Of' at the beginning of lines, and the extra emphasis accorded to
the final image of 'soldiers slain' give the speech great rhetorical
and emotional force. These battlefield images are counterbalanced
by the delicate natural one Kate finds for the beads of sweat on
her husband's brow, 'like bubbles in a late-disturbèd stream'. This
speech exemplifies the particular strength of the *Henry IV* plays in
the variety and quality of their language. The dramatic situation of
Kate and Hotspur has inherent pathos, but the performer who can
take advantage of the linguistic richness of this speech will get the
greatest impact from the scene.

65–77   After this long and emotional appeal from his wife,
Hotspur's first response is to ignore her: 'What ho!' he calls abruptly
to a servant. How far he has been moved by her pleas, and what
prompts him to turn suddenly to other matters, is up to the actor –
but the change of tone will surely be startling, whether it comes
across as comic or brutal. Hotspur transacts some business with his
servant in brusque and specific terms, even naming two offstage
servants, Gilliams and Butler. He makes particular enquiries about
a roan horse that seems to be a favourite of his, and allows himself
a rhyming reflection – 'That roan shall be my throne' – that could
be self-mockingly sing-song or gravely prophetic. When at last he
turns his attention to his wife, she has been driven to such a state
of exasperation that her outburst turns the scene toward comedy:
'Out, you mad-headed ape!'

78–88   The actor of Lady Percy may try to maintain a sense of
grievance or pathos throughout the scene, particularly in a performance highlighting the marginalized position of women within
the world of the history plays. But the impulse toward comedy is
strongly coded in the lines. Kate adopts a tone of testy informality
toward her husband, dropping 'my lord' in favour of 'Harry,' and
comparing him to an ape, a weasel and a 'paraquito'. In the most
striking moment of the scene, she threatens to break his little finger
if he will not reveal his plans to her, and the line seems to indicate
that she actually does get the better of him physically for at least

a moment. How long she has hold of his finger, and how broadly
the physicality of the scene is played, can vary in performance. But
there is at least the possibility of a quite farcical moment here, as the
powerful warrior is physically subdued and brought to the mercy of
his furious wife.

89–117 Hotspur's response is to reject her, and love, which he
decries as effeminate in lines 90–2. Nonetheless, some warmth and
physical affection between the couple usually returns by the end of
the scene, and Hotspur has many opportunities to mix tenderness
with his teasing of her. His final lines to her, in particular, have a
marked emotional weight, borrowed from the faithful words of
Ruth in the Old Testament (Ruth 1:16, 'Whither thou goest, I will
go'), which they invert and paraphrase: 'Whither I go, thither shall
you go too.' But the scene does not end on this pledge, and Kate
gets the last word. Shakespeare introduces a device here that he
uses often in his middle and later plays: providing what seems to
be a conclusive rhyming couplet, then qualifying or undermining
it with an unrhymed final tag line. In the present case, in response
to Hotspur's enquiry as to whether his plan of meeting up with her
later contents her, Kate gives a terse reply: 'It must, of force.' This
could be a joking submission, or a bitter protest. At any rate, Kate's
final line can speak volumes about her marriage and the general
position of women in her world.

Act II, scene iv

The longest scene in either part of *Henry IV*, Act II, scene iv of *Part I*
is one of Shakespeare's greatest achievements. Falstaff's account of
his battle with the hydra-headed buckram men is one of the play's
funniest episodes; the 'play extempore' that rehearses Hal's eventual rejection of Falstaff can be one of its most poignant. The scene
begins with a sort of prologue, the baiting of Frances the drawer,
that shows Hal's political education in action; it ends with a coda
that returns us to the world of rebellion and civil war. But the scene
depends mainly on the two great set-pieces of Falstaff's version of
Gadshill and the role-playing games with Hal. The scene has great
comic moments throughout, but it also engages with the issue of
Hal's future kingship, and regularly brings in the ideas of Hotspur

and the rebellion, as well as of Hal's relationship with his father. All of these moments can be given a good deal of weight. Further, the question of Hal and Falstaff's relationship can be played quite seriously. If the play is given in tandem with *Part II*, the role-playing scene will prefigure the final rejection; if *Part I* is performed alone, then Hal's promise to banish plump Jack – 'I do, I will' – may stand in for that rejection, and represent the most serious moment in the relationship between the young Prince and his companion.

The Tavern is plainly one of the play's dominant imaginary worlds. The playground of Falstaff and his friends must exert a powerful pull on Prince Hal, and contrast markedly with court and countryside. The physical demands of the scene are not great. In a way, the most important part of the setting is the door to the outside world, which would have been represented by one of the two permanent doors of the Elizabethan stage. Access to the stage is carefully controlled throughout the scene, but the world outside is always threatening, first with news of the court and the rebels, then with the hue and cry following the robbery. Besides the doors, there must be a joint-stool for the 'throne' of the play extempore, and an arras for Falstaff to fall asleep behind. Modern designers generally go far beyond this in creating an atmosphere brimming with local colour, with overstuffed chairs, oaken beams, pewter plates, and the like. However much or little the stage is altered by the introduction of furniture, Shakespeare's language serves to give the tavern a local habitation, if not a name (the only allusion to the Boar's Head by name is Hal's question 'does the old boar feed in the old frank?' in *Part II*, II.ii.138–9). Many cups of sack are ordered and drunk; we hear of other rooms called the Half-Moon and the Pomegranate; reference is made to hogsheads, pints of bastard, pennyworths of sugar, the clinking of pewter, anchovies and sack after supper, and so forth. One notable fact about the setting of the tavern is that it seems, in some sense, to be outside time. At the beginning of the scene it is twelve midnight, according to Hal; in the middle of the revelry, when a nobleman from the court tries to intrude on the proceedings, it is still said to be midnight; but when the sheriff finally breaks up the party in the search for Falstaff, it is revealed to be two in the morning. The drunkard's sense of time suspended, as the night slips away, is nicely suggested by Shakespeare's time references in the scene.

1–33   The first part of the scene introduces the tavern through Hal's account of his drinking with the drawers. In a long prose speech, Hal demonstrates his ability to adapt himself to different companies, and to adopt their dialect and manners: 'I can drink with any tinker in his own language during my life.' The speech can be played as evidence of Hal's democratic good-fellowship, getting on a first-name basis with the lowly drawers who will one day be his subjects. It could also be interpreted as a rather cold-blooded ethnographic mission: Hal learning to manipulate people of all classes by 'recording' their language, in Stephen Greenblatt's terms. Or it could be played as a rather distasteful and patronizing mockery of the 'puny drawer' Francis and his friends. The element of contempt comes through when Hal brings Francis to the stage – though the scene may still be very funny indeed.

34–79   The basic joke of the Francis scene is of the cruel sort described in Henri Bergson's famous essay on laughter, in which humour is derived from 'the mechanical encrusted on the living' – a human being reduced to the status of a machine. Francis's automatic reaction of the shrill cry 'Anon, anon, sir!' whenever Poins calls him from offstage is just such an instance of mechanized behaviour, resulting from the short-circuit created by Francis's conflicting impulses to be courteous to the Prince and to attend his customers. Audiences share in this kind of humour as much as princes do, so the scene should certainly get laughs; though depending on how pathetic Francis is, the laughter may be cut with a good deal of sympathy, and some feelings of reproach toward the Prince and Poins. The Prince's teasing offer of a thousand pounds in exchange for a pennyworth of sugar, an offer he withdraws when Francis seems to defer it with an involuntary 'Anon', seems a rather cruel joke on the poor drawer. ('A thousand pound' is the standard marker of great wealth in *Henry IV*; it is the amount of the Gadshill robbery, of Hal's alleged debt to Falstaff, and of Falstaff's debt to Shallow in *Part II*.) While Francis is rather an easy mark, he does allow Hal to indulge his love for lists, in his abusive characterization of the Vintner in lines 69–71. Francis himself, though a minor character with 'fewer words than a parrot,' is a great role for a comic actor, and usually makes a memorable impression. For Hal, the episode reveals not only his playfulness but his manipulative powers and mercurial temperament: he describes himself as a kind of Protean gamester, of all humours 'since the old days of Goodman Adam'.

80–111   Hal ends the episode by comparing Francis, with his limited vocabulary, to his rival Henry Percy; the Prince evidently has Hotspur on his mind. In some ways it seems an odd comparison, given Hotspur's reputation for uncontrolled speech; but Hal's performance of Hotspur is on target in many ways. Like the real Hotspur of the previous scene, Hal's burlesque version pays more attention to his roan horse than to his wife. The actor of Hal may choose to imitate Hotspur's manner very closely; or his performance may be a grotesque parody that registers as unfair. (Hal is certainly unfair to Lady Percy, who is no enthusiastic supporter of her husband's warlike ways.) In conceiving of an impromptu performance in which he will play Hotspur and Falstaff 'Dame Mortimer his wife' Hal anticipates the upcoming 'play extempore', which will dramatize offstage events very differently. Hal's love for role-playing can certainly come through in this brief episode, as he mocks his rival through exaggerations of voice and manner.

112–218   Falstaff and the Gadshill crew enter, their garments torn and bloodied from their supposed fight. Falstaff immediately takes command of the stage. Going on the offensive, he wishes a plague on all cowards, and laments the world's decline – a typical pose for him. He speaks mainly in short, explosive phrases – 'a bad world', 'a king's son' – but nonetheless monopolizes the conversation, pausing only to drink (twice). It takes him forty lines or so to get to the point of his tirade – that Poins and Hal are cowards for avoiding the tremendous combat that he and the others have survived. How seriously he expects to be taken is a substantial interpretive question throughout this scene, but at the beginning, at least, he seems to wish to be believed.

The scene is relatively crowded and animated, with Poins, Hal, and the four Gadshill robbers onstage, and the Hostess and Francis coming and going. In production, other colourful tavern denizens are often present to heighten the atmosphere of the scene and the reaction to Falstaff's antics. As soon as Falstaff introduces the stolen thousand pounds at line 156, the stage is set for the story of the robbery. The humour of the scene, obviously, comes from Falstaff's exaggerations, and from Hal's encouragements of them: 'What, fought you with them all?', 'Pray God you have not murdered some of them' and so forth. It is possible that these exchanges indicate some private or half-acknowledged communication between the two, as though Hal is directly urging Falstaff to outdo himself in his extravagant lies. Such an interpretation would suggest a kind of complicity between Hal and Falstaff, as though the two of them were enjoying a joke on everyone else. It is hard to resist the idea that Falstaff has some consciousness of what he is doing, particularly in the episode of the multiplying men in buckram. Hal and Poins actively play along – Poins confirms Falstaff's assertion that there were four, whereas in fact he had said two, and Hal observes aside that 'we shall have more anon.' The actor of Falstaff can convey a sense of consciously pushing the limits of his storytelling by pausing slightly and giving each new number added emphasis: 'These … *nine* in buckram that I told thee of – '. On the other hand, he could just be getting carried away and upping his estimate of the opposing forces each time, with the exaggeration typical of a tavern *raconteur*.

219–62   When, however, at lines 219–22 Falstaff adds the detail about fighting men in Kendal green when it was too dark to see his own hand, he seems to be begging to be contradicted. (He is also, perhaps, glancing at the conventions of the Elizabethan stage, where every nighttime conflict, no matter how obscure it was supposed to be, took place in broad daylight.) Hal interrupts, and though Falstaff initially refuses to give a reason upon compulsion, Hal pursues him with a torrent of prose invective to which Falstaff responds in kind. The exchange at lines 239–46 is typical of the 'flyting' that marks their relationship, with Hal's four colourful insults matched by eight from Falstaff, quenched only when the fat knight theatrically runs out of breath. These 'base comparisons', as Hal calls them, reveal the wit and verbal facility of both characters. They may also contain some real malice or sensitivity, as the more serious conflict between Hal and Falstaff builds underneath their playful sparring, to emerge later in the scene.

263–80   When Hal reveals the deception, Falstaff pulls off his greatest coup. As all on the stage wait eagerly to hear how he will excuse himself, he says with relish, 'I knew ye as well as he that made thee.' Falstaff turns his fault into a virtue – he was a 'coward on instinct', the valiant lion would not touch the true prince. Falstaff's answer presumably gives immense satisfaction to the company – possibly, but not necessarily, including Hal and Poins – and will likely be greeted with a shout of triumph and applause. Falstaff is at the height of merriment and calls for a 'play extempore', though Hal cools his mood slightly by proposing the topic of his running away.

281–322 The sudden intrusion of the Hostess with news of the court is the first of two crucial incursions of the outside world into the world of the tavern. Mistress Quickly is one of Shakespeare's most enduring creations, the only character besides Bardolph, Queen Margaret, and Humphrey of Gloucester to appear in four of Shakespeare's plays. She offers a range of characterizations, depending on her relative levels of shrewdness and gullibility, innocence and carnality, gentility and fishwifery. In this first appearance she plays a rather limited role, and one of her chief sources of humour, her tendency toward unconsciously lewd malapropisms, is not much in evidence. Her news, that a nobleman of the court is at the door, temporarily interrupts the revelry, but Hal doesn't seem much disturbed initially. While Falstaff investigates, Hal has a chance to tease the other Gadshill robbers, notably Bardolph, who gets his first significant characterization as he excuses his cowardly behaviour: 'Faith, I ran when I saw others run.' The exchange with Bardolph dwells mainly on his most distinctive characteristic, his red face, but it also allows for a foreshadowing of the future relationship of Hal and his cronies. When Bardolph blusters that the colours of his face portend 'choler ... if rightly taken', Hal's reply – 'No, if rightly taken, halter' – threatens his friend with the hangman's noose. Shakespeare may or may not have known that two plays later Hal would sanction Bardolph's death by hanging, for robbing a church in France in *Henry V*; but most actors know it. Hal's offhand joke can be a chilling moment anticipating Bardolph's execution; at the very least, it revisits the question of the future king's dispensing justice to thieves, a question Falstaff first raised in I.ii.

323–68 Falstaff enters to relate the news of Glendower, Douglas and the rebellion. For once, Falstaff is apparently more serious than the Prince, who turns away Falstaff's concerned reports with light or frivolous answers. When Falstaff says that with the approach of war, land can be bought 'as cheap as stinking mackerel', Hal replies that maidenheads will come cheaply too – a coarse offhand remark that hints at the social disorder occasioned by civil war. Hal can certainly be played as more serious than his lines suggest; he is making flippant remarks not because he is heedless of the rebellion, but because his deeper thoughts are fully occupied with it. It is an advantage to the actor of Hal to be able to convey that his mind is working on two levels at once: this double nature is a feature of the character as it develops through these two plays, and is especially important in *Henry V*. In the present scene, Hal's genuine gravity at the threat can come through in his cool reply to Falstaff's query as to whether he is afraid: 'Not a whit, I' faith. I lack some of thy instinct.' Alternatively, of course, this can be a genuinely carefree rebuff.

369–426 Falstaff's suggestion that Hal prepare for his father's chiding prompts Hal to propose an improvisational performance, and this sets up the second of the great set-pieces in this long scene. Falstaff's preparations glance at the simple representational strategies of the Elizabethan theatre: a chair stands in for a throne, a cup of sack provides the red eyes of passion. The 'throne' may be placed on top of a table to give it visual prominence; it may also echo the position and orientation of the King's throne from earlier scenes, creating a parody of the *locus* of the Court. Falstaff's performance alludes to two prominent literary styles of the time, ranting Elizabethan tragedies like Thomas Preston's *Cambyses* and the exaggeratedly balanced style of John Lyly's *Euphues*. The second is the primary influence on Falstaff's enactment of the displeased King Henry IV, chiding his son for his misbehaviours. Falstaff may parody the voice and behaviour of King Henry, but from a linguistic standpoint his Henry IV has little in common with the character the audience has met. Euphuism is a highly wrought prose style that depends on alliteration and antithesis, balancing one thought against another in sometimes painfully elaborate ways: 'For, Harry, now I do not speak to thee in drink, but in tears, not in pleasure, but in passion, not in words only, but in woes also.' Falstaff's King chides Hal for the villainous company he keeps, excepting only one virtuous man. Hal, playing along, inquires what manner of man, allowing Falstaff the pleasure of a flattering self-portrait. In this speech Falstaff is clearly playing to his audience, perhaps enacting his own 'cheerful look' and 'noble carriage' as he goes. His assertion that he is fifty often draws protests from the onlookers, prompting his revision of his age to 'inclining to threescore'. In the Welles film *Chimes at Midnight*, Falstaff is so in control of his audience that he doesn't even need to announce his own name: it is supplied by the crowd, followed by a general cheer.

427–54　Finally Hal has had enough: he interrupts, and demands that they switch roles. He may be genuinely offended at Falstaff's burlesquing of his father. Or he simply be eager for his turn, or miffed that Falstaff seems to be besting him in the exchange. He may be resentful at Falstaff's ability to sway the crowd; if so, his assertion of regal authority at this point may be a kind of rehearsal for the eventual coronation and rejection. At any rate, Hal's 'deposition' of Falstaff is a key turning point in the scene, and moves it closer to being a serious challenge to Falstaff's position vis-à-vis the Prince.

　　Like Falstaff, Hal may imitate King Henry's mannerisms; but Falstaff takes the opportunity to one-up him by mocking the 'young Prince', perhaps using a high voice or a pert manner in his reply. Hal's response may carry genuine anger at the mockery. The biggest interpretive question pertaining to this speech, and indeed the entire scene, is whether, and at what point, the game becomes earnest. It might be as early as the beginning of Hal's long speech criticizing Falstaff; or it might come as late as Hal's 'I do, I will' at the end of the exchange. Alternatively, the scene may never turn serious, or Falstaff may never realize its seriousness; even after the Sheriff interrupts them, Falstaff wants to play out the play, as he has 'much to say on behalf of that Falstaff'. In performance, of course, much will be determined by the response of the onstage audience, and Falstaff himself, to Hal's taunts. The Prince launches into an attack on Falstaff that contains both hyperbolical mockery and cutting moral opprobrium. He starts with a list of the exaggerated metaphors for Falstaff's person that we have heard before, culminating in 'that roasted Manningtree ox with the pudding in his belly'. Then he switches to attacks on Falstaff's character, comparing him initially to the allegorical figures from medieval morality plays: 'that reverend Vice, that grey Iniquity'. Whether this switch indicates a change of outlook or intention on the part of Hal is up to the actor. He concludes the speech with a series of rhetorical questions as to Falstaff's worth, concluding his assessment with one of Shakespeare's power-ful keywords: 'nothing.'

455–76 Falstaff is game enough to evade this blow through a posture of ignorance at lines 455–6. In performance, Falstaff may be rattled or confident, but he is certainly in no doubt as to whom Hal/Henry means. The question in his mind, or the audience's, is who is speaking? To what extent is Hal revealing feelings of his own through the performance of his father? Falstaff manages, regard-less, to mount a spirited defense, though whether he speaks with blithe confidence or desperate panic is up to the actor. The onstage audience's reactions are again critical: do they recognize any under-current of real feeling, or are they simply applauding Falstaff's self-aggrandizement, as during the 'buckram men' scene?

Falstaff concludes with a grand and perhaps oracular pronounce-ment: 'Banish plump Jack, and banish all the world.' Does this convey pride, bitterness, despair? The Prince's simple, monosyllabic reply is potentially crushing: 'I do, I will.' The possibilities for both actors are legion. Each of Hal's two-word phrases can be given any number of inflections, and they may contradict each other. Hal may, in one breath, break Falstaff's heart, and in the next try to comfort him; or he may treat the first phrase as a huge joke, and then slip in the second as a grave promise. There may be a pause before, or after, or between, the two phrases. Regardless, these stark, sim-ple statements, coming at the end of a pair of long and elaborate prose speeches, have great dramatic force. In the theatre, this tense moment is suddenly broken by knocking from offstage: an effect Shakespeare would reuse powerfully in *Macbeth* (just after the mur-der of Duncan, in II.ii and II.iii). Whether the knocking comes in silence or in tumult, whether it follows a pause or comes just on the heels of Hal's words, whether it is matter-of-fact or startlingly vio-lent: these choices determine much about the impact of the scene. Whatever the interpretation, the moment is a crucial one: just as Hal and Falstaff have rehearsed a decisive point in their relationship, the outside world intrudes on them, demanding attention and action.

477–520 The Sheriff's entrance brings an abrupt halt to the play within the play, leaving audiences to speculate on what Falstaff might have said in his own behalf, or what direction the improvisation might have taken. In another sense, the knocking forces the issue the play raised: the relationship of Hal to his criminal cronies. Falstaff and company are wanted for a robbery, and Hal suddenly is in the position of abetting their escape or turning them over to the law. Falstaff's lines to Hal (486–94) may be pure bluff and bravado, or they may reveal real anxiety that his friend will turn him in for what is, after all, a hanging offense: Falstaff mentions being 'strangled with a halter'. Does Hal pause for a grave moment of decision before sending Falstaff to hide behind the arras, or does all happen in a scrambling hurly, with no more seriousness than a school prank? In either case, the Carrier's description of Falstaff – 'As fat as butter' – probably returns the play to comedy, at least for a moment. Hal may adopt a haughty tone in his exchange with the Sheriff; his order to leave the house carries the weight of his high rank, and bides no question. On the other hand, when the dismissed Sheriff (chastened or angry?) bids Hal good night, his reply – 'I think it is good morrow, is it not?' – suggests a more friendly type of condescension, evidence of Hal's common touch. The Sheriff's observation that it is now two o'clock in the morning feeds into the weary tone of the final part of the scene.

521–45 Falstaff is found to be asleep behind the arras, and 'snorting like a horse'; if he is seen by the audience, it is an inevitably comic tableau, though perhaps not without pathos also. The reading of Falstaff's tavern reckoning is also almost certainly funny, probably Peto's best moment in the play. But there is a sense of exhaustion at the end of the scene, as the stage, which has been crowded with people and action for nearly half an hour, is now populated by only three characters, one of them asleep. The end of II.iv is close to the midpoint of the play; modern productions usually take an interval here. 'I'll to the court in the morning', Hal observes; 'We must all to the wars.' The temporary escape into the timeless world of the tavern has ended.

ACT III

Act III, scene i

The story of the rebels continues with a meeting of the principal leaders in Wales. The first half of the scene derives comedy from the friction between Hotspur and Owen Glendower, the testy Welsh magician, but the proposed division of England into three parts emphasizes the political stakes of the rebellion. The second half of the scene draws pathos from the relationship of Mortimer and his wife, Glendower's daughter. Hotspur and Kate provide a lively contrast, but the scene of the rebel leaders and their wives, accompanied by the mystical music provided by Glendower, serves as a melancholy prelude to the upcoming scenes of civil war.

The atmosphere of the Welsh scene is unlike any other in the play: characters speak and sing the Welsh language, music plays as if by magic, the moon is said to shine fair, and there is talk of fiery shapes in the heavens and spirits in the deep. Hotspur's prosaic dismissal of this 'skimble-skamble stuff' may or may not be enough to break the romantic mood of the scene; but clearly Shakespeare is at pains to suggest a world very different from any of those yet seen in the play. Modern designers often take pains to create a realm of Celtic mystery through lighting, sound, and costume. Even in an Elizabethan performance, Glendower and his daughter would presumably have looked and sounded different from the other characters – though it is notable that Glendower is the only one of Shakespeare's Welsh characters not to be saddled with a comic Welsh accent (cf. Sir Hugh Evans and Fluellen, who always use 'p' for 'b', and so forth). Glendower makes a point about speaking English like a native, though Welsh rhythms can still be found in his lines.

1–66   The four rebel leaders gather around a table, perhaps brought on for this scene, perhaps remaining from the tavern. The scene is unusual in requiring that the characters sit – though how long they remain seated, as their conflicts escalate, remains a question. The business and order of seating may itself be a form of veiled aggression, as both Hotspur and Glendower urge the other to sit first; Shakespeare depicts similar gamesmanship between Antony and Octavius as they sit for an ill-fated conference in *Antony and Cleopatra*, II.ii.29–33.

The scene introduces two new characters: Mortimer and Glendower. Though Mortimer is the one with a claim to the throne, he seems to be the weakest of the three would-be triumvirs, constantly having to mediate between the squabbling Hotspur and

Glendower. Glendower, though he appears in only this one scene, is a very distinctive and memorable figure. Plainly, he is at least partly comic – no character can twice declare that at his birth 'the front of heaven was full of fiery shapes' and expect to be taken wholly seriously, particularly if Hotspur is constantly calling him on it. But the actor of Glendower may also create some real sense of magic out of the character's other-worldly demeanour, powerful natural imagery, and rhythmic, alliterative verse. Glendower's speech uses heavily aspirated consonants, especially 'F' and 'S' sounds, in evoking the portents attendant upon his birth: 'the frame and huge foundation of the earth', 'The front of heaven was full of fiery shapes', 'strangely clamorous to the frighted fields'.

Hotspur's impatient nature can bear very little of this, and he scores some points, and probably wins laughs from the audience, with his retorts at lines 48 and 52–3. How justified Hotspur's mockery is, and how angry or forbearing Glendower is in response, determines much about the audience's assessment of the rebel leaders: but such conflict is hardly an encouraging sign, particularly when the parceling out of England becomes the topic.

67–142   Glendower returns them to business, focusing attention on the map with which they will divide the kingdom. The creation of the 'indenture tripartite'; the agreement between the three rebel leaders, is based on a historical event recorded in Holinshed, but the division of England into three parts has the force of folk myth, as it will again years later in *King Lear*, I.i. The physical prop of the map, especially if it is large enough to be seen clearly by the audience, reinforces this impact. Presumably everyone in Shakespeare's audience would have felt such a plan would lead to catastrophe, and there is much in the scene to support this view. The casual talk of diverting rivers and reconfiguring landscape can easily be played as thoughtless and doomed hubris. The conflict of temperament between Hotspur and Glendower becomes an open quarrel over land (though the territory in dispute is actually Mortimer's, south of the Trent river). Worcester, the most pragmatic and cool-headed of the rebels, is notably silent during most of this scene: his stony presence in the midst of their squabbles can foretell the rebellion's failure. In the end Glendower yields the point, whether through intimidation, exasperation, or boredom, and leaves the stage.

143–87 Mortimer chides Hotspur for baiting his father-in-law, prompting an outburst of mockery. Hotspur catches Glendower pretty exactly, burlesquing his prophecies of the moldwarp and the ant, 'a dragon and a finless fish', and so on. If Glendower speaks with a Welsh accent, Hotspur may imitate the sounds as well as the manner of his speech. His coarse and colourful language in lines 154–60, with its memorable image of living 'with cheese and garlic in a windmill', probably wins audience laughter, but also a stern rebuke from Worcester that lays out clearly some of the political disadvantages of Hotspur's choleric temperament.

187–223 The second half of this scene, when the rebels are joined by Lady Percy and Lady Mortimer, allows for a wide range of moods, encompassing doomed romance, faerie mysticism, sparkling sexual comedy, and sour realism. The scene will certainly take on a different physical character: instead of a group of men gathered around a table, we have two couples reclining 'on the wanton rushes'. The linguistic divide between Mortimer and his wife – he speaks only English, she only Welsh – can be charming, pathetic or ridiculous. The Welsh dialogue presents something of a production challenge: Shakespeare gives no more help beyond stage directions like '*The lady speaks again in Welsh.*' Presumably Shakespeare's company found actors who could ad-lib in Welsh or some near approximation; or else they merely muttered in gibberish. Modern productions often write touching endearments for Lady Mortimer to address to her husband, which must be learned phonetically if a Welsh-speaking actress is not available. The song gives a good opportunity for haunting Celtic threnody, accompanied by whatever equivalent the producer can find for Glendower's mystical airborne music.

224–62 In their dialogues, Hotspur and Kate have the opportunity to develop their relationship from the point where they left it earlier in the play. Their exchanges, though sharp, appear affectionate, but Kate's refusal to sing, for instance, can indicate jealous resentment, on the one hand, or a premonition of doom on the other. Their scene together, like the previous one, ends with Hotspur charging eagerly offstage to put his plans in action, and Kate's reaction is again an important commentary. Are the two ladies left alone together for a moment as the men go off 'to horse immediately'? If so, how do they respond to each other, and how do they exit the stage? The scene affords a rare opportunity for displaying female solidarity in the masculine world of Shakespearean history: it is the only point in *Part I* when there is more than one woman onstage.

Act III, scene ii

The interview between the King and the Prince has been anticipated since the first scene of the play, discussed by both parties, and even rehearsed onstage. It falls more or less in the middle of the play, and is a kind of hinge for the action, as Hal leaves behind the world of the tavern and prepares himself for the world of battle. It provides a focal point for the volatile father/son relationship that constitutes the psychological spine of the two plays. The scene also reaches out across the Lancastrian tetralogy, recalling the relationship of Bolingbroke and Richard in *Richard II* and anticipating the kingship of Henry V. In Hal's protestation that he will 'redeem all this on Percy's head,' he anticipates the conclusion of the play. Hal's misadventures with Falstaff, his anguished relationship with his father, and his rivalry with Hotspur – all of the major plot strands of the play intersect in this decisive and highly dramatic duet scene.

1–28 After clearing the room, King Henry confronts his son. He begins in measured tones, building his speech with the even rhythm of the lines, but the longer clause of lines 8–11 suggests that the King is unleashing considerable emotion. The hendiadys of line 10 is a violent image combining Biblical grandeur with the brutality of corporal punishment. The sense-break in the middle of line 11 doesn't halt the rhythm of the King's admonition, but allows it to surge onward, brooking no reply, with renewed energy. Henry pounds through the repetitive, demeaning 'such' clauses of the following lines, finishing with the bitterly ironic aspersion on Hal's 'princely heart'. What is unclear is how much of the speech is directed inward as well. Henry suggests that his misbehaving son may represent divine punishment, but he doesn't acknowledge the nature of his fault: the deposition and murder of an anointed king. The actor, in pronouncing such euphemisms as 'some displeasing service I have done' may convey a sense of deep personal regret, but it is just as possible that Henry has genuinely blinded himself to his guilt.

Hal's speech in response may show genuine remorse, though it seems to contain a degree of equivocation; he deflects much of his guilt onto the 'smiling pickthanks and base newsmongers' who have misreported him. In any event, Hal's initial apology clearly does not satisfy Henry.

29–128   The King's next speech is the longest in the play, and, at over sixty lines, one of the longest in Shakespeare. Recalling the events of *Richard II*, Henry recounts the circumstances by which he allegedly won the hearts and minds of the English people away from their lawful king. Henry may or may not be a reliable source; one of the interesting features of both Shakespearean history cycles is the way previously dramatized events are recounted with subtle or not-so-subtle variations. Here, Henry's attacks on Richard as one who 'Enfeoffed himself to popularity' sound oddly like descriptions of Bolingbroke's own past behaviour (see *Richard II*, I.iv and V.ii). Even audiences unfamiliar with *Richard II* may notice the ambiguity of Henry's self-descriptions in lines 50–2, with their heavy element of thievery and theatre: stealing courtesy, dressing in humility, plucking allegiance from men's hearts. In any event, Henry creates a vividly powerful, if potentially misleading, contrast between himself and Richard. He concludes the speech with a damning identification of his son with the King he deposed – one of the strange psychic projections the scene is full of. The speech leads Henry to what may be his most emotional moment in the play – he acknowledges a longing to see Hal, and weeps with 'foolish tenderness' at line 91. But he pushes on with the invidious comparison, likening himself to his son's rival Hotspur, and renewing the identification of Hal with the deposed and murdered Richard. Henry's praise of Hotspur becomes so hyperbolical – 'Mars in swaddling clothes,/ This infant warrior' – that it could be played ironically, but it could just as easily be sincere. The passage ends with Henry forcefully returning the scene to the present crisis, reminding Hal (and the audience) of the exact extent of the rebellious conspiracy, enumerating the five principal opponents.

129–59   Apart from one faltering promise to be more himself, the Prince of Wales has remained silent for nearly one hundred lines of fatherly abuse. Is he fuming, crestfallen, aghast? To what extent does he feel himself susceptible to the accusations? Does he remain in one place, perhaps kneeling, or pace the stage in mute fury? When he does speak out, it is with his longest speech in the play, and one that apparently erases all of his father's doubts in one fell swoop. His language is the most violent we have heard from the Prince: 'I will wear a garment all of blood/ And stain my favors in a bloody mask', he claims. His speech zeroes in on Hotspur, whom he treats with what could be played as respect ('this same child of honour and renown') or contemptuous sarcasm ('this Northern youth'). Notably, Hal doesn't dwell on the past or try, as before, to excuse his behaviour; rather, he focuses on how his confrontation with Hotspur will restore his tarnished name, recalling his plan for 'redeeming time' in his first soliloquy.

160–80 Henry seems to respond positively to Hal's fervour, though he could express lingering doubts in his final speech, or in subsequent scenes. For the most part, however, the remaining text of the play suggests that Hal has already redeemed himself in his father's eyes. This creates problems if the two parts of *Henry IV* are being staged together, as Hal must revert to scapegrace status after having enjoyed royal favour for much of *Part I*.

The hurried entrance of Blunt hastens matters forward and makes mention of characters and places that will be important in the scenes to come: John of Lancaster, the Earl of Westmorland, the Douglas, and especially the town of Shrewsbury, here named for the first time. All of the succeeding scenes will direct the audience to anticipate the coming battle.

Act III, scene iii

Back at the tavern, Falstaff squabbles with Bardolph and Mistress Quickly. The Prince enters with news of the coming war, for which he has procured Falstaff a military commission. This relatively brief scene shows Falstaff in his accustomed surroundings and behaviours: lying, wheedling, lamenting his fallen state, and wittily abusing his companions. The location is understood to be the Eastcheap tavern from II.iv. The presence of Mistress Quickly establishes continuity, and Falstaff complains of having fallen asleep 'here behind the arras' and having his pocket picked, a clear reference to the earlier scene. Beyond the arras, there are no specific scenic requirements, though some furniture would be appropriate: Falstaff's deflated attitude at the beginning suggests a seated posture.

1–51 Falstaff begins in full repentant mode, bemoaning his dwindled condition: depending on how fat Falstaff appears, the line can be more or less humorous. He may be affected by genuine melancholy, or it may all be part of a pose. Bardolph's grim prognosis at line 11 suggests that Falstaff is sincerely depressed. Falstaff's second speech, however, has a self-conscious playfulness about it, as he notes how he 'diced not above seven times – a week,' and so forth. An expansive Falstaff may move into a more performative mode here, perhaps winking at the on- or offstage audience. When Bardolph makes a passing comment on his fatness, he responds with disproportionate force, subjecting Bardolph's red face to more than twenty lines of sophisticated prose mockery. Abusing Bardolph seems to improve Falstaff's mood, as he moves from thoughts of death to reminiscences of the robbery and of walking 'betwixt tavern and tavern'.

52–79 The Hostess enters, and Falstaff accuses her of collusion in the picking of his pocket. She has enough sense, at lines 66–7, to assess his motives as deceptive and mercenary. The scene affords the Hostess good opportunities to display outraged dignity, notably through her insistent repetition of the name 'Sir John.' Falstaff puts up a lame resistance, derogating the shirts the Hostess bought him and pushing some of the debts onto Bardolph. The Hostess provides Falstaff with a classic comic set-up when she mentions that the Prince said his ring was copper. Falstaff declares he would 'cudgel him like a dog' for saying so, just as the Prince walks in the door. Falstaff, once again, gets the chance to make creative excuses for himself, providing much of the scene's humour.

80–152 The Prince's entrance is given an oddly specific stage direction: he is said to be '*marching, and Falstaff meets him playing upon his truncheon like a fife*'. The Prince enters with Peto, but is he also accompanied by soldiers, or a drummer? Both seem out of place in a tavern. Yet if he isn't, his marching would seem to be in the playful or parodic manner of Falstaff's response to it – which would seem out of character for the newly reformed Prince. It is hard to know exactly what would have happened on Shakespeare's stage, though the general sense of Falstaff's military burlesque is clear enough.

The Prince greets the Hostess by name, Mistress Quickly; it is the only time she is named in the play. (She seems to be married at this point – both she and the Prince refer to a husband – but in *Part II* she seems to be a widow.) The Prince takes her side in the quarrel with Falstaff, though his involvement could be played as either chivalric or patronizing. Falstaff soon has to defend himself from charges of threatening and slandering Hal, which he does with brio, though whether Hal is amused or angered is up to the actor. Hal could become momentarily serious when challenging Falstaff to be as good as his word and fight him, creating a moment of stage danger in their charged relationship. Falstaff has an opportunity to get his own back when he mocks Hal as the 'lion's whelp', laughing off the suggestion that Hal should be feared as much as his father. Depending on how it is played, it could be a tense exchange: another moment that prefigures the eventual rejection.

153–206 Hal chooses ridicule over conflict, revealing that it was he who picked Falstaff's pocket, which contained nothing of value. This revelation sends Falstaff back into his mode of sorrowful repentance in lines 165–9. To Mistress Quickly, Falstaff adopts a posture of unearned magnanimity: 'Hostess, I forgive thee. Go make ready breakfast.' In such moments, there is a question as to how self-conscious Falstaff is of the ironies of his position – is he really such a monster of egotism, or is he consciously making a joke on himself? The answer is possibly both.

The Prince relates that the money from the robbery has been paid back, and that he is good friends with his father 'and may do anything' – a rather glib comment that might raise questions about the sincerity of his reformation. His procuring Falstaff 'a charge of foot', first mentioned in II.iv as a practical joke on his fat friend, comes up again, but now under the threat of impending combat. By the end of the scene, Hal seems more serious than he has been at any time except during the interview with his father. His penultimate line – 'The land is burning' – expresses the horrors of civil conflict more vividly than anything yet spoken in the play. Falstaff, for his part, looks to the future with regret, as the action of *Henry IV: Part I* leaves the setting of the Boar's Head tavern for the last time. His final lines mark his unwilling transition from one world to another: 'Oh, I could wish this tavern were my drum!'

ACT IV

Act IV, scene i

Hotspur meets with the Douglas, and learns of two major setbacks, as the forces of his father and Glendower are unable to join with them. Hotspur's fervent and perhaps naïve optimism contrasts with Worcester's gloomy political wisdom. The chief interpretive question of the scene has to do with Hotspur's state of mind: how clearly does he grasp the situation? Does he proceed from courage, or foolhardiness, or both?

This scene opens the 'outdoor' phase of the play, the remainder of which will take place largely on the road, in military camps and on battlefields. An Elizabethan stage wouldn't change physically, but the disposition of the actors could indicate a larger and more open space. There may be some suggestion of the rebel camp; or the military tenor of the scene might be established by drum and colours, or by the characters wearing armour or other battle gear.

1–85 Hotspur seems to have found a kindred spirit in the Douglas, his former adversary; he goes out of his way to flatter him, while twice denying he is doing so. Douglas responds with reciprocal admiration. Douglas is a small but memorable character, probably distinguished by a Scots accent and some form of Highland dress. He provides an enthusiastic counter to the otherwise demoralizing reports Hotspur receives from the messenger, Worcester and Vernon. Hotspur's response to the news of Northumberland's illness is characteristically mercurial: he first declares it 'a very limb lopped off', but soon argues that his father's absence is actually a benefit, since it will give them reserve forces for future battles. Whether Hotspur actually believes this, or is simply trying to put a brave face on the situation for the benefit of his followers, is up to the actor. Worcester's political sagacity puts a grimmer construction on the situation. In coolly precise verse, Worcester analyzes how the Earl's absence will appear to 'the eye of reason.' Throughout the Shrewsbury sequence,

Worcester's dour Machiavellianism contrasts with Hotspur's blustery valour and casts doubt on the rebels' hopes.

86–137 Sir Richard Vernon appears for the first time, reporting the approach of the King's forces. In response to Hotspur's question about 'The nimble-footed madcap Prince of Wales', Vernon launches into a Pindaric paean to the Prince that uses language unrivalled in the play for decorative grandeur. Hal and his followers are associated with May and Midsummer; the Prince leaps from the ground like 'feathered Mercury', mounting his horse as though it were Pegasus. Vernon's language elevates Prince Hal, at least temporarily, into the realm of the mythic; productions that focus on the gritty realities of war will have a hard time accommodating this speech. (The vaguely sexual nature of the language, with its comparisons to goats and bulls, may provide one alternative reading.) Vernon's classical tribute is unexpected and unwelcome to Hotspur, but he rises to the occasion with allusions of his own to Bellona and Mars. The further news of Glendower's delay impels Hotspur to a courage that could be seen as valiant, fatalistic, or even suicidal: he leaves to muster his armies with the line, 'Doomsday is near: die all die merrily.'

Act IV, scene ii

1–47 Falstaff is on the march with his ragged soldiers. This is another outdoor scene, this time given precise geographical placement. Falstaff and his men are in Warwickshire, approaching the town of Coventry; they will march through to Sutton Coldfield on their way northwest to Shrewsbury. Falstaff mentions that they have already been through St. Albans and Daventry. The plethora of place-names is striking in so short a scene, and gives dramatic concreteness to the soldiers' long march.

Falstaff's interaction with Bardolph demonstrates his gluttony, avarice and duplicity in quick succession: Sir John dupes his lieutenant into refilling his bottle of sack at Bardolph's own expense, using a play on words to evade responsibility for the costs he has already incurred. In a prose soliloquy, his longest speech of the play, Falstaff details how he has 'misused the King's press damnably' in accepting bribes to release well-to-do soldiers from service, conscripting instead a company of 150 ragged paupers. Falstaff outdoes himself in describing both the cowardly 'toasts and butter' who have bought their way out of service, and the 'slaves as ragged as Lazarus' who have been forced to replace them. His account of the poor soldiers can come across as either funny or alarming, though his report about 'a mad fellow' accusing him of impressing corpses from gibbets has an almost irresistible horror to it, suggesting a Bosch-like nightmare. Do Falstaff's soldiers actually appear onstage? If so, they could suggest either comic decrepitude or abject misery. Whether the soldiers appear or not (and on Shakespeare's stage they probably didn't), the scene's mixture of comedy and corruption anticipates the more fully-developed recruiting scenes of *Part II*, and their successors in such plays as Fahrquhar's *The Recruiting Officer* and Brecht's *Mother Courage*.

48–80   Hal and Westmorland hasten Falstaff towards the battle, and provide a pragmatic assessment of the recruits' unworthiness for military service. Falstaff's response, lines 64–6, is so astringently cynical that it could be read as a critique of the whole military enterprise: the men are 'good enough to toss, food for powder'; they'll 'fill a pit as well as better'. Falstaff's attitude is monstrous, and can be played as such; but it also, in a Brechtian way, exposes the ideological underpinnings of conscription and armed combat. *All* foot soldiers are, in a sense, food for powder, and Hal and Westmorland may not have any nobler concern for their troops than Falstaff does for his. On the other hand, this episode may give Hal an opportunity to distance himself from his corrupt companion through an attitude of grave disapproval. This scene is filled with sharp humour and can get its fair share of laughs, but it has a mordant, bitter edge.

Act IV, scene iii

A quarrel over strategy among the rebels is interrupted by Sir Walter Blunt, representing the King's forces in a parley. Hotspur details the rebels' grievances in a long and angry speech, rehearsing much of the action of *Richard II* and the early part of *Part I*. The scene takes place at the rebel camp near Shrewsbury; if the camp was represented scenically in IV.i, that setting may be repeated here. The number of relatively short scenes in Acts IV and V would have required a lot of coming and going on the Elizabethan stage. Probably, as Falstaff delivered his closing couplet of IV.ii to the audience and made his way to one of the upstage doors, the other door was already opening and the rebel captains were bursting in, in mid-argument.

1–31   The scene begins dramatically *in medias res*, with the rebel leaders already in vigorous disagreement over their strategy for fighting the king. In the opening speeches, Shakespeare uses shared verse lines, distributed among the four captains, to evoke a quarrel that has already passed the bounds of civility and become a shouting match. Hotspur and Douglas, the more bellicose party, begin the lines, with the more reluctant Worcester and Vernon shouting them down. These two shared lines, like most in the quarrel, are strongly end-stopped, and the short words and strong stresses give the whole exchange passion and punch. The pragmatic Worcester finally reduces things to their very simplest form, perhaps over-stressing his words as though talking to a child: 'The number of the King exceedeth our.'

32–53   At this point '*The trumpet sounds a parley*', the first of several military horn calls in the play, part of a communications code that might well have been intelligible to many in the Elizabethan audience, who had done service in the Low Countries or elsewhere. Sir Walter Blunt enters, and Hotspur speaks graciously to him, but Blunt maintains a tough stance against the rebels, though he indicates that the King is prepared to consider their grievances. In an earlier scene Blunt had spoken up in defense of Hotspur, and the actor might register some of that sympathy now in his voice or bearing; it is not wholly clear whether Blunt is speaking for himself or delivering a pre-scripted *communiqué* from the King.

54–107   Hotspur assumes the latter is the case, and in the first line of his response he mockingly says 'the King' twice as though he is addressing him formally in the third person. For the rest of his long speech he refuses to grant Henry this title, referring to him instead as 'a poor unminded outlaw sneaking home' and reserving the royal honorific for the deposed Richard. His speech relates many events from *Richard II*, and if that play has been staged along with *1 Henry IV*, audiences will have a chance to evaluate Hotspur's account of

Bolingbroke's behaviour based on their memories of the other performance.

Regardless, Hotspur's speech provides an alternative to King Henry's own recollections of his return to England, as detailed in III.ii of the present play. Hotspur's Henry more openly manipulates his adoring public, gauges his popularity, 'seems to weep/ Over his country's wrongs', wins the hearts 'of all that he did angle for', and proceeds to judicial murder, usurpation and regicide. How much Hotspur believes his own rhetoric, how far he can go in taking the high moral ground, is debatable; after all, one of his grievances is that he and his family helped Henry to the crown and are now insufficiently rewarded. After a list of his more immediate complaints – Mortimer's imprisonment, the Scottish prisoners, the dismissals of his father and uncle – Hotspur makes his way to the one point on which Henry is vulnerable: his title, perhaps 'Too indirect for long continuance.'

108–15 Blunt's dignity cools Hotspur down, and he defers his answer until the morning (effectively ending the quarrel over strategy with which the scene began). Blunt makes a final plea to Hotspur to accept the King's grace; if he has established a sympathetic relation to the young rebel, these final few lines of the scene can be charged with emotion. Hotspur relents slightly, in words that seem gentler than his previous utterances: 'And maybe so we shall.' Blunt completes his line with words that convey his earnestness and urgency, and the mortal threat of the battle to come: 'Pray God you do.'

Act IV, scene iv

1–41 This brief scene, the shortest in the play, is the only appearance of the Archbishop of York, who was supposed to be one of the key figures of the rebellion, and who becomes significant only in *Part II*. Scholars who argue that the two plays are part of a unified design contend that this scene is here to foreshadow the Archbishop's greater role in the latter play. IV.iv presumably occurs in the Archbishop's palace in York, and is important as the only scene that brings the Church into the play as a potentially consequential force (we learn in *Part II* that the Archbishop 'turns insurrection to religion' through his preaching). Accordingly, in performance this scene might feature some ecclesiastical trappings, such as a crucifix or altar, or at least the Archbishop's vestments.

The Archbishop of York is busily preparing for the failure of the rebels in the battle of Shrewsbury, which is to happen the next day; this scene serves partly to provide a break between the two parley scenes and to indicate the passage of time overnight. The Archbishop directs Sir Michael to bear letters to the Lord Marshall, Thomas Mowbray, and to others who will make up the second wave of rebellion in *Part II*. The chief purpose of the scene seems to be to enumerate the key players on both sides, and to cast doubt on the rebels' success. The Archbishop reminds us that neither Northumberland nor Glendower will be present, and names all of the characters who will fight on the King's side: the Prince, Lord John of Lancaster, Westmorland and Blunt. The scene functions as a kind of programme for the upcoming battle scenes, and a trailer for the second rebellion of *Part II*. It is very often cut in modern performances, especially if *Part I* is being performed alone.

ACT V

Act V, scene i

On the morning of the battle a second parley, this time between the King and Worcester, revisits again the causes for the rebellion. The Prince makes offer of a single combat with Hotspur, which the King forestalls; though he reiterates an offer of pardon to the rebels. Hal and Falstaff prepare for battle, the latter giving his thoughts on honor in an ironic 'catechism'.

1–29   The scene is again outdoors near Shrewsbury, this time perhaps in the King's camp; if so, some royal insignia may be displayed, and troops or supplies may be visible. The first lines of the scene demonstrate Shakespeare's method of establishing time and place through language. It is daybreak on the morning of the battle, and the King's opening words are both descriptive and figurative: 'How bloodily the sun begins to peer/ Above yon bosky hill!' Modern productions will probably make some attempt to recreate this effect through lighting, but Shakespeare's words do the work.

The parley begins civilly enough, as both the King and Worcester make reference to the incongruity of men their age wearing armour and leading troops, rather than enjoying 'quiet hours'. In urging obedience on Worcester, the King again invokes the astronomical metaphors that have been prevalent throughout the play. Hal had earlier conceived of himself as the sun hidden by clouds; Bolingbroke, in his rare public appearances, was wondered at like a comet; now Worcester is compared to a portentous meteor, and urged to return to his fixed orbit in the Ptolemaic cosmos that corresponds to the political order of England. How much such systems of metaphor can be picked up by an audience in performance is arguable: but the uneasy similarity of Bolingbroke-as-comet and Worcester-as-meteor might register for some.

At line 29, Falstaff intrudes into the conversation with a well-timed barb at Worcester. Though he is quickly silenced by the Prince, his interruption here shows his political brazenness; it may also remind the audience of Falstaff's discordance in the world the Prince is entering.

30–82 Worcester presents his version of the rebels' grievances, focusing on the aid the Percy family gave to Bolingbroke and the danger he now poses to them. He three times mentions an oath Bolingbroke allegedly swore to the Percies at Doncaster that he had no designs on the crown. This episode was not depicted in *Richard II*, in which Worcester never appeared, and in which Northumberland was a very active agent in helping Bolingbroke depose Richard. Nonetheless, the King does not really dispute Worcester's account; his response merely casts the rebels as agents of disorder, stirring up 'pell-mell havoc and confusion'. It must be determined in performance who has the high moral ground in this exchange: do Worcester's arguments undermine the King, or does he come across as merely a bitter old man acting out of his own sense of frustrated entitlement?

83–113 Prince Henry graciously acknowledges Hotspur's noble deeds, and admits he has 'a truant been to chivalry'. To spare bloodshed, he offers to resolve the conflict in single combat with Hotspur. He may, of course, be doing this for his father's benefit, knowing the offer will not be allowed to stand; this moment allows the actors of Hal and Henry to extend the relationship they developed in III.ii. Henry could pause teasingly before speaking, or after his first line, as though weighing the possibility of staking everything on Hal's chivalry; or he could reject the offer abruptly or even uncharitably. Henry seems finally to dismiss the notion of single combat, but makes an offer of pardon to the rebels if they will lay down their arms. At the close of his offer he displays a little of the political gamesmanship he showed in Act I, cutting off Worcester's response with 'We will not now be troubled with reply.' His decisive words reestablish his authority, but his final rallying cry, invoking the justice of his 'cause', may put the audience, or Hal, again in mind of his usurpation.

114–40 The coda to the scene has Hal and Falstaff preparing themselves for battle. After the tense political verse of the preceding scene, this quiet prose exchange allows the expression of genuine feeling, as Falstaff exposes his vulnerability: 'I would 'twere bedtime, Hal, and all well.' Hal could be tender, dismissive, or merely preoccupied in his response: 'Why, thou owest God a death.' At any rate, it is not the response Falstaff wanted to hear, and after Hal leaves the stage he launches into his most celebrated soliloquy, his interrogation of the concept of honour as a motive for mortal combat. Falstaff would have addressed the audience in an Elizabethan theatre, so his questions – 'Can honour set to a leg?' – could have been asked directly to individual spectators, who had their own opinions and might well have responded. His conclusions – that honour is simply a word, air, a trim reckoning – might have gone against Elizabethan ideology, but would no doubt have found many supporters among the groundlings, as they do in almost all theatres today. The speech builds through what Falstaff describes as a 'catechism' of rhetorical questions and blunt answers to its triumphant rejection of honour: 'Therefore I'll none of it.' In spite of his scruples, however, Falstaff proceeds to the battle.

Act V, scene ii

Worcester and Vernon agree not to tell Hotspur of the King's offer of pardon. Vernon describes the Prince's offer of single combat in glowing terms, to the extent that Hotspur's jealousy is roused. Hotspur makes a brief exhortation to his comrades, and they go off to the battle.

The scene occurs in or near the rebel camp, like IV.i and IV.iii. The two doors of the Elizabethan stage might have been localized to the extent that the rebels always came and went from one side, the King and his forces from the other. The battle scenes of *Richard III* are located in this way, with Richard and Richmond's 'tents' on opposite sides of the stage. It is just as likely, however, that the alternating scenes merely entered from whichever door was available, coming and going swiftly as the battle approached.

1–40 Worcester's unwillingness to convey the King's offer of pardon to Hotspur can be played at least two ways, and its impact differs depending on whether the two parts of *Henry IV* are played together. On the one hand, Worcester can be ungrateful and untrusting, a man so corrupt that he can't believe in good faith in others. He even seems to resent and belittle Hotspur's good reputation, and effectively to condemn him to death in consequence. On the other hand, his Machiavellian assessment of the place of former rebels in a government is apt, 'For treason is but trusted like the fox.' And if *Part II* is performed, the fate of the Gaultree rebels will seem to vindicate Worcester's scruples, and justify his reluctance to put his trust in the King's 'grace'.

41–74 Vernon resumes his habit of earnestly praising the Prince of Wales, describing how 'modestly' he challenged Hotspur with a 'princely tongue', recalling his 'blushing cital of himself', and concluding with praise of him as England's hope. As in IV.i, Vernon's language is so fervid that the audience may tend to concur with Hotspur's response: 'Cousin, I think thou are enamorèd/ On his follies.' Regardless, Vernon's speech is a necessary stage in the restoration of Hal's reputation, and a reminder to the audience of his future successful kingship. It may give Hotspur momentary pause before he resumes his dismissal of the Prince. Hotspur himself flirts with a kind of battlefield homoeroticism in his pledge to 'embrace' Hal 'with a soldier's arm'. Hotspur and Hal never meet until their fatal duel in the penultimate scene of the play, and their lines there suggest it is the first time they have ever laid eyes on each other; but they speak about each other in nearly every scene in which they appear. Depending on how the actors play these moments, they can convey the sense of an emotionally charged and dynamic relationship between two men who are strangers, rivals and mortal enemies. Shakespeare will develop something similar with Coriolanus and Aufidius much later in his career (see *Coriolanus* I.x, IV.v).

75–100   Turning to his comrades, Hotspur excuses his inabilities as an orator, before making one of the most memorable battle orations in Shakespeare. His observation that 'the time of life is short' recalls the theme of time that has been woven through the play since the second scene. The rhetorical grandeur of line 85 suggests a ringing confidence, although Hotspur could be played at this moment as a man who knows he is doomed. The Percy motto, '*Esperance!*' means hope, but whether Hotspur is upbeat or fatalistic, an elated pregame athlete or a dead-eyed berserker, is to be determined by the actor in performance. His speech calls for dramatic stage action: he draws his sword at line 92, perhaps followed by his men; he calls for trumpets and drums at line 97; and the speech ends with embraces as the rebels part for the final time before battle.

Act V, scene iii

1–29   The Quarto and Folio texts make this scene continuous with the last, though editors since the eighteenth century have marked a new scene here. The stage direction '*The King enters with his power. Alarum to the battle*' indicates some formal establishment of the battle sequence beyond what is demanded by the play's action, since the scene opens with Blunt and Douglas. A military procession with supernumerary soldiers, drawn weapons, fluttering pennons, and trumpets and drums would have made an impressive spectacle on the stage of the Theatre; modern theatres often create an analogous effect with amplified explosions, strobe lighting and machine-made smoke.

The King's stratagem to have 'many marching in his coats' is well documented in Holinshed and elsewhere, and was not unusual military practice; nonetheless, it may cast some doubt on Henry's heroism and reinforce audience perceptions of him as a Machiavellian schemer. The audience may, in fact, mistake Blunt for Henry for the first few moments of the scene, or even until Hotspur identifies the body at line 20. Blunt gains stature from the dignity with which he fulfils his kingly role, even to the death. However, Douglas's frustration can easily lead the scene toward humour, especially if, as is often the case, his Scots accent and dress are broadly marked. His anger against the King's 'coats', and his threat to 'murder all his wardrobe' are certainly comic.

30–61   Falstaff enters, exhausted from the battle and alarmed for his own safety. His discovery of the dead Sir Walter seems to confirm his previous doubts about the value of honour. The sounds of battle probably continue around him as he prays to God to 'keep lead out of me'. He reports (with what emotions?) that he has led his 'ragamuffins' to their deaths, though under what circumstances is not clear. His actions could be interpreted as selfless heroism or deliberate murder, but probably fall somewhere in between.

Falstaff hears someone coming, and is relieved to find that it is Hal. Hal's focus is on the battle, and he twice asks Falstaff to lend a sword. Falstaff, buying time, brags of brave deeds, and offers his pistol case to Hal by way of a joke. When '*The Prince draws it out and finds it to be a bottle of sack*', it is clear that the two can find no common ground in the crisis: the Prince rebukes Falstaff and returns to the fight. Falstaff, in soliloquy, musters some courage, but makes it clear that the battle must come to him; he will not seek it. Calling the audience's attention to Blunt's rigid corpse, he rejects the 'grinning honour' Sir Walter has found. He will save his own life if he can, and he exits the stage, presumably heading away from the battle.

Act V, scene iv

The battle gives Hal the opportunity to redeem himself in the eyes of his father: he saves the King from Douglas, then defeats Hotspur in single combat, as he had earlier wished and promised to do. This victory, and the presumed death of Falstaff, leaves Hal bereft of two of the formative influences of his life: he goes forward alone to his new role as the future king. Falstaff's resurrection disconcerts Hal and reminds the audience of the inevitability of a break between them.

1–58   The battle is now reaching its height, marked by stage effects – '*Alarum. Excursions*' – movements of soldiers, sounds of cannon, etc., and possibly the business of removing Blunt. If his body remains onstage, unnoticed by the entering King and his party, it contributes to the overall sense of a violent and costly conflict.

The King and his troops are stained from combat; Hal is wounded and his face is probably covered with blood. Holinshed records that the Prince was wounded in the face by an arrow, and Hal had earlier promised to wear 'a bloody mask'. He refuses offers of help, eager to return to the fighting, but pauses long enough to praise his brother, Lord John of Lancaster, who makes his first significant appearance in this scene. He will be a decisive player in *Part II*, more through policy than through the valour he displays here. Douglas enters, having finally found the real King after killing at least two of his substitutes; there may be a note of comedy in their exchange. The King is clearly bested in their fight, but Hal enters and drives off Douglas. Father and son have a tense and probably emotional moment together, as Henry acknowledges his son's rescue of him and Hal, perhaps with some resentment, defends his conduct and his motives.

59–76   As the King leaves by one door, Hotspur enters by another; probably Hal has his back to him at first (the moment resembles the 'Turn, hellhound, turn' confrontation of Macbeth and Macduff, *Macbeth* V.viii.3). They exchange single, near-formal lines of challenge; then Hal makes explicit what both have long recognized, that England isn't big enough for the both of them. Hotspur gloats briefly over his greater military reputation, perhaps rousing Hal to fury. There are several points in *Part I* where Hal might show sudden anger, anticipating his father's description of him in *Part II*: 'being incensed, he is flint.' Here, he throws himself into the combat. How long and skillful the fight is will vary from production to production. Shakespeare's actors were practiced swordsmen and his audience connoisseurs of the art; the duel might have been a virtuoso display. From a realistic perspective, of course, both Hal and Hotspur are exhausted at the end of a long battle, and if they are fighting in plate armour with broadswords, the fight will be a painful and heavy affair rather than a swashbuckling duel.

Strikingly, Shakespeare divides the audience's attention even during this climactic combat. Douglas enters and fights with Falstaff, '*who falls down as if he were dead*'. Any production must make choices as to what the audience is supposed to be watching at each moment, and exactly what they are supposed to see. Is the audience meant to believe Falstaff is actually killed? Or are they allowed to watch a comic pratfall? Does the faked death occur while the audience is focused on a key moment of the Hal/Hotspur fight, so that they never notice Falstaff fall?

77–110   Regardless, the end of the fight is the climax of the play, and will necessarily reclaim focus. As Hal is the underdog, he might be initially at a disadvantage, and then win through a final surge of effort. Perhaps Hotspur's confident bravado causes him to leave himself momentarily exposed. Whatever the fatal blow, the speeches afterwards are crucial. They will be a physical challenge for the actors, winded from the fight and probably kneeling on the stage. Hotspur begins, characteristically, thinking of his lost honours, but soon moves to metaphysical reflections on time and life, and tantalizingly threatens to prophesy before his breath runs out. What would his prophecy concern? The resurgent rebellion of *Part II*? Or perhaps Hal's future as Henry V? Unable to speak further, Hotspur dies in mid-line, after declaring himself 'dust, /And food for – '. After seven beats of silence, indicated by the incomplete verse line, Hal finishes the thought: 'For worms, brave Percy.' Olivier, whose Hotspur stammered on 'w' sounds, was unable to say 'worms', and Hal had to give the word for him. Even without such a gimmick, Hal's completion of Hotspur's final sentence is a magnanimous gesture and a moving moment on stage. The simple, monosyllabic valediction – 'Fare thee well, great heart' – overweighs the sanctimonious lines about 'ill-weaved ambition' that follow. Hal probably lowers Hotspur's body to the ground, and uses some part of his own costume to cover his face.

As he stands up, he notices Falstaff. His reaction to the apparent death of his friend is critical to the audience's final assessment of Prince Hal in this play. Is he able easily to dismiss his companion? Does he force himself to deny feelings of loss? His speech contains at least three conscious jokes about Falstaff's fatness ('all this flesh', 'a heavy miss', 'so fat a deer'). Several of his lines, however, could also contain deep feeling. Hal's mixed emotions are possibly best expressed in the line, 'I could have better spared a better man.' When he leaves the stage, he thinks, and perhaps the audience thinks, that he is leaving a part of his life behind him. If *Part I* is performed alone, his departure here marks a critical and final change in his relationship with Falstaff.

110–28   'Falstaff *riseth up*.' This may be a sudden and surprising resurrection, or Falstaff may proceed slowly, first opening his eyes to make sure he is unobserved, then beginning the laborious process of getting himself to his feet. He can't take too long, however, as his line must follow Hal's in fairly quick succession for its full effect. This moment represents Falstaff's greatest triumph; for the end of *Part I*, at any rate, he has managed to defeat death. His contention (lines 119–20) that 'The better part of valour is discretion' is likely to win over even the most disapproving audience members. His wounding of the dead Hotspur in the thigh, however, may be either comically macabre or morally shocking: Falstaff challenges the audience's sensibilities yet again.

129–63 When the Prince reenters, he must convey a complex mixture of emotions on seeing Falstaff again alive. Is he overjoyed, disappointed, or perhaps angry that he has made himself emotionally vulnerable over a fraud? His attitude as he listens to Falstaff's tale, and as he agrees to support Falstaff's claim of killing Percy, will reveal much about Hal's changing relationship to his friend. Falstaff's exit – carrying Hotspur on his back – is likely to be a rather grotesque spectacle, though it may be comic as well.

Act V, scene v

The King's forces have prevailed; Worcester and Vernon are sent to execution, while Hal enlarges the Douglas as a chivalrous gesture. The King splits his forces to confront the remaining rebels, ending the play with victory, but with future conflicts in mind.

The play's brief concluding scene probably demands a final tableau, with the King's power assembled and in control of the battlefield, and Prince Hal occupying a new position of authority by his father's side. However, the amount of battlefield debris that remains from previous scenes, and the level of combat fatigue and injury evinced by Henry's troops, can undermine the sense of victory and call attention to the problems the King has yet to face.

1–16 King Henry starts the scene with high-handed moralizing – 'Thus ever did rebellion find rebuke' – choosing to forget the better success of his own rebellion. His chiding of Worcester for not bearing his offer of pardon may be motivated by genuine grief at the resultant loss of life on both sides, but Worcester may well win this final round through his steady dignity. The King's execution of Vernon, who has served mainly as spokesman for Prince Hal's virtues, may come across as overly harsh. How the prisoners are treated, and how they comport themselves, as they are led off to their deaths can have a good deal of influence on the audience's perception of the play's conclusion.

17–44   The Prince counters his father's severity through his plan to release Douglas without ransom. Shakespeare conceals the nature of Douglas's injuries – Holinshed reports that he 'brake one of his cullions' (testicles) – perhaps out of decorum toward the Prince's gesture. The Prince speaks in language of heraldic dignity, calling both Douglas and Percy 'noble' and referring to the 'valours' and 'high deeds' of his adversaries. The text does not call for Falstaff to be present: the Prince, for the purposes of this play, has cast off his past and realigned himself with the values of chivalry and royalty.

The impact of the ending may depend much on whether *Part II* is also to be performed. If it isn't, then the victory at Shrewsbury and the reformation of the Prince may come across as more conclusive. If it is, this ending may have something of a 'To be continued' quality about it. The King's final lines refer to his remaining enemies, Northumberland and the Archbishop on the one hand and Glendower and Mortimer on the other. Rather than dwell too much on his present victory, the King must divide his power to deal with these remaining threats.

The final effect, of course, can vary from production to production depending on the overall interpretation of the play. The natural imperative toward narrative closure, the decisive nature of the final combat, and the stately language of the King and Prince can certainly create a sense of victory achieved and order secured. The Prince has risen to his personal challenge, 'redeeming time' as he has promised throughout the play that he would. On the other hand, the distasteful aftermath of Hotspur's death, and Falstaff's renewed position in consequence, slightly sully Hal's ostensible reformation. For his part, the King has temporarily won victory by force of arms, but hasn't answered any of the charges levied by the rebels about his unjust title, or assuaged any of the guilt of his opening soliloquy. The King's two closing couplets ring with confidence, but the bearing of the actors, the manner of their exit, and the final tableau of the battlefield may erode this sense of closure and remind the audience of the painful costs of civil war – the images with which the play began.

Henry IV: Part II

Induction

1–40 Who or what is Rumour? The prologue figure was probably, in Shakespeare's theatre, a single actor in some sort of allegorical costume, grotesquely 'painted full of tongues' (such personages appeared in various Tudor pageants). Rumour could be an actor who is about to take another role in the play, perhaps related to the ideas expressed in the Induction. Lord Bardolph, who begins the play's action with a false report, would be a likely candidate. Prince Hal, who both suffers from and manipulates the vicissitudes of public opinion, might be another. In modern productions, when the Induction is included (it often isn't), it may be shared among members of the company; there might also be shifting tableaux illustrating the various events recounted, true and false.

Rumour begins aggressively, with a command to the audience. His opening words emphasize his universal power and influence, encompassing the whole world with 'continual slanders' in 'every language'. His language is grand and confident, but assumes a tone of menace by lines 9–10, with sinister sibilants and cynical alliteration. He may take a confrontational tone with regard to the audience, whom he addresses as his own 'household'. His references to 'the blunt monster', the wavering public, are filled with contempt.

At line 22, he begins to explain his presence, first recounting the true events of Shrewsbury, then the false report that will reach Northumberland. He speaks disdainfully of Northumberland's castle ('this worm-eaten hold') and impugns the integrity of his character ('crafty-sick'); both images create a feeling of disease and corruption. Rumour's final lines, rhyming and balanced, but harshly paradoxical, set the tone for a disorienting scene of 'smooth comforts false'.

ACT I

Act I, scene i

The opening scene extends the sense of sickness, haste and confusion established in the Induction. In rapid succession, Northumberland gets false good news, uncertain alarming news, and certain, crushingly bad news. The second half of the scene is animated by a new urgency – at first desperate and feverish, then increasingly confident – as the rebels gather their energies for a new revolt.

1–59 The setting, Northumberland's castle, has been established by Rumour. The stage directions in the 1600 Quarto (hereafter Q) indicate that Lord Bardolph enters by one door, the Porter at another; a third entrance, perhaps the central opening, seems to be indicated by the Porter's reference to an orchard gate (line 5). The scene begins, strikingly, with three questions, establishing a mood of uncertainty. There are 16 questions asked in the first 67 lines of the scene, before Northumberland ascertains the fates of his son and brother. The sense of confusion is perhaps not alleviated by the fact that Lord Bardolph, introduced by name in line 3, shares that name with one of the low-life tavern figures from *Part I*, who will turn up only a few scenes later.

Northumberland makes a striking, almost emblematic figure of sickness, with a crutch and a nightcap; his demeanour may or many not corroborate Rumour's suggestion that his sickness is a sham. His opening lines conjure a violent image of civil war as a runaway horse, reinforcing the haste and confusion of the Induction. Lord Bardolph's confident reply fleshes out the false exposition given by Rumour, adding numerous circumstantial details, including one true one – Blunt's death at the hands of Douglas. Northumberland responds with three more questions (lines 23–4), perhaps betraying doubts about Lord Bardolph's report. The arrival of Travers further erodes the false comforts. His speech, filled with hard-spurring riders and panting, bloodied horses, builds the scene's atmosphere of breathless alarm. Lord Bardolph's pompous certainty provides for a few moments of mild comedy, as he glibly offers to give his barony 'for a silken point' and dismisses the 'hilding fellow' who brought the bad news.

60–135 The appearance of Morton establishes the grimness of the real situation. Northumberland's speeches give precise clues to Morton's behaviour, both in their grave and measured cadences, and in details of expression and gesture: a furrowed brow like a wrinkled seashore, a white cheek, trembling, sighing, shaking the head. These speeches both delay and magnify the bad news, invoking the image of Priam awakened at the fall of Troy. Northumberland protracts the moment still further, begging at line 93 to be spared the report of his son's death. His speech concludes with the onomatopoeic, echoing tones of a 'sullen bell ... tolling' Hotspur's end.

Morton's thirty-line account of events at Shrewsbury begins with Hotspur's death, but concentrates on the demoralizing influence this had on the rebel troops, and on their subsequent flight. Again, images of haste are prevalent, as the panicked soldiers fly like arrows. Morton ends with the news that 'a speedy power' is on its way to encounter Northumberland, injecting an immediate urgency into the mournful tone of the previous 75 lines.

136–60 Northumberland then undergoes a striking transformation that serves as the hinge point of the scene. The paradox he expresses in lines 137–9 may be merely a rationalization, if he has in fact been shamming illness. But the image that follows, of the fever-weakened wretch suddenly breaking 'like a fire/ Out of his keeper's arms', has visceral power; and the dynamic gesture of throwing away the crutch and coif is a potent visual emblem. The lines that follow explode with passion, in short, choppy imperatives that threaten the very destruction of the earth. His language mixes the harsh realities of war – a scaly gauntlet, joints of steel, brows bound with iron – with universal personifications of Time, Spite, Nature and Order. His repeated use of the rare third-person imperative, borrowed from Biblical Greek – 'Let Order die' – gives his speech oracular weight. Northumberland's outcry takes on cosmic dimensions, expressing a cataclysmic nihilism closer to the world of *King Lear* than to the history plays. The final image, recalling *Lear*'s great stage of fools, is one of theatre as a spectacle of the apocalypse.

161–215 His comrades recognize the incongruity of his 'strainèd passion', and urge him to wisdom and fortitude in seeing the rebellion through. Northumberland remains silent until the end of the scene, as Morton and Lord Bardolph counsel him to accept the loss of Hotspur as 'th'event of war' and to prepare for the next phase. Their measured, rational arguments contrast with Northumberland's apocalyptic vision. Lord Bardolph's image of a merchant on a commercial voyage – he uses the verb 'venture' three times – turns family tragedy and destructive war into a calculated matter of risk and profit. Morton invokes the moral authority they will gain from the Archbishop, and calls attention to the semantics of political action. His observation that the very word 'rebellion' made Hotspur's soldiers fight with 'queasiness, constrained' smacks of modern spin doctoring, though his image of fish frozen in a pond is eerie and apt. Morton's triumphant assertion that the Bishop 'Turns insurrection to religion' – a single, paradoxical verse line of breathtaking cynicism – would surely have raised a moral alarm in an Elizabethan audience. The 'supposed' sincerity of the Archbishop (line 202) subtly undermines Morton's rallying speech, which nonetheless effectively deploys the rhetoric of a bleeding land, a heaven-sanctioned quarrel, and, most importantly, the blood of Richard II, 'scraped from Pomfret stones'. The events of *Richard II* weigh much more insistently on *Part II* than on *Part I*; this image sets in motion an obsessive pattern of recollection and even direct quotation.

When and how Northumberland is brought to focus on the task at hand depends on the actor, but his final lines suggest a new urgency in their project of 'safety and revenge'. His final few lines are all imperatives, short and purposeful commands that finish the scene with energy and propel the play toward a new conflict.

Act I, scene ii

Falstaff appears, his purse and his health having declined since *Part I*. He encounters the Lord Chief Justice, who will be his opposite throughout the play. Trading on the false report of his valour at Shrewsbury, be evades immediate censure, but he will plainly need all of his wits to maintain his standing in the difficult world of *Part II*.

1–53   The scene opens with a visual joke, as the huge Falstaff and his diminutive Page enter together. Falstaff may be limping, from the gout or pox, in which case his entry echoes and parodies the earlier one of Northumberland with his crutch. Q specifies that the Page bears his 'sword and buckler', perhaps as an advertisement for Falstaff's heroism at Shrewsbury; if the weapons are large and ungainly they offer a further opportunity for physical comedy.

With the exchange about Falstaff's 'water', Shakespeare achieves the difficult feat of opening a scene with two successive laugh lines.

The humour is of a rather low sort, and picks up the idea of disease that has been present from the beginning of the play; in the modern theatre the Page sometimes has Falstaff's urine sample with him. Falstaff embarks on a characteristic speech, filled with parallel phrases, rhythmic movement and surprising changes of direction; as in *Part I*, he speaks prose almost exclusively throughout the play. This speech, though addressed to the Page, may also be directed partly to the audience, whom Falstaff seems to chide for laughing at his girth. Yet he transforms his resentment into a kind of self-glorifying pride (lines 9–10). The physical difference between himself and the Page feeds Falstaff's imagination, inspiring colourful comparisons: a sow and a piglet, a mandrake, a tiny jewel. His thoughts flit from one idea to another, often led by plays on words: 'jewel/juvenal', 'royal' in relation to both kings and coins, 'grace' as both an honorific and as personal favour. By line 19, however, Falstaff's thoughts all revolve around the Prince. While grumbling about Hal as a beardless and thoughtless youth – a pose familiar from *Part I* – Falstaff may reveal anxieties about their future relationship.

His question to the Page about an order for satin leads to an out-burst against tradesmen for demanding 'security'; evidently Falstaff's prodigality has run him into debt. The tirade reveals Falstaff's pen-chant for citing scripture – he invokes Dives and Achitophel within two lines – and his withering sarcasm. Through five repetitions of 'security', he gives the word the character of an obscenity, and he ends by impugning Master Dommelton as a cuckold in a compli-cated play on 'horn', 'lightness', and 'lantern/lanthorn'. The refer-ence to Bardolph in Smithfield is another straightforward set-up for Falstaff's wit, providing him with a satisfying if heavy-handed play on a proverbial warning to gullible Londoners.

54–90 Suddenly a worthy opponent appears. The Page spies the Lord Chief Justice, with a servant, entering upstage. His costume and bearing will identify him as a person of stature and a major new figure in the play; his robes also mark him as a personification of the Law. On the Elizabethan stage, the two pairs of characters would initially be far enough apart for them to carry on independent paral-lel conversations. The Page alludes to the story, not dramatized by Shakespeare but important to the play, that the Lord Chief Justice imprisoned Prince Hal for striking him. Falstaff at first tries to avoid him; the spectacle of a very fat man trying to slip away unnoticed provides easy humour, but also registers Falstaff's attitude to law, which will eventually lead to his downfall. Falstaff's quick stratagem of feigning deafness adds to the comedy, as does his unwarranted belligerence to the servant who tries to accost him. This exchange reveals Falstaff's mastery of the aggressive rhetorical question (lines 71–3), his amoral attitude toward the rebellion (lines 73–7), his opportunistic wit (line 79), his willingness to pull rank (lines 80, 86–7), and finally, his physical cowardice (lines 87–9).

91–121 When the Lord Chief Justice addresses Falstaff directly and unavoidably, however, he instantly changes his attitude to one of unctuous bonhomie. The repeated 'your lordships' quickly become patronizing, as does the feigned concern with the Justice's health. In addressing the Justice as though a vigorous young man were speaking to a weak old one, Falstaff repeats the posture he took against the victims of the Gad's Hill robbery in *Part I*. Whether this posture is purely a conscious rhetorical game, or reflects some self-deception on Falstaff's part, is up to the actor.

When the Justice attempts to confront him about Gad's Hill, Falstaff employs another strategy he will use throughout the scene; simply refusing to heed the person speaking, and carrying on an entirely different conversation from the one his interlocutor wishes to initiate. After successfully deflecting the Justice's conversational thrusts four times, Falstaff seems to leave himself exposed by characterizing the King's apoplexy as 'a kind of deafness'. Seizing the opportunity with some wit, the Justice accuses Falstaff of just such a disease – but Falstaff is too quick for him. He ends this round of conflict with a solid victory: he hears the Justice very well, but is troubled only by 'the disease of not listening'.

122–76 For the next ten speeches, Falstaff uses another characteristic approach; taking his opponent's words, turning them around and throwing them back at him. He mocks the justice's metaphor of being an administering physician, punning on two senses of the word 'patient'. He then converts the Justice's language of law to his own defense. He plays on the word 'great', transforming a moral observation, as he often does, into a joke about his own fatness. The double inversion of lines 139–42 is almost too easy, and after sustaining one more direct rebuttal, the Chief Justice withdraws from the field. Evidently the story of Falstaff's valour at Shrewsbury has had enough currency to cancel out the Gad's Hill robbery; the Lord Chief Justice gives up on prosecuting the crimes of the past. His attempts to advise Falstaff about appropriate behaviour for his age meets with no more success, as Falstaff fends off every overture with wordplay, the most egregious being that on 'gravity' and 'gravy'. His next long speech leads Falstaff into a nexus of double meanings involving coins, weight, and value that few audiences will follow; but the general gist, that true valour such as Falstaff's is unregarded in 'these costermonger's times', is clear enough. It is an attitude familiar from *Part I*, when Falstaff claimed there were but 'three good men' left in England. He leaves this melancholy vein at line 172 by again asserting his prerogatives of youth against the Chief Justice's age.

177–226 The Lord Chief Justice responds with incredulity and considerable wit, elucidating 'the characters of age' as they appear in Falstaff using a series of short parallel phrases, often antithetical: 'a decreasing leg, an increasing belly'. His exasperation is apparent in the repeated 'fie' with which he concludes; but on the whole he has been more successful than most of Falstaff's opponents. Falstaff's reply undercuts him with a polite 'My lord' and a disarming picture of an infant Sir John, white beard, round belly and all. After further asserting his youth – while saying that he will not – Falstaff seems to take the Lord Chief Justice's part in his quarrel with the Prince, adopting a posture of mediation and reconcilement, though not without a final playful pun on 'sack'. The Justice, accepting that Hal and Falstaff will be separated by the wars, changes the subject to military matters, giving Falstaff one more opportunity for mock-heroic self-aggrandizement. On the one hand, he has no wish to sweat in battle; on the other, he contends that his reputation for valour puts him at the center of every 'dangerous action'. In lines that appear only in Q (213–19), he laments the English habit of making good things common, and regrets that his name is 'so terrible to the enemy'. Ironically, his reputation does turn out to be effective in combat, at least with the rebel Coleville in IV.iii.

227–48 After refusing to give a loan of a thousand pounds – the same sum Falstaff later borrows from Justice Shallow – the Lord

Chief Justice exits, having maintained some dignity throughout the scene. Falstaff, discovering the advanced state of his 'consumption of the purse,' dispatches the Page with various letters, some of them presumably angling for money (the letter to the Prince will be read aloud in II.ii). As he starts to exit, Falstaff winces and limps – his big toe suffers from the gout or pox. This final speech can be played a couple of different ways. It could show the irrepressible power of Falstaff's wit, able to turn any situation to advantage. But if the actor wants to show Sir John as coming down in the world – through age and sickness, cynicism and corruption – these final lines provide ideal material, as Falstaff vows to 'turn diseases to commodity'.

Act I, scene iii

The rebel leaders evaluate their chances, reckoning their troop strength and considering the uncertainty of Northumberland's aid. As in the previous scene, their attitudes range from rational caution, here voiced by Lord Bardolph, to passionate exclamation, expressed in the Archbishop's contempt for the wavering public. Though hardly of one mind, the rebels decide to press on in their attempt.

1–62 The staging, like many of the political scenes in both plays, seems relatively straightforward: a group of men stand on the stage and deliver verse speeches to one another. There are no indications of place, no necessary props or implied stage action. The Archbishop probably enters first, and in his robes of office he presents a striking figure. The incongruity of his appearance with his role as a rebel leader is discussed throughout the play, by his friends and foes alike. He speaks first in the scene, seeming to chair the meeting, but then is mostly silent as the other lords give their opinions on the prospects for the rebellion.

Two of these lords are new characters, Hastings and Mowbray; the latter is never identified by name, so his connection to the banished Mowbray of *Richard II* remains unexpressed in this scene. Lord Bardolph is plainly the most cautious of the four, invoking judgment and certainty, rejecting hope and promise. It is ironic, given his rumour-mongering role in I.i, that he warns against 'conjecture, expectation and surmise' so vigorously here; that irony may or may not be apparent to an audience, but he is unlikely to inspire much confidence as a rebel leader. He dismisses Hotspur contemptuously as a kind of madman, 'eating the air' and 'flatt'ring himself' in suicidal delusions. Lord Bardolph's image of rebellion as an architectural project exemplifies his rational pragmatism, his insistence on a 'sure foundation' for their enterprise. This complex metaphor, extended for twenty lines, suspends the action of the scene; most of it is cut in Q, and many modern productions follow this lead. Nonetheless it is a vivid image, and concludes with a memorable picture of the half-completed building standing exposed to 'churlish winter's tyranny'.

63–110 Hastings eagerly encourages his fellows, reminding them (and the audience) that the King must divide his forces against multiple threats, as the end of *Part I* showed. The Archbishop casts the deciding vote for proceeding with the rebellion. His assertion that public opinion has turned against Henry IV turns into a scathing attack on the fickle populace, recalling Rumour's contempt for 'the still-discordant wavering multitude.' The Archbishop characterizes the public, which has come to regret its rejection of King Richard, as a dog eating its own vomit. This ugly image anchors a lengthy apostrophe that the actor might well deliver directly to the theatre audience. The scathing vitriol that the Archbishop unleashes may alarm or inspire his comrades, and may arouse discomfort or resentment in the audience. Regardless, the speech has the effect of bringing the events of *Richard II* forcefully back into the theatrical present. It animates the rebels, who leave the stage committed to action; they will not reappear until the encounter in Gaultree Forest in Act IV.

ACT II

Act II, scene i

Mistress Quickly attempts to have Falstaff arrested for debt. Despite the intervention of the Lord Chief Justice, Falstaff manages not only to avoid imprisonment, but to secure additional funds, as well as an evening in the tavern with the Hostess and Doll Tearsheet.

1–59 The aspersions cast on the common people at the end of the previous scene are perhaps borne out by the Londoners who begin II.i: the boisterous but pliable Hostess and 'an officer or two' (Q),

Fang and Snare. The lower worlds of *2 Henry IV* get much of their
local colour from the distinctive comic names of characters, both
seen and unseen. Here the names suggest not only the characters'
profession, but a degree of grotesquerie. Fang and Snare are probably not very impressive officers; indeed, Snare can't be found at the
beginning of the scene, and perhaps pops out from a stage curtain
or behind a pillar at the last moment. (It is possible that the original
Snare doubled one of the rebels in the previous scene, and needed a
moment for a quick costume change.) Their plans to arrest Falstaff
involve them all in a rich series of bawdy double entendres: words
like 'stand', 'enter', 'weapon', 'foin' and 'thrust' pile up rapidly in the
first twenty lines of the scene. The actors may reinforce some of
these with gestures, but it seems plain that the sexual meanings are
not consciously intended by the speakers, the Hostess in particular.
Her long speech beginning at line 22 represents her as a paragon of
wronged virtue and quivers with righteous indignation. Her zeal,
first expressed in misused and mangled words ('infinitive', 'continu-
antly', 'indited'), inevitably leads her to statements that can be taken
in a sexual sense – as when she declares that her 'case' is 'openly
known to the world'. Her emphatic triple repetitions ('borne,'
'fubbed off') make even relatively innocent words sound obscene,
and the use of the ethical dative rounds the speech off with the
unavoidably suggestive cry of 'do me, do me, do me your offices.'

Falstaff's entry provokes a sudden flurry of stage action, as the
officers attempt to grab him, Bardolph draws his sword, and even
the Page gets involved in some sort of physical fracas. The officers
call out for rescue, while the Hostess delivers shrill malapropisms
('thou honeysuckle villain!') and bursts of grunting dialect ('Thou
woo't, woo'ta?'), and even the diminutive Page shouts hilariously
inflated invective. Only the entry of the Lord Chief Justice contains
the farcical energy onstage.

60–133   The Justice makes an initial attempt to turn the conversation to serious political matters – Falstaff is supposed to be on his
way to York to join the royal forces – but he is soon drawn into medi-
ating the Hostess's quarrel. Given a platform, the Hostess reveals her
sentimental side, making it clear that Falstaff's breach of promise
means at least as much to her as his debts. In a long sentence full of
colourful circumstantial details, she asserts that he swore to marry
her (lines 84–90); and in a series of parallel questions, she adds

damning corroborative evidence (lines 90–100). The parcel-gilt goblet and the sea-coal fire might be figments of Quickly's romantic imagination; goodwife Keech's prawns might belong to another occasion; but the kiss followed by a request for thirty shillings is pure Falstaff. Faced with this accusation, Falstaff adroitly takes the Justice aside and tries to give him a stake in silencing Quickly; but he will have none of it. In balanced and dignified prose, the Justice insists on Falstaff's satisfying the Hostess; so Sir John has no recourse but to try his luck with her directly.

134–93   In the few moments it takes for the Lord Chief Justice to receive and read a letter delivered by Gower, Falstaff gets the better of the Hostess. Within three lines of stage time (lines 131–3), he has not only erased his debts, but prevailed on her for additional sums. Their body language while they talk aside should reveal something of the progress of the argument. The first few spoken lines show Falstaff soothing and cajoling; the Hostess protests momentarily ('Faith, you said so before') but she has, in effect, already yielded. Lines 128–9 show her trying to limit the damage she will incur in pawning her goods to meet Falstaff's wants. Falstaff, with some élan, tries to convince her that she will be keeping up with the fashion in parting with her plate and tapestries. When she protests, Falstaff shows his mastery of reverse psychology, threatening to walk out on the deal, at which point the Hostess is ready literally to give him the clothes off her back (line 156).

The Lord Chief Justice and Gower remind Falstaff, and the audience, of the ongoing rebellion and royal preparations to meet it. The short, pointed sentences, filled with names, places, and numbers of troops, change the scene's tone to one of military seriousness. Nonetheless, Falstaff's indignation at being shut out of the conversation, and his subsequent trick of flattering 'Master Gower' and ignoring the Lord Chief Justice, allow him to have the last laugh, if not the last word. Falstaff's fencing metaphor aptly characterizes his ongoing duel of wits with the Lord Chief Justice. Falstaff feels he has won this round, triumphing over both Hostess and Justice.

Act II, scene ii

In this scene Prince Hal appears for the first time in *Part II*, with his tavern-companion Ned Poins. Amid some sour jesting, the Prince reveals that though he is upset about his father's illness, he can't reveal his feelings for fear of being thought a hypocrite. Bardolph brings a letter from Falstaff that warns the Prince against Poins. Learning that Falstaff is in London, the Prince and Poins decide to disguise themselves and spy on him.

1–65 Like *Part I*, *Part II* introduces the Prince outside of his princely role, speaking prose in an informal setting with a friend. In this case the friend is Poins rather than Falstaff, and the tone of the scene is rather darker. Prince Hal announces that he is 'exceeding weary,' and his vocal quality and body language will likely reinforce this sense of ennui through much of the scene. Stools or other furniture may be useful for the lounging and slouching postures the language suggests. As in the equivalent scene of *Part I*, modern productions often use a tavern setting; though as before, the Prince and Poins are plainly not in the Boar's Head, as they plan to ambush Falstaff there that evening.

As the scene begins, the pair may be drinking 'small beer', playing cards, or engaging in other time-wasting activities. Poins twits the Prince with the inappropriateness of his behaviour for 'one of so high blood', and for the next several lines Hal reflects moodily on the baseness of his appetites, surroundings, and acquaintances, including Poins. In *Mimesis*, his classic 1946 study subtitled *The Representation of Reality in Western Literature*, Erich Auerbach makes 'The Weary Prince' the eponymous motif of his chapter on Shakespeare. Hal, jesting with Poins about foul linen and whores' bastards, exemplifies for Auerbach Shakespeare's mixture of styles, his insistent juxtaposition of the low, incongruous and grotesque with that which is lofty and consequential. Hal's language in this scene is daringly coarse, and his attitude to Poins, who 'for fault of a better' he calls his friend, distastefully cynical. The tone can vary in performance – the exchanges between the two might be played as light-hearted, brotherly banter – but there is an underlying seriousness to the scene, which soon emerges.

The King's sickness – an important motif in the play – has been mentioned once before, in passing, in I.ii. Here it is Poins who brings up the subject, though Hal may have been thinking of it already. Hal's response suggests that he wishes to confide in Poins but doesn't fully trust his attitudes on this subject. Has Poins insinuated, in asking about the King's illness, that Hal should be happy about it, as it brings him nearer to the crown? (There is a similar moment in *Antony and Cleopatra*, I.ii.168, when Enobarbus cynically rejoices over the death of Antony's wife Fulvia, assuming that Antony will be happy to be a widower.) Hal is guarded at first, speaking in the conditional about his feelings – he 'could be sad' – but there are moments where he seems to let genuine emotion through, saying his heart 'bleeds inwardly.' This inner pain may inflame his hostility toward 'such vile company' as Poins, although, as both recognize, expressing his sorrow would make Hal appear a 'princely hypocrite'. The original meaning of 'hypocrite' as an actor may not be irrelevant to this characterization of Hal, the player-king.

66–169   The entrance of Bardolph and the Page lightens the mood of the scene, and perhaps dissipates the tension that may have built up. The Page's precocious wit earns him some coins and laughter at the expense of Bardolph's face. Falstaff's letter, which the Prince reads aloud in a spirit of mockery (and probably with exaggerated imitations of Sir John), may touch a nerve in the Hal/Poins relationship, perhaps already strained. Has Poins, in fact, intended his sister for Hal? He denies it, but in production that denial may ring false; Hal's response to the suggestion, in turn, may indicate either resentment or affection. The Prince changes the subject to Falstaff, who is 'at the old place' in Eastcheap; Hal's reference to 'the old boar' probably alludes to the Boar's Head Tavern, established there since medieval times. The mention of Falstaff at the tavern, in company with Mistress Quickly and Doll Tearsheet, seems to reanimate Hal. For the remainder of the scene (lines 141–69), he speaks in eager questions and short, authoritative statements, his mood of melancholy apparently past as he plans a new trick on Falstaff. Poins's plan, to disguise themselves as drawers in order to spy on Falstaff, returns Hal to the reflections on social incongruity with which the scene began – 'from a prince to a prentice?' However, the jokes seem lighter now, punning questions with snappy rejoinders; and the Prince leaves the stage with eager energy, bidding Poins follow.

Act II, scene iii

In another scene with echoes of its counterpart in *Part I*, II.iii deals with the Percy family at home. It is now a desolate household,

haunted by the memory of the slain Hotspur, who is conjured up
in idealized form by his grieving widow. Persuaded by his wife and
daughter-in-law to abandon the rebellion, Northumberland resolves
to take refuge in Scotland.

1–45   If there are seats on the stage remaining from II.ii, they may
be used here by Northumberland or his wife; some scenic gesture
toward domesticity seems appropriate. The scene requires no
props, but some physical memento of Hotspur may be carried, or
even worn, by Lady Percy. As the scene begins, an argument has
apparently been going on for some time. Northumberland's lines 3
and 4 describe the angry faces the two women wear, and in her lines
Lady Northumberland seems to be abandoning the discussion in
frustration. After this stormy opening, Lady Percy launches into an
appeal to her father-in-law that mixes anxious pleading with grief,
resentment and blame. Her first line is a strong and simple plea. In
what follows, however, she insistently returns to Northumberland's
past fault in not supporting her husband. She describes Hotspur, in
a haunting detail, on the battlefield of Shrewsbury, throwing 'many
a northward look' in search of his father's help; the statement that
closes line 14 is stark and accusatory. Her discussion of the 'two
honours lost' at Shrewsbury dismisses Northumberland's in a single
line; she then spends fourteen lines glorifying her husband. His
honour is like the sun, an image associated with royalty throughout
the tetralogy; he is a mirror to noble youth, who imitate his gait and
speech. She describes him as 'speaking thick', probably meaning
rapidly and impulsively – a detail often used to characterize Hotspur
in *Part I*. Even this apparent defect adds to the luster of her idealized
portrait, which gets its rhetorical payoff at lines 32–3.

Having built up this shining image of her slain husband, she
swings the speech around to attack her father-in-law for abandoning
Hotspur. Repeating 'him' three times, interspersed with hyperbolic
exclamations – 'O miracle of men!' – she finally gets to the subject
of the sentence: 'him did you leave ….' Her damning accusation
gains force from its placement at the emotional core of the speech;
the interjection 'O', often used in Shakespeare as a release point
for passionate feeling, occurs twice in as many lines. The speech
alternates long sentences of praise or condemnation with simple
monosyllabic phrases, which usually occupy the latter half of a

line: 'he did long in vain,' 'him did you leave', 'so you left him', 'Let them alone'. These blunt, insistent phrases drive home Lady Percy's derogation of Northumberland's appeals to honor. Oddly, much of this speech is cut in Q, and some have speculated that its portrait of an ideal chivalric hero might have fallen foul of the censor because it seemed identifiable with the Earl of Essex, the Queen's troubled favourite and rival.

45–68   As bitter as Lady Percy's attack is, its goal is to persuade Northumberland to protect himself, and not to participate in the rebellion. Her chiding plainly has an effect; Northumberland's weak defense of himself for his 'ancient oversights' and his pragmatic assertion of the need for action both sound half-hearted. Lady Northumberland renews the argument with the practical, if shameful, suggestion of flight. Lady Percy, joining up with her, provides Northumberland with a hollow rationalization in lines 53–5, though her thoughts immediately turn back to her husband. The joined power of the two women is evidently more than Northumberland can withstand; the actor could well play this moment with the relief of someone who has been looking for an excuse to back out. On the other hand, Shakespeare has provided the image of the tide at a still-stand, and the actor may take this as a cue for motivation, or even physical movement. Northumberland may start the speech at a point of absolute indecision, still wavering between two possible courses of action; but by the final two lines he has resolved for flight. He leaves the stage decisively, and the women, given no lines to express their reactions to his yielding, hurry off after him.

Act II, scene iv

The tavern scene, the longest in the play, has a similar placement and function to its counterpart in *Part I*, also II.iv. Falstaff inflates himself among his cronies only to be exposed by Hal, and their relationship is left unsettled as news of the rebellion breaks into the space of the tavern. Falstaff's awareness of mortality, together with his intimacy with the prostitute Doll Tearsheet, gives the scene added pathos.

1–96   Two drawers, one recognizable as the shrill-voiced Francis of *Part I*, scurry about making preparations for Sir John and Doll.

Francis, now a co-conspirator with Hal rather than the victim of his jokes, eagerly announces the plot; the drawers might remove their jerkins and aprons at this moment. Presumably the drawers, along with a third identified as 'Will', bring on such tables, stools and so forth as the scene requires. Falstaff is clearly sitting by line 203, perhaps for much of the scene. The tavern room in which the scene takes place is understood as upstairs, though this would not necessarily have been indicated on the Elizabethan stage. Probably entrances came from one of the upstage doors, rather than, for instance, through the stage trap.

The Hostess enters with Doll Tearsheet, a new character who has twice been mentioned previously. Her name leaves little doubt as to her profession, and her appearance will probably reinforce the identification (though in Elizabethan productions she would of course have been played by a boy, and she is evidently quite well-dressed, wearing a ruff). She has evidently had too much to drink, and has perhaps just been sick offstage. She now feels 'better than [she] was' and her 'Hem!' may represent a range of physical actions: throat-clearing, a belch or hiccup, even a new spasm of vomiting. The earthiness of the tavern world, its concern with what Bakhtin, in his classic 1965 study *Rabelais and his World*, calls the 'lower bodily stratum', is reinforced by Falstaff's entering command to 'Empty the jordan.' Unsubtle productions may have the chamber pot brought onstage. The conversation dwells on topics of 'Gluttony and diseases,' important topics in the play; in coarse prose, Doll and Falstaff squabble about the causes and effects of syphilis and obesity. The Hostess's intercession brings them into accord, and Doll introduces a note of bitter pathos in anticipating Falstaff's departure for war.

The mention of the 'swaggering rascal' Pistol sends Mistress Quickly into an indignant tirade against 'swaggerers'. Her insistent repetition of the word is comic and increasingly bizarre. Her account of a conversation with two Dickensian local authorities – Deputy Tisick and Minister Dumbe – suggests that she may not be altogether sure of the meaning of the word 'swagger', but its mere mention leads her into fits of nervous shaking. The thirty-line digression on swaggering builds anticipation for Pistol's blustering entrance.

97–185   From the moment of his shouted greeting, Pistol brings an intrusive theatrical presence that temporarily eclipses even Falstaff's dominance. He is usually outlandishly dressed, loud, and physically disruptive, related to the same braggart-solider tradition from which Falstaff partly derives. He immediately antagonizes the two women with his salacious offers to drink their health. He and Falstaff work through several bawdy double entendres on Pistol's name, which continues to furnish lame jokes throughout the life of the character. Doll, who evidently has a history of conflict with Pistol, vilifies him with eager relish, using salty and scornful language: 'filthy bung', 'moldy chops', 'saucy cuttle', 'bottle-ale rascal'. When he threatens to 'murder' her ruff, she derides him at length for his pretensions to military standing, attacking his title of 'Captain' through a series of incredulous questions (lines 138–45). By turns, Falstaff, Bardolph and the Page try to get him to leave. His outraged response is to launch into a bombastic performance of stagy rhetoric, cobbled together from half-remembered fragments of Peele and Marlowe. The sudden eruption of bombastic blank verse stands out from the scene's prose, adding an absurd touch of the exotic and mythological in references to Asia and cannibals, Erebus and Cerberus, Caesars and 'Trojan Greeks', together with a garbled mix of Spanish and Italian. Pistol seems momentarily to be pacified, laying down his sword and kissing Falstaff's hand, but Doll is unwilling to let him remain, and the quarrel blows up again. Evidently Bardolph is unable to get rid of him, and the brawl reaches its height as Falstaff draws his sword. After some moments of boisterous combat, Pistol is driven out, 'downstairs', as the text repeatedly insists.

186–322 Whether Falstaff's fighting is effectual or farcical, it is enough to impress the ladies, who fawn over him and fuss over possible injuries. Doll's flattery is laced with affectionate allusions to Falstaff's fatness – 'whoreson chops', 'Bartholomew boar-pig' – but she seems to show genuine concern for him. In the calm aftermath of the fight, with Doll sitting on Falstaff's knee and appropriate music provided by Sneak's noise, the scene takes a turn for the sentimental, or even the sombre. Doll's admonition to Falstaff to 'patch up thine old body for heaven', and his unwillingness to 'remember mine end', can be played with a good deal of gravity. It is one of the points in this play, like 'I do, I will' in the last, where Falstaff's impending tragedy can be most strongly foreshadowed; it can serve as a *memento mori* for the audience as well as Falstaff. Lest the scene become too mournful, however, Shakespeare chooses this moment to bring the Prince and Poins on in their drawer disguises, after line 231. Doll immediately begins questioning Falstaff about the Prince, raising the question of whether she, perhaps, is in on the joke. If she is, it will likely lighten the tone of the scene, especially if she is making eye contact with Hal over Falstaff's shoulder; however, it may also sully the tenderness of Doll's interaction with Falstaff, and perhaps make the voyeurism of the scene even creepier. Further, Hal seems in II.ii not to know Doll, and it is not apparent how they could have coordinated the scheme together.

Falstaff plays right into trick, insulting Hal and Poins, respectively, with patronizing faint praise and blunt force. His account of the mutual interests of the two younger men (lines 242–53) may betray some sour-grapes longing for the mindless vigour of youth. How much the spies are amused or affronted at hearing themselves described may vary in performance. In a way, the joke can be either on Hal or Falstaff. It is on Hal if he puts himself in the position of hearing uncomfortable truths about himself spoken aloud – a disguising episode has similar results when he goes among the soldiers on the night before Agincourt in *Henry V*, IV.i. The joke is on Falstaff if his dishonesty and ingratitude is exposed in obvious and mean-spirited lies he tells about his supposed friend. With which character does the audience vicariously identify? Falstaff probably has the edge, through prominence of place on the stage, and through the vulnerability and intimacy of his relations with Doll. The juvenile insults of the Prince and Poins about desire outliving performance may seem voyeuristic and distasteful as Falstaff, mindful of his mortality, shares a moment of tenderness with Doll, who ruffles his white hair (lines 257–8). 'I am old, I am old', he says, bringing her near tears. The gravity of her homely counsel – 'well, hearken o' th'end' – gives a weight to their encounter that is not wholly dissipated when the Prince and Poins burst in at line 281.

Their entrance, parodying Francis's 'Anons' from *Part I*, lightens the tone immediately, and Falstaff seems quickly to rise to the familiar occasion of defending himself. One of the key interpretive questions of this scene is how it differs from its counterpart in *Part I*, if the two plays are given together. Do Hal and Falstaff have a similarly playful relationship? Or is there a greater edge to this interrogation of Falstaff, and do his self-excusing lies fall a little flatter this time? Falstaff's allegation that he dispraised Hal before the wicked so they wouldn't love him is never wholly accepted or rejected; as in *Part I*, a knocking at the door interrupts before Falstaff can say all he would on his own behalf. The news from outside transforms the scene immediately and irrevocably, breaking the tavern fellowship for the final time.

323–57 Peto, formerly one of the Gad's Hill riff-raff, enters speaking urgent and dignified blank verse. His speech conveys haste and disorder in its image of sweating captains knocking on tavern doors looking for Falstaff. The Prince's reply, also in verse, reveals his guilt over idling in the tavern while a 'tempest of commotion' threatens the kingdom. His brief farewell to Falstaff may include an acknowledgment that they will not enjoy this kind of relation again.

Falstaff expresses an eloquent sadness at leaving 'the sweetest morsel of the night … unpicked'. Whatever his mixed emotions, he can't resist taking advantage of the sudden elevation of his status, telling his 'wenches' how 'men of merit are sought after'. The farewells of Doll and Quickly are amusing but affecting, particularly with the homely detail by which the Hostess measures her association with Falstaff, 29 years 'come peascod time'. When Bardolph reappears to bid Doll come to Falstaff for a final farewell – or a final tryst – her emotion overcomes her, and 'she comes blubbered'.

ACT III

Act III, scene i

The King laments the burdens of his office in a tortured soliloquy, then reflects on Richard II's prophecy of Northumberland's treachery. Warwick, refuting the notion of a malevolent fate, reassures Henry, who resolves to confront the present crisis in the hopes of a future crusade.

1–31 The King appears, probably in his nightgown; on Shakespeare's stage the scene would of course be played in daylight, so the time must be established by the King's costume and behavior, and perhaps some such property as a candle. A modern production will make full use of atmospheric lighting, and may include some suggestion of the royal bedchamber. After a few words to an attendant – often cut in performance – the King begins a soliloquy that contains the most famous and resonant lines of his part. The opening lines, with the emphatic 'thousands', doubled 'O's, and repeated 'sleep's, convey an anguished longing for rest. The idea of sleep as a unique boon – gently and euphoniously rendered as 'nature's soft nurse' – is one Shakespeare will return to in *Macbeth*; the similarities of this speech and II.ii.39–47 of that play may give some sense of the depth of feeling the King's speech is meant to express. The whispering alliterations of line 8 are similarly evocative of sleep's welcome oblivion. In lines 9–17, the King sets up an elaborate comparison between the easy-sleeping poor and the insomniac ruler, a repeated motif in the history plays, from Henry VI's molehill speech at Taunton (*3 Henry VI*, II.iv) to Henry V's 'Upon the King' meditation the night before Agincourt (*Henry V*, IV.i). Here the comparison is drawn out with elegant precision, with three lines about the poor detailing, respectively, the dwelling, bed, and sounds pertaining to their rest, followed by three exactly equivalent lines on the 'perfumed chambers of the great.' It is a notable feature of the speech that the images associated with the sleeping peasant are ugly and harshly discordant ('buzzing night-flies'), while those linked to the king are softly harmonious ('lulled with sound of sweetest melody'). On the one hand, of course, this is part of the rhetorical point of the speech – the untroubled poor can sleep in the harshest conditions. But this language serves a further purpose in providing an outlet for the King's tormented psyche. This becomes apparent in the next extended metaphor, at lines 18–29, when the King speaks of a ship-boy sleeping in a crow's nest in the midst of a stormy sea. The speech gives little attention to the boy or his rest, but focuses instead on the cloud-shaking power of the storm – which stands in, of course, for the tempest in the King's own mind. The essence of the metaphor is completed by the end of line 20, but the King goes on obsessively for another five lines, escalating the storm to such proportions 'That, with the hurly, death itself awakes.' After this almost apocalyptic climax, the speech decrescendos to a quietly despairing conclusion, capped off by Shakespeare's oracular aphorism about the burdens of power.

31–79 Three lords enter, though only Warwick speaks to the King. His cheerful greeting may break tactlessly into the scene's somber mood, or he may approach the King cautiously, tempering his voice and manner. The King may be resentful or relieved at the lords' intrusion; in any event he quickly turns to business. His mention of the kingdom's sickness raises one of the principal metaphors of the play, and his language – 'foul', 'rank diseases' – anticipates the poisoned world of *Hamlet*. Warwick, as he does throughout the scene and the play, offers comfort and reassurance in confidant, almost paternal tones.

The King breaks out in a despairing groan: he uses the interjection 'O' repeatedly through the scene, here as part of a vocative appeal to God. His speech on 'the revolution of the times' expresses a grim pessimism, a sense of inevitable mutability and inscrutable, malign fate. The imagery is cataclysmic, with mountains leveled and continents melting into the sea. The posture of defeat at the end that closes this conceit – the disillusioned youth going to 'shut the book, and sit him down and die' – may be matched by the King's physical demeanour. The next, short line (57) may indicate a weary pause. But the speech continues, with a kind of desperate energy, as the King details the speed with which alliances were broken in the civil conflicts of the preceding ten years. With startling precision, the King recalls the words of Richard II to Northumberland, quoted nearly exactly from *Richard II*, V.i.55–9. The moment has the feeling of an authentic memory, especially as the King appeals to Warwick for corroboration; yet oddly, neither Bolingbroke nor Warwick was in the scene in which Richard made the speech in question. The King's memory – or honesty – is called into question also by his assertion that he 'had no such intent' at the time, as to ascend Richard's throne, when in fact he had already done so in IV.i of the earlier play. It can be played, of course, that King Henry actually believes that 'necessity' compelled him to kiss greatness; but his insistence on this point, in the middle of his despairing speech, can also be a clear place for an actor to express his guilty conscience.

80–108 Warwick's speech in reply is meant to reassure the King, and seems to succeed; but it incorporates a change of attitude that runs throughout the history plays and that, in its deepest meanings, must have been troubling to Elizabethans. This is the shift from a Providential to a Machiavellian view of historical causation, as outlined by Phyllis Rackin in her 1990 book *Stages of History*. The

King's speech on the 'book of fate' indicates that human affairs are controlled by Providence, which, though it might appear malevolent and implacable to a usurper like Bolingbroke, nonetheless has meaning and purpose. Warwick's view – that 'there is a history in all men's lives' which, properly studied, allows one to make a 'perfect guess' about future events – corresponds to the 'politic history' of Machiavelli and his Elizabethan followers like John Hayward and Francis Bacon. This view means that the future, though predictable, is alterable; but it also means there is no ultimate meaning to human events. Warwick emphasizes the positive side of this view in his comforting lines, and King Henry shows a new resolve as he prepares to face the 'necessities' of the rebellion, but the conversation is unlikely to have given much comfort to Elizabethan audiences.

The scene ends with some reassurances. Warwick, downplaying the threat of Northumberland and recalling the play's opening, correctly states that Rumour has doubled the number of the enemy. He gives news of Glendower's death, and expresses solicitude for the King's sickness and sleeplessness. The King, in allowing himself to be led off to bed, seems to have overcome some of his anxieties; but he probably reveals a lingering guilt in his desire to transcend 'these inward wars' through the long-desired pilgrimage to the Holy Land.

Act III, scene ii

Two country justices recall the past and assist Falstaff in his recruiting duties. The comic peasants who appear at the muster undermine the seriousness of the war effort, while the corrupt practices of Falstaff and Bardolph allow able-bodied men to evade service. In a final soliloquy, Falstaff cynically mocks Justice Shallow and reveals his plans to fleece him.

1–53 If the King's exit from III.i has suggested a new purpose and the possibility of altering future events, the next scene undermines it with an image of two old men dwelling on death and the past. Shallow and Silence are two new characters, markedly different from any met so far in the play, and they lead the audience into a different world. Yet as in _Part I_, the juxtaposition of contrasting worlds has expressive meaning in building up the play's whole picture of life, and the picture here, though moving and often comic, is not a heartening one. Aging, sickness and death haunt the play, catching up with Falstaff in the tavern, the King in his perfumed chambers, and the justices in the orchard of Gloucestershire.

A modern production may alter the setting to establish the rural atmosphere of the scene – Terry Hands' 1975 RSC version famously had bare branches and croaking ravens – but on Shakespeare's stage the action was probably continuous, with Shallow and Silence entering from one door as the King left by another. Shallow's insistent repetitions and exhortations give an impression of energetic, if shuffling, movement, and piping but quavering speech. Shallow is usually played by a thin actor with a grey beard and high voice, and contrasts in appearance and temperament with his cousin Silence. The repeated 'Come on' of Shallow's opening lines suggest that Silence is slower moving, and he is certainly less loquacious. The reasons for Silence's relative silence may vary – he may be extremely old, or foolish, or annoyed, or simply unable to get a word in next to his exuberant cousin. Orson Welles gave him a stammer in his film. At any rate, his reticence here sets up his surprising volubility in V.iii. In performance, the pair of justices can come across as anything from sprightly old duffers to cadaverous grotesques.

The opening conversation is one of cozy familiarity and some of the warmer qualities of domestic life in the country: early rising, family news, nature and education. Silence is modestly deprecating of his daughter's beauty – he compares her to a blackbird – and his son's industry, complaining of the expense of Oxford. The mention of university life at line 10 propels Shallow into the past, and the scene, probably, into comedy; certainly the inappropriateness of the sobriquet 'lusty Shallow' will raise a laugh. In rambling prose, Shallow revisits the Inns of Court in remarkable detail, enumerating the 'swinge-bucklers' of his acquaintance, including one 'Will Squele, a Cotswold man', perhaps an avatar of Shakespeare. Shallow even conjures up the surprising image of a boyish Falstaff at line 25. But these recollections of youth inevitably turn to thoughts of mortality: 'Death is certain.' The oscillation in Shallow's thoughts between the homely concerns of country life and the passing of his old acquaintances has long been one of the most admired passages in the play. In the eighteenth century Colley Cibber's Shallow was celebrated for the 'solemn insignificancy' with which he turned from the price of livestock to reflections on mortality and back (Wells, 2000, p. 20). These juxtapositions may provide occasions for laughter, but the conversation contains pathos as well; the combination of poignancy and banality in the Gloucestershire scenes gives them something of the atmosphere of the plays of Anton Chekhov. Like many of Chekhov's characters, Justice Shallow often dwells in a sepia-tinted past. The details of his anecdotes, remembered or embellished at a distance of 55 years – the fact that Sampson Stockfish was a fruiterer, young Falstaff fighting at the court gate, Double's ability to shoot an arrow nearly three hundred yards – are what give the conversation its poignancy. Almost incidental mentions of Thomas Mowbray and John of Gaunt keep the world of *Richard II*, raised in the last scene, a spectral presence in the play.

54–95 The entry of Bardolph '*and one with him*' (so Q; perhaps the Page, following F), brings the scene to its essential business of recruiting. Bardolph's portrait is fleshed out here with airs of military bluster and linguistic pretension. Shallow's enthusiasm for the word 'accommodated' leads Bardolph to go a little out of his depth, but he may put Shallow in his place for describing it as a 'phrase'. Their encounter can be either friendly or contentious. Falstaff enters; he can either support or disprove Shallow's assertion, 'you bear your years very well', though his complaint about the hot weather suggests that he has not been enjoying his time on the march. After a brief exchange of pleasantries, Falstaff gets down to business with surprising initiative (he later, amazingly, 'cannot tarry dinner'). It eventually becomes clear that Falstaff's business is to 'misuse the King's press damnably', as he characterized it in *Part I*; we get here a demonstration of the corrupt recruiting practices he only described there.

96–186 The old men sit, probably at a table whereon Shallow, after some repetitive fussing, spreads out the roll. Each of five peasants is called forward and pricked for service. They may all be onstage from the beginning of the scene, lurking in a cowering huddle; or they may enter one at a time as called. They are characterized only briefly but are usually memorable in performance. Their comic names – Mouldy, Shadow, Wart, Feeble and Bullcalf – probably are reflected in their appearances, and provide Falstaff with material for fairly rudimentary puns. His jokes are usually less funny than Shallow's sycophantic laughter and pedantic explanations ('Things that are mouldy lack use'). The recruits can evoke a range of responses from laughter to pity to contempt. Mouldy's talk of 'husbandry and drudgery' may be leering sexual innuendo, or it may honestly reflect the difficult situation of peasant farmers when the man of the house is called off to war. Shadow's name calls attention to other 'shadows' that 'fill up the muster book' in Falstaff's corrupt practice. Wart, probably the most subhuman of the lot, is given no other characterization beyond his raggedness, but Feeble, the woman's tailor, shows bravery unexpected in one of his maligned profession. Bullcalf is plainly a coward, feigning an illness caught while bell-ringing, but Falstaff's cold-blooded promise that 'thy friends shall ring for thee' – i.e., at his funeral – probably gains him momentary sympathy from the audience.

187–219 Before the final choices are made, Shallow seizes another opportunity for reminiscing with Falstaff, whom he treats as a crony from his Clement's Inn days. Interestingly, Falstaff resists – 'No more o' that, Master Shallow' – perhaps from playful teasing, but perhaps also from the unwillingness to reflect on aging and mortality that he showed in the earlier conversation with Doll. His replies to Shallow's long-winded memories are brief and grave, perhaps recognizing more in the passage of time than Shallow himself does. Certainly Falstaff's line about the chimes at midnight (line 214) can carry a weight of mournful poetry, as Orson Welles recognized in choosing it for the title of his Falstaff film.

220–97 Bardolph's acceptance of bribes from Mouldy and Bullcalf is carried out with an ease suggestive of much previous practice: 'Go to, stand aside.' Feeble, surprisingly, passes up the attempt to buy his way out, and his simple courage and stoicism – 'A man can die but once' – put the others, including Falstaff, rather to shame. When Falstaff reenters, he seems fully cognizant of Bardolph's scam ('Go to, well'), and releases the able-bodied Mouldy and Bullcalf just as Shallow has picked them out as the best men. To justify his choices, Falstaff launches into a disquisition on the virtues of soldiers like Wart that provides a triple opportunity for physical comedy: as first Bardolph, then the troglodytic Wart, and finally the doddering

Shallow perform maneuvers with what is ostensibly a loaded mus-
ket. Having achieved his objective in soldiers and cash, Falstaff
quickly quits the scene. In his voluble farewell, Shallow lets slip
that his unctuous attentions to Falstaff have not been disinterested:
'Peradventure I will with ye to the court.'

298–331   Left alone, Falstaff reveals that Shallow's sycophantic
ambition is no match for his naked predation. Falstaff effortlessly
and mercilessly takes apart the nostalgic world of 'lusty Shallow',
establishing that 'every third word' has been a lie, and substituting
a no less funny, but more distasteful version of Shallow as a contemptible wretch 'like a forked radish'. The images are rather gross,
but effective, and we are forced to dwell on the image of Shallow
as a naked homunculus, a Vice's dagger, a mandrake root. Falstaff
is himself, of course, an old liar, as he reminds the audience, but
the withering detail of his account of Shallow has the ring of truth,
and we may rather regret having the old man's illusions punctured,
even in his absence. Falstaff, whose greed and cynicism have been
highlighted throughout the scene, resolves to return and prey on the
justices, and his final lines reveal a view of social life that anticipates
the Darwinian struggle for existence: 'I see no reason in the law of
nature but I may snap at him.' Falstaff speaks in a privileged position
here, as he does at two other times in the play: delivering a soliloquy
at the close of a scene, giving his own take on events directly to the
audience. How far that enables him to keep the audience on his side
depends on the performance; but in this case his sour joking at
Shallow's expense, together with the openness of his larcenies, may
weigh against him somewhat.

ACT IV

Act IV, scene i

The first two scenes of Act IV, concerning the rebels in Gaultree
Forest, are essentially a single continuous action; the first scene
centered on the Earl of Westmorland's encounter with the rebels,
the second on that of Prince John. The Folio in fact treats the whole
action at Gaultree, IV.i–IV.iii, as one long scene, a practice followed
by the New Cambridge Shakespeare; but most editions follow the
eighteenth-century practice of dividing Act IV into five scenes. IV.i

begins and ends with discussions among the rebels that reveal their military weakness and political disunity; Westmorland's parley provides a strong case for the King's position, and sets up the trick by which the rebels will eventually be defeated.

1–25   The rebels enter, establishing the location in the first two lines. The forest setting is appropriate to the murky moral maze of this sequence, and modern productions often make full use of shadowy lighting and twittering birds. Presumably there are few, if any, supernumerary soldiers; throughout the sequence the *offstage* presence of the armies is an important factor, but this conflict is decidedly one of words rather than blows. Nonetheless, the rebels are in armour, and the incongruity of this costuming, in the Archbishop's case, is repeatedly commented on in the scene; he presumably also wears some portion of his clerical robes. The scene begins with a setback for the rebels: the Archbishop barely has time to reveal Northumberland's unsurprising truancy before a messenger enters announcing the approach of Westmorland with the King's forces.

26–52   Westmorland is a commanding presence in the scene, and his opening address to the Archbishop, while somewhat formal and rhetorical, is forceful and effective. The speech is built on contrasts between peace and civil war. The opening lines, concerning rebellion, have a relatively loose and colloquial structure, and are filled with coarse and unpleasing words, centered on 'b' and 'g' sounds: 'base and abject routs,' 'guarded with rags,' 'boys and beggary,' 'ugly,' 'base,' 'bloody.' At line 42, Westmorland switches to smooth and euphonious anaphora, as self-contained verse lines express the orderly world that should be inhabited by the Archbishop, 'Whose beard the silver hand of peace hath touched,' and so on. The final part of the speech juxtaposes these two worlds in succinct phrases, stressing the incongruity of turning 'books to graves' and 'ink to blood,' and demanding the Archbishop's reasons for what the speech has already established as a monstrous violation of proper civil order.

The Archbishop's response, after three brief introductory phrases, emerges as a passionate excoriation of the sickness of the kingdom. Less formal and more urgent than Westmorland's speech, it restates the idea of a diseased land that the King himself used in III.i, but with more sensuous detail and moral outrage. The whole kingdom is guilty of 'surfeiting and wanton hours' that have brought on this 'burning fever'; the late King Richard was himself infected, and died as a result; the cure will require letting blood, purgation of the bloated land, and the dieting of 'rank minds, sick of happiness'. In justifying his course, the Archbishop introduces a second metaphor that he will use throughout the scene, a river flooding its banks, driven by 'the rough torrent of occasion'. Perhaps his delivery conveys some sense of the minister in the pulpit; his speech is animated with sincere intensity, but it is built on metaphors, and contains very little that is concrete about the rebels' political position. The Archbishop ends by mentioning the articles of grievance – never detailed in the play – that will, ironically, become the tool the King's forces will use to crush the rising.

88–182 Westmorland stonewalls him, flatly denying that the appeal was denied, and then denying the Archbishop's right to make an appeal at all. This proves too much for Mowbray, who enters into his own passionate self-justification. Westmorland, in rebutting Mowbray's complaint, reminds him that he was restored to his father's estates by the King, and thus opens another window into the world of *Richard II*. Until this point, even an attentive audience member may not have realized that this Mowbray is the son of the man who was banished in I.iii of the earlier play. In a seventeen-line speech (lines 113–29), Mowbray recreates the climactic moment in the trial by combat of his father and Bolingbroke, when King Richard threw his warder down to stop the joust. This vivid speech, with its neighing coursers, burning eyes and blowing trumpet, halts the action of the play to give a picture of England's lost chivalric past. The audience will likely be drawn in by this, sympathetic to Mowbray and mindful of the disorder that followed Richard's decision to temporize and banish the two men.

Westmorland is unperturbed: he rejects speculation on the outcome of the trial, pointing out Bolingbroke's military valour and Mowbray's unpopularity. Dismissing such talk as 'mere digression from my purpose', he reports, surprisingly, that Prince John is willing to consider the rebels' articles. Challenged by Mowbray that this offer is merely a subterfuge forced by the rebels' rising, he authoritatively states the strength of the King's position. Using anaphora again to powerful effect ('Our battle … Our men … Our armour'), he details his forces' advantages. The rebels are now in disarray, with open disagreements about how to proceed: Mowbray rejects negotiation while the others waver. While seeming to offer a concession, Westmorland has clearly gained the rhetorical high ground in the parley. When Hastings weakly asks whether Prince John has the authority to rule on their grievances, Westmorland can be sardonically dismissive: 'I muse you make so slight a question.' The Archbishop, who from the beginning of the play has been seen as the figurehead of the revolt, takes the decisive step and presents the schedule, a stage prop invested with great significance for these scenes. The handing over of the rebels' grievances is a critical moment of stage action, and will call forth various responses in the different players: Mowbray sullen and defeatist, Hastings blandly hopeful, and the Archbishop benignly pleased at the prospect of reforming the kingdom without shedding blood. The audience should perhaps sense that this is a moment of defeat for the rebels; particularly as Westmorland, with haughty and confident demeanour, receives the schedule and leaves them to debate among themselves.

183–228 Immediately on Westmorland's departure, Mowbray calls the peace into question. Against Hasting's optimism, he presents arguments identical to those advanced by Worcester in *Part I*, V.ii: the King will never truly forgive former rebels. Mowbray's image of winnowing grain adds an ominous Biblical weight to his speech. The Archbishop's hopeful response may reflect his own desire for peace and reconciliation, a desire that perhaps impairs his judgment throughout the episode. He argues, with some justification, that the civil disorders of the preceding years have so compromised everyone in England that it will be impossible for the King to sort friends from foes, and therefore he will 'wipe his tables clean'; but in this he underestimates Henry's ruthlessness. The Archbishop's surprising image, of a threatened wife holding up her baby in the midst of a domestic dispute, serves as a moving reminder of the painful intimacy of civil conflict. Nonetheless, it provides little support for the proposition that close bonds of kinship prevent violence. Hastings assures Mowbray that in terms of military strength, Henry is 'a fangless lion'; he forgets Machiavelli's other symbolic beast, the fox (see *The Prince*, Chapter XVIII). The Archbishop, in his final reassurance, returns to the metaphor of bodily health, in this case, the 'broken limb united' that grows 'stronger for the breaking.' All of these images for the rebels' peace are susceptible to more pessimistic interpretations, and the audience is liable to trust more in the gloomy fatalism of Mowbray: 'Be it so.'

Act IV, scene ii

The rebels, drawn in by Prince John's promises of a redress of their grievances, dismiss their army, and are arrested for treason and sent to execution. The morality of this action – historically carried out by Westmorland – was a matter of debate from the moment it occurred, and Shakespeare critics have questioned it since the eighteenth century: Dr. Johnson condemned 'this horrible violation of faith' (Knowles, 1992, p. 28).

1–42 The action of this scene seems continuous with the previous one, though the closing lines of IV.i could suggest some kind of march around the stage. Prince John, who had only a few lines in *Part I*, emerges as a major character and a formidable politician. He enters with '*his army*,' subtly changing the onstage balance of power from the previous scene, where Westmorland held his own against the three rebel leaders. Prince John's speech to the Archbishop repeats the themes of Westmorland's, harping on the incongruity of a churchman 'turning the word to sword and life to death'. But, in a difference characteristic, perhaps, of the difference in speakers, John dwells not on open military conflict but on 'mischiefs ... set abroach ... In shadow' by one close to the King. His concerns here are not irrelevant to the coming question of Hal's relationship to Falstaff. In place of the ringing denunciation given by Westmorland, John deals in sly insinuation, undermining the bishop's religious authority through the language of sedition: 'intelligencer', 'false favorite', 'deeds dishonorable', 'counterfeited zeal'. John asserts the King's role as 'God's substitute,' upholding monarchical Divine Right against baronial privilege, and avoiding the issue of Henry's usurpation altogether.

The Archbishop, already committed to a course of peace, acknowledges the 'monstrous form' their rebellion has taken, effectively yielding the moral high ground and blaming their actions on 'the time misordered'. While he invokes their inability to have their grievances heard, he does so mainly to promise peace upon redress of them. The direction of the Archbishop's impulses can be felt in his imagery: the war he has started is a monstrous hydra, a kind of madness, and he longs for a peace where 'true obedience' may 'stoop tamely to the foot of majesty'. It is one of the many cruel ironies of the scene that Archbishop's most humane instincts will be used against him.

43–105 The other rebels present a more defiant front, and even the usually weak Hastings conjures up an alarming image of civil war succeeding perpetually, 'heir from heir … While England shall have generation.' This savage prospect recalls the Bishop of Carlisle's prophecy at Richard's deposition (*R2*, IV.i), and the apocalyptic diatribe of Northumberland in the opening scene of *Part II*. It invokes the terror of civil conflict promulgated in the Tudor homilies. The Prince, rejecting this prophecy, shows something of the cool Machiavellianism of Warwick in III.i; history can be anticipated, but not by the likes of Hastings. John's speech may be laced with irony, informed by his knowledge of the trap he is about to spring; or it may represent a flaring-up of genuine emotion. In any event, Westmorland keeps Prince John on task, reminding him of the articles. The Prince utters a surprisingly bland speech of conciliation (lines 54–65). This speech is so out of character with everything he has said before that both audience and rebels may be astonished at it. It presents a difficult task for the actor of Prince John: how sincere should he try to make it, how much should he alter the tone of supercilious dislike with which he has heretofore addressed the rebels? If he is too unctuous, it is not credible that he will be believed. Should the audience suspect the treachery, or should they also be taken in by the prospect of peace? How much time passes, and how do the rebels behave, before the Archbishop steps forward decisively to accept John's princely word?

The text suggests that the rebels and the royal party embrace and drink to each other, behavior that may strike the audience as incongruous for armed warriors. The emergence of waiters with trays of goblets from among the royal army may even have a comic dimension, and may serve as a clue that all is not as it seems. Again, a production will have to make choices about how fully to give the game away. Westmorland's lines are charged with sinister double meanings. Mowbray's sudden illness at line 80 seems premonitory; he may stand apart from the drinking. The scene is awash in ironies, from the cheerful shouting of the soldiers, to the Archbishop's mild pronouncements about the virtues of peace, to the Prince's ominous assurance that they shall lie that night together. The Prince and Westmorland seem to play with the rebels as cats with mice, openly discussing their own army's unwillingness to disband (lines 98–101). Hastings's enthusiastic description of the departing soldiers as young steers or exuberant schoolboys makes a final, painful irony, as the naiveté of the rebels costs them their lives.

106–23   The arrest is swift and shocking, and the rebels barely get a chance to protest before being led off to their deaths. John's speech justifying his action mixes legalistic punctiliousness with a kind of high moral indignation about rebellion. How it plays in performance depends both on the actor and the whole previous scene. Prince John has, after all, saved thousands of lives and prevented a probably disastrous civil war. Yet his swearing by his honour, his promise to redress the rebel's grievances 'with a most Christian care,' and his ascription of the victory to God may read as malicious gloating, especially as he is condemning an Archbishop. If his words are accompanied by an action such as stripping a cross from around the Archbishop's neck, John may come across as dangerously sacrilegious. Similarly, the spectacle of the rebels being marched off to their deaths may communicate a sense of justice achieved, or of a brutal war crime (Michael Bogdanov had the rebels shot onstage in his 1986 English Shakespeare Company production). The Gaultree sequence's essential action, of rebels being outsmarted and tricked into their own defeat, provides a basic kind of dramatic satisfaction, but the icy *Realpolitik* of Prince John has generally done little to endear him to audiences.

Act IV, scene iii

The rebel Coleville surrenders to Falstaff, and on Prince John's orders is sent to execution. A contretemps between the Prince and Falstaff leads the latter into a soliloquy enumerating the virtues of sack for inculcating wit and courage. This scene seems to follow more or less immediately on the one preceding, though the stage is cleared in the interim. The alarums and excursions presumably illustrate the royal army's pursuit of 'the scattered stray' from the rebel forces, ordered by John at the end of the scene before.

1–84   Exactly how Falstaff and Coleville meet, and how and why the latter surrenders, must be determined in performance. Falstaff attributes his triumph to the reputation for valour he earned at Shrewsbury, and to his immediately recognizable belly. Nonetheless, nothing that Coleville does elsewhere in the scene suggests that he is particularly foolish or cowardly, so his submission to Falstaff seems rather unmotivated. He may be counting on lenient treatment, in which case he is sorely disappointed.

Prince John and Westmorland fit rather awkwardly into this comic prose scene, with their terse verse speeches about orders and executions. The Prince's antipathy to Falstaff emerges in a grim jest about hanging (line 29). Falstaff does his best to lighten the tone with a self-important account of his capture of Coleville, which quickly expands, in Falstaff's mind, into an illustrated ballad. In claiming his deserts, Falstaff lures John into something like an exchange of wit, in which the Prince, surprisingly, seems to get the better of Falstaff, at least for the moment. The relationship between the two men can be one of amused tolerance or outright hostility. As was the case with the Lord Chief Justice, the Prince upsets Falstaff most by simply ignoring him. At line 75, after dispatching Coleville to execution, the Prince turns his attention to what will become the preoccupation of the remainder of the act: the King's sickness and imminent death.

85–129   Falstaff, having received some grudging acknowledgement, berates the departed Prince for his cold-bloodedness and lack of wit. These faults he attributes to sobriety, and this realization leads Falstaff into his longest sustained utterance in either play, his encomium on the virtues of sack. His opening criticisms of 'this same young sober-blooded boy' may find sympathetic response from an audience still troubled by the Gaultree treachery. Gradually, in the leisurely prose of which he is master, Falstaff leads the speech into comic territory, belittling John and his ilk through deftly-chosen images: 'demure boys', 'thin drink', 'fish meals', 'male greensickness'.

Eventually he switches to his true subject, for which he selects the elegant euphemism, 'inflammation'. The bulk of the speech is structured by the 'twofold operation' of sack in begetting wit and courage. Discussing the former (lines 96–101), Falstaff illustrates it through language as 'nimble, fiery and delectable' as what he describes. For the latter quality (lines 102–15), he explores the extended metaphor of 'this little kingdom, man' aroused to valour through the 'warming of the blood'. Falstaff's delight in language is evident throughout the speech, notably in the use of words like 'pusillanimity' and 'illumineth' that allow a virtuoso display of verbal adroitness.

Though the speech is mainly about sack and Falstaff's love for it, it is book-ended by a comparison of Prince John with Prince Hal that may reveal much about Falstaff's anxieties and preoccupations, and that certainly calls the audience's attention to the remaining matter of the play. Falstaff ends the speech praising Hal's courage, noting in passing that Hal shares John's inheritance of cold Lancastrian blood, which he compares to 'lean, sterile and bare land'. While Falstaff goes on to praise Hal for having 'manured, husbanded and tilled' this land with sack, the reference to the Lancastrian inheritance, and the association of Hal with his father and brother, give a serious weight to the end of the speech – though it may be one that Falstaff doesn't realize himself. Certainly, his closing line has a ringing confidence devoid of any anxiety. And his determination, in his speech to Bardolph, to forget military life and set his sights on fleecing Shallow, suggests that he is not greatly concerned about events at court. In thinking of his next victim as a mere bit of wax that he is warming between his finger and thumb, Falstaff takes on an inflated self-regard that the audience may recognize as hubris.

Act IV, scene iv

The sequence of the King's sickness and death is treated as a single scene in the Folio, though most modern editors have divided it into two. If it is two scenes, the first, IV.iv, could be presumed to take place in the Jerusalem Chamber, where the King initially swoons, the second in the King's bedroom; though the action could be played through in a single space. The first scene deals with King's illness and the resolution of the various uprisings, the second with the King's final reconciliation with Prince Hal.

1–80 Whether the two scenes are thought of as separate or continuous, it is apparent that there must be somewhere for the King to swoon between lines 111 and 129; in IV.v he must be in bed. Having a bed onstage throughout seems likely, and would immediately establish the King's weakened condition. He might even be in bed from the beginning, pushed out from behind the curtains in the discovery space, or revealed by lighting in a modern theatre. His appearance may also indicate the decline in his health mentioned by Prince John a scene earlier; he is probably in nightclothes, perhaps carried in a chair or supported if he is able to walk. On the other hand, his speech begins with a tone of confident resolution, expressed in even and parallel end-stopped lines, that may belie his physical condition. Only at line 8 does he admit the want of 'a little personal strength' that will doom his dreams of crusade to failure. If he has been standing, he probably sits or lies down at this point, and remains so for most of the scene.

The King asks of Prince Hal's whereabouts, recalling his very first inquiry about his 'unthrifty son' in *Richard II*, V.iii.1. Gloucester and Clarence, two other sons introduced here for the first time, are placed in the awkward position of covering for their brother. At any rate, Clarence knows that Hal is not at Windsor when Gloucester tells the King he is (line 14); perhaps the two brothers exchange a look revealing something of their relationship. Shakespeare does not do much to characterize these brothers, either here or in *Henry V*, but some in Shakespeare's audience might recall that Gloucester is the good Duke Humphrey of the *Henry VI* plays. The King's speech to Clarence about Hal's personality is an elegant set-piece, full of memorable details: the tear for pity, the hand 'open as day' for charity, the flinty temper capable of sudden wintry storms, the passions exhausting themselves 'like a whale on ground'. Not all of what Henry says here corresponds to the Hal portrayed so far in these two plays, but the account is balanced and more generous than the King has sometimes been. The speech may be played as wish-fulfillment on the part of the King, who wants to bind the brothers together, through Clarence's agency, as a leak-proof vessel for the Lancastrian blood (lines 43–8). Though disappointed by Hal in the past, the King wishes to believe the best of him, and to get his brothers to support and sustain him: Henry knows first-hand the dangers of a divided royal family.

At any rate, as soon as Clarence gives away that Hal is dining in London with Poins 'and other his continual followers,' the King changes his tune, bitterly decrying the 'weeds' that overspread Hal, and prophesying the 'unguided days/ And rotten times' that will succeed him. Warwick immediately steps to Hal's defense, producing an argument comparable to Hal's 'I know you all' speech from *Part I*: the Prince studies his companions like a foreign language, but will reject them in due time (lines 67–78). Warwick's established role as a wise and forthright councillor gives the speech firm conviction, but Henry is unconvinced, and expresses his doubts in a gruesome image of rottenness and sweetness, the honeycomb in the dead carrion (lines 79–80).

80– 132 Westmorland's entry clears away one part of the King's fears with his report of Prince John's success in York. The language takes on an exalted, nearly sacred tone, as 'Peace puts forth her olive everywhere.' In response, the King's mood again changes – the sudden shifts in this scene give the actor of the King good opportunities to convey his fever-weakened emotional state. In one of the play's loveliest images, he casts Westmorland as 'a summer bird' singing in a wintry dawn. When Harcourt, arriving with choric timing, brings word of the defeat of Northumberland, it is too much for the King. The paradox of his sickness, upon the receipt of good news (line 102), reverses the situation of Northumberland at the beginning of the play. The King's swoon may be a sudden collapse, or merely the final expression of the weakened state he had been denying throughout the scene. The older lords take action to revive the King, but his two sons assume the collapse will be fatal. Their lines, invoking portents and prophesies and the wisdom of 'the old folk, time's doting chronicles,' give the scene an eerie solemnity, as they speak over their father's prostrate body. When the King recovers, he asks to be borne 'into some other chamber'; whether he leaves the stage for a scene change, or is moved to another part of the stage, or is merely replaced in his bed, will vary from production to production.

Act IV, scene v

The King's dying encounter with the Prince of Wales, and the Prince's early removal of the crown, is one of the oldest and most enduring parts of the Henry V legend. In most earlier versions, including Holinshed, the King is assumed by several onlookers to have died, and is covered by a linen cloth, before the Prince takes the crown; the Prince is forgiven fairly easily. Shakespeare, following Daniel's *Civil Wars* (see Chapter 3), makes the scene more personal, a searing encounter between father and son, concerned as much with filial betrayal as with political succession.

1–47 The King begins the scene by calling for music, and its offstage accompaniment can add atmosphere and pathos to the scene. The crown, set on the King's pillow, is a crucial property, and needs to be visible to as much of the audience as possible. The Prince enters with inappropriate high spirits; it may take him awhile to absorb the gravity of the royal sickroom. This discordance can come across as merely upbeat vitality or tactless lack of feeling; his brothers can be understanding or resentful, and Warwick can come close to chiding him. His determination to sit and watch by the King may reestablish his filial sincerity, although this action will backfire on him momentarily.

The scene of the Prince with his sleeping father is one of hushed stillness, one of the most theatrically charged moments in the play. Prince Hal's focus immediately falls on the crown, which leads him to reflect on the burdens of royalty in terms recalling his father's sleepless monologue in Act III, and anticipating his own nocturnal soliloquy in *Henry V*, IV.i. In his grave apostrophes to the crown, he seems to consider his own imminent responsibilities, and this may lead him subconsciously to the conviction that his father has already died. The detail of the feather, lines 31–4, gives a precise focus to the moment of the King's supposed death. There is no suggestion in the speech that the Prince snatches the crown away over-eagerly; but he does move rather quickly from a reflection on his dues of grief to his obligations of rule. The moment of his self-crowning is one of iconic power; the Prince's lines 43–47 have the force of a sacred oath.

48–88 Does the audience believe that the King has actually died? If so, his sudden awakening can induce horror-film shock, followed by a dawning realization of the probable effects of the Prince's gaffe. There is perhaps a childlike pathos in the King's question, 'Why did you leave me here alone, my lords?' How quickly do the lords piece together what has happened, and what motives do they impute to the Prince? They may be at pains to dissociate themselves from his misdeed, though Warwick later speaks to excuse him. The King's displeasure certainly falls on his other sons as well as Hal. In a speech that mixes self-pity and self-righteousness, the King speaks on behalf of all 'foolish overcareful fathers' against the thoughtless predations of their issue. The thrice-repeated 'For this' opening is rhetorically forceful but rather stagy; and the audience may feel that the King's comparison of himself to an industrious bee 'murdered' for his pains goes rather too far. In any event, the speech sets up the final confrontation between father and son, probably gaining some anticipatory sympathy for the latter.

89–136 Hal enters, still with the crown, which he is forced to hold guiltily for much of the scene. The King sends the other lords away, heightening the tension. Hal's line 92 probably breaks into a stony silence, but the King is ready for him, delivering a damning riposte, line 93, that invokes the theme of fatherhood even as it accuses Hal of mental patricide. The King's speech begins in terms of sardonic bitterness that nonetheless convey deep personal hurt: 'I stay too long by thee; I weary thee.' The 'thousand daggers' Henry accuses his son of harbouring in his thoughts may recall the dagger that, in Holinshed, the Prince brings into his father's presence in their scene of conflict and reconciliation. From his personal resentment – 'Canst thou not forbear me half an hour?' – the King moves to a mocking invocation of the chaos he believes will plague his son's reign. 'Up, vanity!/ Down, royal state!' the King cries, mortifying Hal through his showy and sarcastic apostrophes. The speech is charged with energy, and demands expressive playing; the actor will need to balance this theatricality against the King's illness, and may represent this as the last outburst of the King's fading life. The words are full of nasty vigour: 'apes of idleness', 'purge you of your scum'. The repetitions of verbs of profligacy, balanced by the rewards of corruption, enliven the latter part of the speech. In the final lines, the King moves toward a vision of national devastation, where 'the wild dog/ Shall flesh his tooth' on the innocent, with England a wilderness peopled by wolves.

137–76 The Prince, at last given a chance to speak, kneels to his father, and probably remains kneeling throughout the speech. He finally returns the crown at line 140, and begins to disavow any dishonorable intent in taking it, even hinting at the 'noble change' he is preparing to make. As part of his excuse, he gives an account of his address to the crown – one that differs significantly from the speech the audience heard him give. This raises questions – does Hal in fact believe that he is accurately reporting the substance of his earlier speech? Should the audience believe he is now stretching the truth in order to excuse himself? Or do we feel that in putting on the crown, he was in fact, as he says, contending with an enemy that he felt had murdered his father?

177–219   In any event, whether or not the speech convinces the audience, it convinces the King. His first line in response is only three syllables, perhaps indicating an emotional pause for reflection or decision, perhaps putting Hal in suspense for a moment as to the effect of his appeal. In the next three lines, however, the King dismisses forever his doubts about his son, and turns, with the urgency of dwindling breath, to advice on statecraft. This speech includes some of Henry's most explicit acknowledgment of the guilt he bears for his usurpation, as well as more pragmatic reflections on the political difficulties that guilt has occasioned (lines 183–98). The scene is both an affectionate deathbed reconciliation of father and son, and a kind of crash course in Machiavellian expediency: any performance will need to strike a balance between these two aspects. The King shrewdly analyzes the successes and failures of his reign; he perceives that his death 'changes the mood', and that Hal will likely have an easier time than he did. Nonetheless, Hal must watch out for the treachery of the King's former friends. Here Henry reveals, astonishingly, that the cleansing pilgrimage he has been talking about since the end of *Richard II* was actually a political ploy. This expedition, which at various times has been described as a pilgrimage of atonement and a holy war, is now characterized as a stratagem to distract any nobles who might look 'Too near unto my state.' Henry's advice to his son to 'busy giddy minds/ With foreign quarrels' may, in this context, come across as the height of Machiavellian cynicism. On the other hand, Henry's imminent death may lead him to a degree of honesty and closeness to his son greater than the audience has ever witnessed. The final lines of his speech indicate both a painful physical vulnerability – 'my lungs are wasted so' – and a spiritual anguish as he prays for God's forgiveness.

220–40   The momentousness of the King's death and the succession of the crown is conveyed by a series of three rhyming couplets, one ending the King's speech and two making up the Prince's. The short intervening line ('My gracious liege') may indicate a pause of emotion or decision on the Prince's part. The arrival of Prince John calls forth another image of birds, now heralding departure and death. The reference to the Jerusalem chamber can arouse a variety of responses in King Henry, depending on the final image of him a production wishes to create. His praise of God seems to reveal a spiritual humility, but there can also be an element of self-mockery, or even bitter frustration, at the cruel joke fate has played him. On the other hand, the revelation that Henry expected to die in Jerusalem casts another light on the pilgrimage: it was intended as his final act, almost a kind of ceremonial suicide. Accordingly, the discovery that this purifying death is as near as the next room may provide for Henry a surprising and blessed relief from the incessant troubles of his embattled reign.

The gravity of this moment is tempered, in production, with a considerable logistical challenge – getting the dying King and his bed offstage. In Shakespeare's theatre, the bed was perhaps pushed back behind a curtain with the King in it, or the King was led off and the bed removed by supernumeraries. A modern theatre could use a blackout, but the sense of the King being bodily transported to another chamber seems important here, and the stage should probably be cleared. Some funereal sound effect – bells tolling, sombre chanting – can help cover the transition, which needs to give the sense of a fundamental change in the action of the play.

ACT V

Act V, scene i

This strange little scene – easily and frequently cut in performance – may have served Shakespeare in some practical way to do with stagecraft, but it certainly demonstrates his commitment to the method of alternating scenes from different worlds and registers of action. As Shallow and his servant fuss over trivialities and make plans for dinner, Falstaff assesses his next victim and plans to entertain Hal with his observations. The prosaic world of Gloucestershire seems very far indeed from the sonorous gravity of the King's death chamber; though perhaps not far enough from the coming showdown between Falstaff and Hal.

1–58   Shallow is given some of his characteristic repetitive blather to establish the comic tone, using every possible variation on the notion that Falstaff will not be excused from dinner. His conversation with his servant Davy, a new character, conveys the mundane concerns of country life: sowing wheat, mending buckets, plow irons, young pigeons and Hinckley fair. At line 28, however, Davy draws Shallow aside for more private talk, revealing a calculating and mean-spirited side to this rural idyll. Shallow is attempting to take advantage of Falstaff as 'a friend i' the court,' despite his contempt for his followers. Davy, for his turn, wants to use Shallow's influence on behalf of his knavish friend William Visor. Both seem willing to 'bear out a knave against an honest man' when it is to their advantage to do so. The self-serving and short-sighted behavior that the play has depicted in court, tavern, and battlefield parley is present as well in the countryside.

59–87   Falstaff has presumably been engaged in some business with the otherwise needless Page and Bardolph while this conversation proceeds, but he may manage to eavesdrop on Shallow and his servant. At any rate, he has observed them sufficiently to anatomize them upon their exit. Falstaff's final soliloquy of the play reveals little new about him, but paints effectively the kind of banal and mediocre world that most of England has become, and that provides Falstaff with endless material for mockery. Yet in his expectation that such jesting will 'keep Prince Harry in continual laughter', Falstaff reveals his blind spot; the audience knows that the Prince has moved very far from such concerns. Falstaff believes himself master of the situation, and goes into dinner eager to tease and observe Shallow; the audience's superior knowledge here continues the erosion of Falstaff's dramatic standing.

Act V, scene ii

The death of the King has created deep anxieties among the members of the court, from his younger sons to the Lord Chief Justice; anxieties the new King attempts to allay.

1–62   The scene begins in a mood of sombreness and fear. Warwick euphemistically reports the old King's death to the Lord Chief Justice, who at once begins to reflect on the dangers of his own position. While no one in the scene (including, later, the new King), seems to begrudge the Justice this concern for his own welfare, it does weaken his standing slightly, and gives the King the opportunity to take the moral high ground later on. As the princes enter, it is revealed that no one – not even Warwick, who always stood up for Prince Hal – has high expectations of Henry V. The gloomy feelings of all are caught in short and simple verse phrases: 'We meet like men that had forgot to speak.' All focus their misgivings on the Lord Chief Justice, who, all agree, stands 'in coldest expectation.' Though defeatist, he is able to summon his dignity just in time for the King's entrance: it is he who first greets him as 'Your Majesty' and he probably leads a bow or some other gesture of obeisance.

The King's first lines establish both his new seriousness and the anxieties he himself feels upon his accession. Yet he quickly hits a more personal tone, coming close to a reassuring joke with lines 47–9: the informality of 'Harry' in this instance is well-judged to put his brothers at their ease. Lest he come across as glib, he embraces their sadness, then draws all together with the notion that it is 'a joint burden laid upon us all'. Instinctively, Hal comes close to the language with which his father, in IV.iv, urged Clarence to seek the unity of the brothers, and their shared line of response suggests that he may have succeeded in that aim. Depending on how they are characterized, the princes may resist this unity to varying degrees; and 'We hope no otherwise' is admittedly not a ringing endorsement. Nonetheless, the issue of the King's relationship with his brothers is tabled as Henry turns to his purported nemesis, the Lord Chief Justice.

63–101   This encounter marks the first onstage meeting between these two characters, though their past history – another key element in the 'wild Prince' legend – has been referred to repeatedly. The Prince's boxing of the Justice's ears, and his subsequent commitment to prison, is a key moment in *The Famous Victories of Henry V*, but for whatever reason Shakespeare chose not to dramatize it; perhaps it would have been out of character for his essentially sober Hal. The episode now, in retrospect, becomes a touchstone in Hal's relationship to the Lord Chief Justice and the law in general: now the scene's essential subject, and an important theme of the play. Variations on the words 'just' and 'justice' occur some twenty-five times in *Part II*, nine of them in this scene.

Hal initially speaks severely to the Lord Chief Justice. His blunt 'No?' stands by itself in a blank verse line, suggesting nine beats of tense silence before he begins a series of aggressive rhetorical questions about the 'great indignities' he has endured. His language contrasts the elevation of his position with the harsh treatment he received: 'What? Rate, rebuke and roughly send to prison/ Th'immediate heir of England?' Is his resentment genuine, or is this a bit of manipulative role-playing, or a Gadshill-style joke, or all of the above? Certainly, he puts the Lord Chief Justice to the test. It is, apparently, a test the Justice passes. In a measured and dignified speech, he defends his action, invoking the abstractions he has embodied, abstractions the King himself will now need to uphold. 'Majesty', 'power', 'law' and 'justice' all ring out nobly in a single line (78). Much of the speech is taken up with a hypothetical case of the new King's son similarly misbehaving, presented in language that greatly impugns the royal dignity. This account uses triple repetitions to magnify the misdeeds: the anaphoric infinitives of lines 85–7, and the 'Hear … See … Behold' openings of lines 93–5. At lines 97–8, after building up the severity of the offense, the Justice succinctly characterizes his own act as one of mildness and restraint, 'soft silencing' the miscreant. He concludes the speech with another triple formulation, defending the appropriateness of his action to his place, person, and 'liege's sovereignty'.

102–45   The King may pause for effect, but once he speaks he keeps the Lord Chief Justice in no further suspense. Indeed, he equates him with the very principle he upholds: he is 'right Justice,' weighing the matter impartially in the balance that he will continue to bear. Hal's speech is itself very balanced, divided equally between praise for the Lord Chief Justice, for committing him, and himself, for obeying. Perhaps he still bears a little resentment, or perhaps he doesn't wish to imperil his own new dignity by dwelling on his wrong-doing; at any rate, he takes care in lines 108–12 to defend his own conduct while praising that of the Justice. At line 113, he may speak metaphorically, or he may give an actual sword of justice into the judge's hand (perhaps one he gave up earlier). At line 117 he certainly gives his hand to the Lord Chief Justice, who shakes or kisses it, perhaps kneeling; if so, the King probably raises him up again soon after.

Having dealt with the Lord Chief Justice, the King expands the focus of his speech, addressing the whole group. After the striking image of his father 'gone wild into his grave,' taking Hal's unkingly inclinations with him, the new King builds his speech with oracular grandeur. His transformation is elemental, a turning of the tide that invests him with the majesty of the sea (lines 129–33). He calls his Parliament in a single weighty line; his concerns are now of national and international scope. With the final couplet, he may return to a more jocular tone, again using the informal 'Harry,' rounding the speech off with apparent confidence and optimism. Whether his brothers, and the Lord Chief Justice, are wholly convinced remains open to question, but there are few openings for doubt in the language itself.

Act V, scene iii

With the surging motion of the previous speech, it would seem that the play is in its final movement toward the King's coronation, but Shakespeare puts on the brakes one more time with another scene in Gloucestershire. Time is nearly at a stop for an evening of wine and song in Shallow's orchard, enlivened by the bizarre outbursts of Silence. Into this idyll bursts Pistol with news of the King's death. Falstaff's mounting excitement, and his hubristic celebrations of his new importance, set the stage for his first and final meeting with the new King.

1–59 Shallow's invitation specifies the place and time very concretely – it is in his orchard, after dinner, on a fine evening when all can appreciate the 'good air' and the apples he has grafted himself. With characteristic repetitions, he settles the guests in their places, probably on benches around a table, and exhorts Davy to spread a cloth. The scene is heavy, even fussy, with props and business, again showing Shakespeare's audacity in not hurrying the play to its conclusion after the King's death. As before, it may take some time for this scene to establish its atmosphere after the seriousness of the preceding one, but drunkenness onstage is usually a guaranteed source of laughter. Here the characters have evidently been drinking

already, and many healths are drunk over the course of the scene. It
is Silence, however, who uncharacteristically is the life of the party,
with his merry *carpe diem* songs. Depending on how Silence has been
portrayed, these can come across as jolly, absurd, or pathetic, but
they are almost sure to be funny, particularly when Falstaff comments on their incongruity: 'I did not think Master Silence had been
a man of this mettle.' His reply – that he has been merry 'twice and
once ere now' – is a certain laugh line, whether or not, as is often the
case, he takes a pause after 'twice'. On the other hand, his observation
that 'now comes in the sweet o' th' night' may recall Falstaff's II.iv
evocation of 'the sweetest morsel of the night', and arouse a similar
melancholy. It does seem important that this scene have a distinctive
rhythm, relaxed and even aimless compared to the forward thrust of
the main plot.

60–121   Foreboding hints are possible; after the songs of wine and
women the conversation turns to London, and the idea of drinking together there as a gesture of faithful companionship. When
Bardolph promises to 'stick by' Davy, Shallow announces, 'Why,
there spoke a king.' One line later there is a knock on the door.
Knocks on the door, in the *Henry IV* plays, invariably mean the intrusion of the world of history on the world of idle leisure; and here the
case is no different. Pistol is announced, 'come from the court with
news.' In showy traveling clothes, speaking loud theatrical verse, he
brings a discordant style and energy into the peaceful rustic scene.
Falstaff, in order to extract his message, has to adopt a similar high-
flown Marlovian style – 'O base Assyrian knight, what is thy news?' –
and Silence bursts in with a song tag to add to the confusion. Pistol
begins to quarrel with Shallow, further delaying the revelation.
Finally, nearly forty lines after his entrance, Pistol makes clear that
'Harry the Fifth's the man.'

122–44   How do Falstaff and the others respond to this news?
His question – 'What, is the old King dead?' – could be shouted
with elation, or whispered with deep emotion, as though Falstaff
were afraid of jinxing the moment of his triumph. Or could the
line convey another sense, an unease or even alarm, a premonition
that this momentous day might have a very different outcome from
that long hoped for. By the time Pistol gives his superbly funny

confirmation – 'As nail in door' – Falstaff seems to be certain of his ascendancy. His exorbitant promises of offices to Shallow, Pistol and Bardolph, and the bustle of clearing props and furniture in preparation for departure, fill the stage with energetic expectation. Silence, presumably having passed out, is carried off by Davy. Falstaff's lawless bravado is evident in his willingness to take any man's horses: 'The laws of England are at my commandment!' All of his final lines look forward to a reckoning with friends and foes, particularly his old enemy the Lord Chief Justice, whom the audience has already seen confirmed in his authority. It is curious that Shakespeare doesn't end the scene with Falstaff's lines; it may be that Pistol's closing tag is designed to highlight the irony. 'Where is the life that late I led', he sings, an old tune once sung by Petruchio in *The Taming of the Shrew* (IV.i.128). The audience knows that the life that he and Falstaff have led is about to change forever.

Act V, scene iv

One more short scene is included before the King's coronation. The arrest of Hostess Quickly and Doll Tearsheet can be a farcical interlude or a scene of brutal police oppression.

1–30 The Quarto stage direction, '*Enter Sincklo and three or four officers*' indicates that a number of men were employed to restrain Quickly and Doll; also that the Beadle was given to John Sincklo, a trusted member of the Chamberlain's Men who had been around playing comic parts since the beginning of Shakespeare's career (he appears in *3 Henry VI* and *The Taming of the Shrew*). However the scene is played, there is a serious accusation at the heart of it; 'a man or two' has been killed, and Doll is implicated. Her exuberant invective directed at the Beadle – 'nuthook, nuthook...thou damned tripe-visaged rascal' – probably pushes the scene toward comedy. On the other hand, the Hostess's wish for Sir John reminds the audience of the question of Falstaff's place in the new state. The arrests may be represented as part of a clean-up connected to the new King's coronation, or even as a deliberate part of his promised reformation. Talk of a possible miscarriage due to Doll's treatment at the Beadle's hands raises serious concerns, unless, as he argues, the pregnancy is revealed to be a sham employing one of Mistress Quickly's cushions. The Hostess's own repeated misstatements, meaning the opposite of what she intends, also suggest a comic atmosphere. But the insistence that 'the man is dead that you and Pistol beat amongst you,' as well as the spectacle of four or five officers dragging two women to prison, allows for a more serious interpretation of the scene. Shakespeare would depict similar arrests in *Measure for Measure* (I.ii and III.iii) as part of Angelo's crackdown on crime. This brief episode reveals both the dangerous underside of the tavern world Hal is leaving, and the severity with which his administration will confront it.

Act V, scene v

The final scene of the play, the long-anticipated meeting of Falstaff and the newly-crowned Henry V, passes in only a few minutes of stage time. The King's rejection of Falstaff is decisive and unambiguous. Falstaff tries to put a brave face on it, but is soon hauled off to prison with his followers, while Prince John and the Lord Chief Justice discuss the possibility of an imminent invasion of France.

1–39 The opening, with two (F) or three (Q) grooms strewing rushes, creates a sense of haste and expectation. The Quarto has a stage direction indicating that '*Trumpets sound, and the King and his train pass over the stage*'; in the Folio the King doesn't enter until after line 40. Having the coronation procession appear before Falstaff and company enter may make the rejection seem more of a foregone conclusion, especially if Hal is notably transformed by his royal panoply. Falstaff and his crew enter hastily, 'stained with travel and sweating' in their eagerness to see the new King. Falstaff's intent to 'leer upon' the King in hopes of favour would not have sounded as bad to Elizabethan ears as it does to ours, but it still suggests that he has misjudged the situation. We learn, in passing, that Falstaff has borrowed a thousand pounds from Shallow; he implies that he has not yet spent it, but we soon learn otherwise. Falstaff's concern about his apparel may betray a degree of anxiety, but otherwise his language expresses certainty and bravado. Shallow's excitement seems to equal Falstaff's, and his rhythmic, repeated 'It doth' lines build the scene to a near-frenzy of anticipation. Pistol interjects, in characteristically histrionic terms, the news that Doll has been arrested, and Falstaff's confident assertion that he will deliver her is the final expression of his presumptive greatness. The crowd roars and trumpets sound, and the King's procession enters.

40–72 Falstaff's lines may be shouted over the noisy crowd, or into a reverent silence inspired by the awesome presence of the King. In either case, they violate the decorum of the occasion, both by their volume and by their inappropriate familiarity: 'my royal Hal', 'my sweet boy'. Nonetheless, the intimate pet names and beatific wishes suggest a depth of genuine feeling on Falstaff's part, as much the proud parent as the greedy hanger-on. At first, the King does not speak to him directly. Perhaps he wishes to avoid the situation, from guilt or pain, or perhaps he is using his new power in an Olympian, impersonal way, delegating to the Lord Chief Justice the problem of rabble in the streets. Falstaff is not deterred, and makes one more personal appeal. He may, at this point, stop the procession in its tracks, perhaps throwing himself to his knees in the King's path; at any rate, something happens that forces the King to confront him head-on.

The King's rejection of Falstaff has long been one of the most debated features of the play: critics have found it inevitable and necessary, or a personal betrayal of the deepest treachery, or both. It may be played with tears in the King's eyes as he turns away his closest friend, or an icy resolve that verges on hatred. Regardless, it is a moment of electrifying theatre, arousing probably the strongest emotions of the play. The King's first line falls in crushing monosyllables, hammer blows on the nails of Falstaff's coffin. It is both noble and cruel: 'I know thee not' has a Biblical grandeur, echoing the rejection of the foolish virgins in Matthew's gospel (25:12); 'old man' highlights the age and mortality that Falstaff has fled from throughout the play. With withering disdain, the King emphasizes the incongruity between Falstaff's appearance and behavior, then reduces him to the shadowy status of a despised dream. The image of the wide-gaping grave is vivid and brutal; but since it touches on one of Falstaff's favourite sources of wit, his size, it may seem to him an opening for the humour that could yet redeem this nightmarish situation. At line 55, Falstaff may be about to speak when Hal abruptly cuts him off: 'Reply not to me with a fool-born jest.' In the lines that follow, the King widens his address to include 'the world,' which shall perceive his transformation. The rejection of Falstaff is, in part, a public declaration, part of the glittering reformation Hal promised in his very first scene in *Part I*. Lines 60–2 could be more intimately directed to Falstaff, and though harsh, they contain an acknowledgement of what the two have shared in their former lives together, and the sense that, for better or worse, Hal has learned from his 'tutor'. Lines 63–5 seem for the public again, an open proclamation of banishment, with the terrifyingly exact detail of 'by ten mile'. Lines 66–70, with their promise of a pension and potential for advancement, may be a sincere attempt to soften the blow – if they are spoken directly to Falstaff. If they are given out to the crowd, they will come across as merely hollow political rhetoric, showing the King's generosity as well as his severity. Finally, in what Falstaff, if he is sentient of it at all, must perceive as a crowning indignity, the King gives charge of his case over to his great adversary, the Lord Chief Justice. With the terse command, 'Set on' – two syllables surrounded by eight beats of silence – the King is gone.

73–110   Falstaff will probably take some moments to recover himself after the stage clears; he and his followers will show postures of visible defeat. Falstaff is unable or unwilling to refer directly to what has just occurred; yet his first line acknowledges the loss of his hopes, and those of his companions. His lines about being sent for in private may be evidence of his clinging to some shred of belief, or they may just be his characteristic manner of brazening out a tough situation. They do not seem to come with much conviction, however, and Falstaff probably deceives himself no more than he does the others. Shallow, in his joke about the stuffed doublet, shows considerable resources of wit; but he also conjures up a rather grim image of a scarecrow Falstaff, a taxidermist's dummy. Shallow also speaks casually of Falstaff's death, and Falstaff's final speech of reassurance flirts with the possibility of a grim double meaning: 'I shall be sent for soon at night' – even at the turning o' the tide, as Quickly will later recall (*Henry V*, II.iii.13). Any degree of composure Falstaff may achieve through his repeated promises is shattered by the entrance of the Lord Chief Justice to arrest him. As officers drag Falstaff and his company to the Fleet prison, Prince John, the sober-blooded hero of Gaultree Forest, declares his approval of the 'fair proceeding'. He goes on to reiterate the King's good intentions for his 'wonted followers,' but quickly turns the brief conversation from the past to the future. The King has called his parliament, and war with France will soon follow. The madcap Prince has completed his transition into the warrior-king, Henry V. The closing words of the play proper, however, go not to him but to the two representatives of the new political order, and their smug self-satisfaction may end the action on a troubling note.

Epilogue

The play, however, is not over; and exactly how it ended, in Shakespeare's time, may have varied from performance to performance. Epilogues are relatively rare in the published texts of Shakespeare's plays, though they might have been spoken regularly in theatrical productions; we have no firm evidence. Much of the epilogue to *Henry IV: Part II* is taken up with conventional appeals for audience forbearance and applause, but it does contain the promise to 'continue the story, with Sir John in it,' along with a vague hint about his death. It also contains a disclaimer about the original name of Falstaff: 'Oldcastle died a martyr, and this is not the man.' Scholars have long speculated about whether Shakespeare really intended to bring Falstaff back in *Henry V*, and why he did not; the departure of Will Kemp from the company, if he played Falstaff, would be one explanation, but such a practical factor is hardly necessary. It certainly seems that after the final scene of the present play, there would have been very little left for Falstaff in the world of Henry V.

In the Quarto version of the epilogue, the line about kneeling to pray for the Queen comes midway through the speech, at the end of the first paragraph (line 15). This, and the redundancy of some of the sentiments, has led many to conjecture that the speech is actually a conflation of two, or possibly even three, epilogues written for different occasions. It could be, for instance, that the first paragraph was used at a performance in the presence of the Queen, and spoken by Shakespeare himself ('What I have to say is of mine own making'). The remainder, or some part of it, might have been spoken by an actor/dancer who performed a jig to close a performance in the public theatre. If, as James Shapiro has argued in his study *A Year in the Life of William Shakespeare: 1599* (HarperCollins, 2005), the speaker of the epilogue was Will Kemp, who was famous for his jigs, then this performance would have meant a lot to the play's final impact. *Henry IV: Part II* has one kind of meaning when, at the end of a court performance, after the coronation of the heroic monarch and banishment of his disgraced favourites, the playwright comes out and speaks deferentially to the Queen. It has another kind of meaning if, after a performance in the public theatre, when the crowd-pleasing Falstaff has been apparently rejected and defeated, the actor of Falstaff comes running back onto the stage to entertain the audience with a lively jig. The play's two dominant and competing concerns, the accession of Prince Hal and the fortunes of Falstaff, persist in the plenitude of its doubled epilogue.

3 Sources and Cultural Contexts

Sources

In almost all of his plays, Shakespeare worked from identifiable pre-existing sources. He took characters, situations, and even dialogue that were already part of his culture and refashioned them to meet the particular demands of his medium, his company and his artistic imagination. In the case of his English history plays, his materials were, by and large, real people and events, documented in a range of sources with varying claims to historical accuracy. For reasons of prudence and censorship, he treated subjects just outside the range of living memory. At the beginning of his career, writing his tetralogy on the late medieval Wars of the Roses, he stopped with the death of Richard III and the accession of Henry VII in 1485; the very oldest in his audience might conceivably have been born under the latter monarch, but none would have had personal experience of the former. At the end of his life, in *Henry VIII*, he concluded with the birth of the Princess Elizabeth, who had been in power during his first decade in London; but all of the political actors represented in that play were long dead. In the case of *Henry IV: Parts I and II*, he was treating of events nearly two hundred years in the past: about the same distance that separates the first readers of this book from the British/American War of 1812. Nonetheless, memories were long enough to have an impact on what could be safely written in a play; as discussed in Chapter 1, Shakespeare changed Falstaff's name from Oldcastle, presumably because of pressure from distant connections of that Lollard martyr.

While Shakespeare certainly felt free to alter and embellish the historical record – as he clearly did in the case of the Oldcastle/Falstaff figure – he was working within a narrative that was generally known and had been retold in a variety of media. Moreover, these sources themselves told the story from a range of different perspectives and Shakespeare often shifted among them from scene to scene or moment to moment. The sense of multi-vocality, of contending points of view, in Shakespeare's history plays derives in part from the range of sources he used, and the differing perspectives on history contained within even a single source. As Phyllis Rackin has pointed out in *Stages of History* (1990), history-writing in Elizabeth's time incorporated both the providential view of medieval chroniclers, who saw history as the working out of God's plan on earth, and the more pragmatic understanding of modern political historians influenced by Machiavelli. In Shakespeare's history play, a single event is often given multiple rival explanations. Henry's usurpation of the throne of Richard II, for instance, is repeatedly revisited over the course of these two plays, and depicted in very different terms each time (*Part I*: I.iii, III.ii, IV.iii, V.i; *Part II*: III.i, IV.i, IV.v). Furthermore, Shakespeare drew on other popular and literary sources that made little pretension to historical truth, but retold the story of the House of Lancaster according to their own conventions and biases. The three principal sources Shakespeare used for the *Henry IV* plays were a narrative chronicle, an epic poem, and a popular historical play. The excerpts that follow illustrate something of the variety of Shakespeare's raw material, and the array of political and personal concerns that he wove together to create the great tapestry of the *Henry IV* plays.

Raphael Holinshed, *The Third Volume of Chronicles*

The primary source for both *Henry IV* plays was the third volume of Raphael Holinshed's *Chronicles of England, Scotland and Ireland*, published in 1577 and reissued in 1587 in an enlarged edition, which seems to have been the text Shakespeare used. Holinshed provided source material, not only for Shakespeare's English history plays, but also for *Macbeth*, *King Lear* and *Cymbeline*. Holinshed included material from the Tudor chronicler Edward Hall and from earlier historical sources like Froissart and Thomas Walsingham.

Holinshed provides Shakespeare with the basic historical material for the rebellions against Henry IV: that of the Percies,

Glendower, and Mortimer in *Part I*, and that of the Archbishop of York and his confederates in *Part II*. Shakespeare's chief alteration of his source is his elaboration of Prince Hal's life away from court, and his relationship with Falstaff and his friends. Shakespeare reshapes Holinshed to provide the strong contrasts that structure both plays, as Hal is placed in a series of oppositions involving figures like Hotspur, Falstaff, the Lord Chief Justice, and King Henry himself. Shakespeare makes Hotspur, in particular, into a clear rival for Prince Hal, a young man of Hal's age who is being compared with him even in Shakespeare's *Richard II*, and who fights a climactic duel with him at the end of *Henry IV: Part I*. In Holinshed, Hotspur is more a rival of King Henry himself: he was actually two years older than the King.

Holinshed's Chronicle, like Hall's before it, though to a lesser degree, includes a certain amount of sententious moralizing on the dangers of civil dissention. Hall's Chronicle interprets medieval history from a providential point of view, justifying the Tudor dynasty as the final outcome of God's plan. He traces the history of the Wars of the Roses back to Henry IV's deposition and murder of Richard II; the subsequent civil strife represented God's curse on the English people for their disobedience, a curse lifted only with the accession of Henry VII and the Tudors in 1485. Holinshed incorporates more alternative views than does Hall, but a fair amount of moral sentiment remains. How much Shakespeare was influenced by this providential view of history – and whether he accepted the 'Tudor myth' that Henry IV's usurpation brought the divine punishment of civil strife upon England – has been much debated by scholars. E. M. W. Tillyard strongly advanced this view of the history plays in 1944, and Shakespeare's historical outlook has been a subject of contention ever since. Many critics have argued that Shakespeare, and even Holinshed, took a more complex and multi-vocalic view of medieval history than the providential view explicitly stated by Hall.

Holinshed's account of Henry IV's reign, after giving the background to the King's troubles with the Welsh, includes a passage reflecting on the precariousness of his position. This passage may have influenced Shakespeare's depiction of the King's insomnia in *Part II*. However, it is worth noting that Holinshed explicitly emphasizes the physical danger incurred by a usurper hated by his people, while Shakespeare attributes the King's sleeplessness more generally to the burdens of power. The moralizing tone of Holinshed creates a certain ambiguity in this passage, as elsewhere in the chronicles. On the one hand, Henry's guilt makes him deservedly fearful; on the other, it was God's will that protected him from the 'naughty traitorous persons' who dared to try to assassinate him. Although Henry had been a usurper, he was the ruling monarch and attempts on his life constituted treason and rebellion. Questions of this kind create conflicts of loyalty throughout Shakespeare's history plays:

> One night, as the King was going to bed, he was in danger to have been destroyed; for some naughty traitorous persons had conveyed into his bed a certain iron made with smith's craft, like a caltrop, with three long pricks, sharp and small, standing upright in such sort that when he had laid him down and that the weight of his body should come upon the bed, he should have been thrust in with those pricks and peradventure slain; but as God would, the King, not thinking of any such thing, chanced yet to feel and perceive the instrument before he laid him down and so escaped the danger. Howbeit, he was not so soon delivered from fear; for he might well have his life in suspicion and provide for the preservation of the same, sith perils of death crept into his secret chamber and lay lurking in the bed of down where his body was to be reposed and to take rest. Oh what a suspected state therefore is that of a king holding his regiment with the hatred of his people, the heartgrudgings of his courtiers, and the peremptory practices of both together! Could he confidently compose or settle himself to sleep for fear of strangling? Durst he boldly eat and drink without dread of poisoning? Might he adventure to show himself in great meetings or solemn assemblies without mistrust of mischief against his person intended? What pleasure or what felicity could he take in his princely pomp, which he knew by manifest and fearful experience to be envied and maligned to the very death?

After reflecting on the difficulties of the King's position, Holinshed gives the background to the rebellion of the Percies, and their affiliation with Owen Glendower and Edmund Mortimer. Holinshed makes the mistake, repeated by Shakespeare, of conflating two Edmund Mortimers: the one who was captured by Glendower and married his daughter, and his nephew, the fifth Earl of March, who asserted a claim to the throne. Holinshed is more explicit than Shakespeare about Henry's attitude with regard to Mortimer; Shakespeare generally allows for a more positive interpretation of Henry's motives.

> Owen Glendower, according to his accustomed manner, robbing and spoiling within the English borders, caused all the forces of the shire of Hereford to assemble together against them, under the conduct of Edmund Mortimer, Earl of March. But coming to try the matter by battle, whether by treason or otherwise, so it fortuned that the English power was discomfited, the Earl taken prisoner, and above a thousand of his people slain in the place. The shameful villainy used by the Welshwomen towards the dead carcasses was such as honest ears would be ashamed to hear and continent tongues to speak thereof. The dead bodies might not be buried without great sums of money given for liberty to convey them away.
>
> The King was not hasty to purchase the deliverance of the Earl of March, because his title to the crown was well-known enough, and therefore suffered him to remain in miserable prison, wishing both the said Earl and all other of his lineage out of this life, with God and his saints in heaven so they had been out of the way, for then all had been well enough, he thought...
>
> Edmund Mortimer, Earl of March, prisoner with Owen Glendower, whether for irksomeness of cruel captivity or fear of death or for what other cause, it is uncertain, agreed to take part with Owen against the King of England and took to wife the daughter of the said Owen.
>
> Strange wonders happened (as men reported) at the nativity of this man, for the same night he was born, all his father's horses in the stable were found to stand in blood up to the bellies...

Holisnhed's report of Glendower's mysterious birth may have affected Shakespeare's presentation of him as a magician; Shakespeare greatly elaborates the character from a few hints in Holinshed.

The scene of the Percies' initial challenge to the King in Holinshed provided a good deal of material for Shakespeare, not least the meddling character of Worcester. Shakespeare altered his source in making the King summon the Percies to explain the disposal of the prisoners, whereas in Holinshed they aggressively go to him 'upon a purpose to prove him'. Shakespeare makes Henry a more authoritative king than the rather weak and calculating figure he is in Holinshed, who puts off the Percies with a 'fraudulent excuse' and is thoroughly conscious of the threat Mortimer represents to him.

Henry, Earl of Northumberland, with his brother Thomas, Earl of Worcester, and his son, the Lord Henry Percy, surnamed Hotspur, which were to King Henry in the beginning of his reign both faithful friends and earnest aiders, began now to envy his wealth and felicity; and especially they were grieved because the King demanded of the Earl and his son such Scottish prisoners as were taken at Homeldon and Nesbit: for of all of the captives which were taken in the conflicts fought in those two places, there were delivered to the King's possession only Mordake, Earl of Fife, the Duke of Albany's son, though the King did divers and sundry times require deliverance of the residue, and that with great threatenings; wherewith the Percies, being sore offended, for that they claimed them as their own proper prisoners and their peculiar prize, by the counsel of Lord Thomas Percy, Earl of Worcester, whose study was ever (as some write) to procure malice and set things in a broil, came to the King unto Windsor (upon a purpose to prove him) and there required of him that, either by ransom or otherwise, he would cause to be delivered out of prison Edmund Mortimer, Earl of March, their cousin german, whom (as they reported) Owen Glendower kept in filthy prison, shackled with irons, only for that he took his part and was to him faithful and true.

The King began not a little to muse at this request and not without cause; for indeed it touched him somewhat near, sith this Edmund was son to Roger, Earl of March, son to the Lady Philip, daughter of Lionel, Duke of Clarence, the third son of King Edward the Third; which Edmund, at King Richard's going into Ireland, was proclaimed heir apparent to the crown and realm; whose aunt called Eleanor, the Lord Henry Percy had married; and therefore King Henry could not well hear that any man should be earnest about the advancement of that lineage. The King, when he had studied the matter, made answer that the Earl of March was not taken prisoner for his cause nor in his service but willingly suffered himself to be taken, because he would not withstand the attempts of Owen Glendower and his complices, and therefore he would neither ransom him nor relieve him.

The Percies with this answer and fraudulent excuse were not a little fumed, insomuch that Henry Hotspur said openly: 'Behold, the heir of the realm is robbed of his right, and yet the robber with his own will not redeem him.' So in this fury the Percies departed, minding nothing more than to depose King Henry from the high type of his royalty and to place in his seat their cousin Edmund, Earl of March, whom they did not only deliver out of captivity but also (to the high displeasure of King Henry) entered in league with the foresaid Owen Glendower. Herewith they, by their deputies in the house of the Archdeacon of Bangor, divided the realm amongst them, causing a tripartite indenture to be made and sealed with their seals, by the covenants whereof: all England from Severn to Trent south and eastward was assigned to the Earl of March; all Wales and the lands beyond Severn westward were appointed to Owen Glendower; and all the remnant from Trent northward to the Lord Percy.

Holinshed's account of the battle of Shrewsbury, based closely on Hall, gave several suggestions to Shakespeare, though the play goes further than either chronicle in making the battle a showdown between Prince Hal and Hotspur. It is just possible that Holinshed's phrase 'the other on his part' could have been taken to mean 'Prince Hal, on his part', as opposed to 'the other soldiers who were fighting on the part of the King'; this reading of the passage might have suggested Hal's slaying of Hotspur, though a final conflict between the two champions seems a natural enough dramatic invention without it.

The prince that day holp his father like a lusty young gentleman; for although he was hurt in the face with an arrow, so that diverse noblemen that were about him would have conveyed him forth of the field, yet he would not suffer them to do so, lest his departure from amongst his men might haply have stricken some fear into their hearts; and so, without regard of his hurt, he continued with his men and never ceased either to fight where the battle was most hot or to encourage his men where it seemed most need. This battle lasted three long hours with indifferent fortune on both parts, till at last the king, crying Saint George and victory, brake the array of his enemies and adventured so far that (as some write) the Earl Douglas strake him down and at that instant slew Sir Walter Blunt and three others apparelled in the King's suit and clothing, saying: 'I marvel to see so many kings thus suddenly arise one in the neck of another.' The King indeed was raised and did that day many a noble feat of arms, for as it is written, he slew that day with his own hands six and thirty persons of his enemies. The other on his part, encouraged by his doings, fought valiantly and slew the Lord Percy, called Sir Henry Hotspur. To conclude, the King's enemies were vanquished and put to flight, in which flight the Earl of Douglas, for haste, falling from the crag of a high mountain, brake one of his cullions and was taken, and for his valiantness, of the King frankly and freely delivered.

Shakespeare spares Douglas the indignity of this injury, and gives Prince Hal the chivalric impulse to free him without ransom.

Shakespeare made selective and limited use of Holinshed in *Part II*, greatly telescoping the events of Henry's reign. He makes the northern rebellion seem to occur within weeks of Shrewsbury, whereas actually it was two years later. He virtually ignores the last five years of Henry's life, after all the rebellions had been put down. During these years the Prince of Wales was an active administrator, and intriguer, within the royal court. Holinshed reports that the Prince tried to get the King, who had fallen ill, to abdicate. As a consequence, the King deprived him of his place in the Council, giving it instead to his brother. Shakespeare makes only the slightest allusion to these matters.

Holinshed's account of the King's death includes his desire to lead a crusade to Jerusalem and the irony of his death in the Jerusalem chamber. It also includes the episode of the Prince's taking away the crown, excused somewhat by the general belief that the King is dead. However, the reconciliation between King and Prince is less full than Shakespeare later makes it.

During this his last sickness, he caused his crown (as some write) to be set on a pillow at his bed's head, and suddenly his pangs so sore troubled him, that he lay as though all his vital spirits had been from him departed. Such as were about him, thinking verily that he had been departed, covered his face with a linen cloth.

The Prince his son being hereof advertised, entered into the chamber, took away the crown, and departed. The father being suddenly revived out of that trance, quickly perceived the lack of his crown; and having knowledge that the Prince his son had taken it away, caused him to come before his presence, requiring of him what he meant so to misuse himself. The Prince with a good audacity answered, 'Sir to mine and all men's judgments you seemed dead in this world, whereas I as your next heir apparent took that as mine own, and not as yours.' 'Well fair son' (said the King with a great sigh) 'what right I had to it, God knoweth.' Well (said the Prince, if you die King, I will have the garland, and trust to keep it with the sword against all mine enemies, as you have done. Then said the King, I commit all to God, and remember you to do well. With that he turned himself in his bed, and shortly after departed to God in a chamber of the Abbot's of Westminster called Jerusalem the twentieth day of March, in the year 1413, and in the year of his age 46, when he had reigned thirteen years, five months and odd days, in great perplexity and little pleasure.

Samuel Daniel, *The First Four Books of the Civil Wars*

Another important source for both *Henry IV* plays was Samuel Daniel's poem *The First Four Books of the Civil Wars*, published in 1595. The events of the battle of Shrewsbury and the character of Hotspur seem to owe much to Daniel. Daniel makes Hotspur a young man, as Shakespeare does, and a figure of courage and nobility. While Daniel doesn't have Hal kill Hotspur he does give prominence to the Prince in the battle scenes, encouraging a comparison of the two young rivals. Daniel's account of Shrewsbury, in the third book, begins with King Henry hastening to meet the rebels:

96
Not to give time unto th'increasing rage
And gathering fury, forth he hastes with speed,
Lest more delay or giving longer age
To th'evil grown, it might the cure exceed:
All his best men at arms, and leaders sage
All he prepared he could, and all did need;
For to a mighty work thou goest O King,
To such a field that power to power shall bring.

97
There shall young Hotspur with a fury led
Meet with thy forward son as fierce as he:
There warlike Worcester long experiencèd
In foreign arms, shall come t'encounter thee:
There Douglas to thy Stafford shall make head:
There Vernon for thy valiant Blunt shall be:
There shalt thou find a doubtful bloody day,
Though sickness keep Northumberland away.

98
Who yet reserved, though after quit for this,
Another tempest on thy head to raise,
As if still-wrong avenging Nemesis

Did mean t'afflict all thy continual days:
And yet this field he happily might miss
For thy great good, and therefore well he stays:
What might his force have done being joined thereto
When that already gave so much to do?

99
The swift approach and unexpected speed
The king had made upon this new-raised force,
In th' unconfirmèd troops, much fear did breed,
Untimely hind'ring their intended course.
The joining with the Welsh they had decreed
Was hereby stopped which made their cause the worse.
Northumberland with forces from the North
Expected to be there, was not set forth.

100
And yet undaunted Hotspur seeing the King
So near approached, leaving the work in hand
With forward speed his forces marshalling,
Sets forth his farther coming to withstand.
And with a cheerful voice encouraging
By his great spirit his well emboldened band,
Brings a strong host of firm resolvèd might
And placed his troops before the King in sight.

101
This day (saith he) O faithful valiant friends,
Whatever it doth give, shall glory give;
This day with honour frees our state, or ends
Our misery with fame, that still shall live,
And do but think, how well this day he spends,
That spends his blood his country to relieve:
Our holy cause, our freedom and our right,
Sufficient are to move good minds to fight.

102
Besides, the assurèd hope of victory
That we may even promise on our side,
Against this weak constrainèd company,
Whom force and fear, not will and love doth guide
Against a prince whose foul impiety
The heavens do hate, the earth cannot abide,
Our number being no less, our courage more,
What need we doubt if we but work therefor.

103

This said, and thus resolved even bent to charge
Upon the king; who well their order viewed,
And careful noted all the form at large
Of their proceeding, and their multitude:
And deeming better if he could discharge
The day with safety, and some peace conclude,
Great proffers sends of pardon and of grace
If they would yield, and quietness embrace.

104

But this refused, the King with wrath incensed,
Rage against fury doth with speed prepare:
And O, said he, though I could have dispensed
With this day's blood, which I have sought to spare;
That greater glory might have recompensed
The forward worth of these, that so much dare;
That we might good have had by th' overthrown,
And the wounds we make might not have been our own.

105

Yet, since that other men's iniquity
Calls on the sword of wrath, against my will;
And that themselves exact this cruelty,
And I constrainèd am this blood to spill;
Then on, brave followers, on courageously,
True-hearted subjects, against traitors ill;
And spare not them, who seek to spoil us all
Whose foul confusèd end, soon see you shall.

106

Straight moves with equal motion equal rage
The like incensèd armies unto blood,
One to defend, another side to wage
Foul civil war, both vows their quarrel good:
Ah too much heat to blood doth now enrage
Both who the deed provokes, and who withstood,
That valour here is vice, here manhood sin,
The forward'st hands doth O least honour win.

107

But now began these fury-moving sounds,
The notes of wrath, that music brought from Hell,
The rattling drums, which trumpet's voice confounds
The cries, the encouragements, the shouting shrill;

That, all about, the beaten air rebounds
Thundering confused, murmurs horrible;
To rob all sense except the sense to fight.
Well hands may work; the mind hath lost his sight.

108

O war! begot in pride and luxury,
The child of wrath and of dissension.
Horrible good, mischief necessary,
The foul reformer of confusion,
Unjust-just scourge of our iniquity,
Cruel recurrer of corruption,
O that these sin-sick states in need should stand
To be let blood with such a boisterous hand!

109

And O how well had thou been spared this day
Had not wrong-headed Percy been perverse?
Whose young undangered hand now rash makes way
Upon the sharpest fronts of the most fierce:
Where now an equal fury thrusts to stay
And rebeat-back that force, and his disperse:
Then these assail, then those chase back again,
Till stay'd with new-made hills of bodies slain.

110

There, lo that new-appearing glorious star,
Wonder of arms, the terror of the field,
Young Henry, labouring where the stoutest are,
And even the stoutest forces back to yield;
There is that hand boldened to blood and war,
That must the sword, in wondrous actions, wield:
But better hadst thou learned with others' blood;
A less expense to us, to thee more good.

111

Hadst thou not there led present speedy aid
To thy endangered father nearly tired,
Whom fierce encountering Douglas overlaid,
That day had there his troublous life expired:
Heroical courageous Blunt arrayed
In habit like as was the King attired
And deemed for him, excused that fate with his,
For he had what his lord did hardly miss.

112

For thought a king, he would not now disgrace
The person then supposed, but princelike shows
Glorious effects of worth that fit his place
And fighting dies, and dying overthrows:
Another of that forward name and race
In that hot work his valiant life bestows
Who bare the standard of the King that day,
Whose colors overthrown did much dismay.

113

And dear it cost, and O much blood is shed
To purchase thee this losing victory
O travailed King: yet hast thou conquered
A doubtful day, a mighty enemy:
But O what wounds, what famous worth lies dead!
That makes the winner look with sorrowing eye,
Magnanimous Stafford lost that much had wrought,
And valiant Shirley who great glory got.

114

Such wreck of others' blood thou didst behold,
O furious Hotspur, ere thou lost thine own!
Which now once lost that heat in thine waxed cold,
And soon became thy army overthrown;
And O that this great spirit, this courage bold,
Had in some good cause been rightly shown!
So had not we thus violently then
Have termed that rage, which valour should have been.

115

But now the king retires him to his peace,
A peace much like a feeble sick man's sleep,
(wherein his waking pains do never cease
Though seeming rest his closed eyes doth keep)
For O no peace could ever so release
His intricate turmoils, and sorrows deep,
But that his cares, kept waking all his life,
Continue on till death conclude the strife.

In the version published in 1595 that Shakespeare probably used,
Daniel proceeds immediately to the scene of the King's death with
the Prince taking away the crown. In the revision of 1609, probably

influenced by Shakespeare's play, Daniel includes the Archbishop's rebellion and then proceeds to Henry's death scene, somewhat expanded from the present version.

What follows is Henry's death scene from the 1595 version that Shakespeare had access to as a source; it follows immediately on the passage previously quoted. It is notable how conscience-stricken Henry is: he even seems to decide to give up his crown 'to whom it seemed to appertain'. It is the Prince who asserts that his own claim to the throne will appear stronger than his father's through the passage of time. Shakespeare adopts much of Daniel's phrasing from this section, including the King's advice to the Prince to distract his subjects from his weak claim through foreign war: 'But some great actions entertain thou still, /To hold their minds, who else will practice ill.'

116

Whose herald, sickness, being sent before,
With full commission to denounce his end;
And pain and grief, enforcing more and more,
Besieged the hold, that could not long defend;
And so consumed that all emboldening store
Of hot gain-striving blood that did contend
Wearing the wall so thin that now the mind
Might well look thorough and his frailty find.

117

When lo, as if those vapors vanished were,
Which heat of boiling blood, and health, did breed,
(To cloud the sense that nothing might appear
Unto the thought, that which it was indeed)
The lightened soul began to see more clear
How much it was abused, and notes with heed
The plain discovered falsehood open laid
Of ill persuading flesh that so betrayed.

118

And, lying on his last afflicted bed,
Where Death and Conscience both before him stand;
Th'one holding out a book, wherein he read
In bloody lines the deeds of his own hand:
The other shows a glass, which figurèd
An ugly form of foul corrupted sand;

Both bringing horror in the highest degree,
With what he was, and what he straight should be.

119
Which seeing all confused trembling with fear,
He lay a while, as overthrown in sprite,
At last, commands some, that attending were,
To fetch the Crown, and set it in his sight.
On which, with fixèd eye, and heavy cheer,
Casting a look; O God, sayeth he, what right
I had to thee, my soul doth now conceive:
Thee, which with blood I got, with horror leave.

120
Wert thou the cause my climbing care was such
To pass those bounds, nature and law ordained?
Is this that good which promisèd so much
And seemed so glorious ere it was attained?
Wherein was never joy but gave a touch
To check my soul to think, how thou wert gained,
And now how do I leave thee unto mine,
Which it is dread to keep, death to resign.

121
With this the soul rapt wholly with the thought
Of such distress, did so attentive weigh
Her present horror, whilst as if forgot
The dull consumèd body senseless lay,
And now as breathless quite, quite dead is thought,
When lo his son comes in, and takes away
The fatal crown from thence, and out he goes
As if unwilling longer time to lose.

122
And whilst that sad confusèd soul doth cast
Those great accounts of terror and distress,
Upon this counsel it doth light at last
How she might make the charge of horror less,
And finding no way to acquit that's past
But only this, to use some quick redress
Of acted wrong, with giving up again
The crown to whom it seemed to appertain.

123
Which found, lightened with some small joy she hies,
Rouses her servants that dead sleeping lay,

(The members of her house) to exercise
One feeble duty more, during her stay:
And opening those dark windows he espies
The crown for which he looked was borne away,
And all-aggrieved with the unkind offense
He caused him bring it back that took it thence.

124

To whom (excusing his presumptuous deed
By the supposing him departed quite)
He said, O son, what needst thou make such speed
Unto that care, where fear exceeds thy right,
And where his sin whom thou shalt now succeed
Shall still upbraid thy inheritance of might
And if thou canst live, and live great from woe
Without this careful travail, let it go.

125

Nay, Father; since your Fortune did attain
So high a Stand, I mean not to descend,
Replies the Prince: as if what you did gain,
I were of spirit unable to defend.
Time will appease them well that now complain,
And ratify our interest in the end.
What wrong hath not continuance quite out-worn?
Years makes that right, which never was so borne.

126

If so; God work his pleasure, said the King:
Yet thou must needs contend, with all thy might,
Such evidence of virtuous deeds to bring,
That well may prove our wrong to be our right:
And let the goodness of the managing
Race out the blot of foul attaining quite;
That discontent may all advantage miss,
To wish it otherwise, then now it is.

127

And since my death my purpose doth prevent,
Touching this sacred war I took in hand
(An action wherewithal my soul had meant
T'appease my God, and reconcile my land)
To thee is left to finish my intent;
Who, to be safe, must never idly stand;
But some great actions entertain thou still,
To hold their minds, who else will practice ill.

128

Thou hast not that advantage by my reign,
To riot it, (as they whom long descent
Hath purchased love, by custom) but, with pain
Thou must contend to buy the world's content.
What their birth gave them, thou hast yet to gain
By thine own virtues, and good government:
And that unless thy worth confirm the thing,
Thou canst not be the father to a king.

129

Nor art thou borne in those calm days, where Rest
Hath brought asleep sluggish Security:
But, in tumultuous times; where minds addressed
To factions are inured to mutiny;
A mischief, not by force, to be suppressed,
Where rigor still begets more enmity:
Hatred must be beguiled with some new course,
Where states are strong, and princes doubt their force.

130

This and much more affliction would have said,
Out of th'experience of a troublous reign,
For which his high desire had dearly paid
The interest of an ever-toiling pain:
But that this all-subduing power here stayed
His faltering tongue and pain reinforced again,
And cut off all the passages of breath
To bring him quite under the state of death.

131

In whose possession I must leave him now;
And now, into the ocean of new toils;
Into the stormy main (where tempests grow
Of greater ruins, and of greater spoils)
Set forth my course (to hasten on my vow)
Over all the troublous deep of these turmoils,
And, if I may but live t'attain the shore
Of my desired end, I wish no more.

The Famous Victories of Henry V

The Famous Victories of Henry V, an anonymous play probably first performed in 1594, provided much of the material for the comic scenes of Shakespeare's *Henry IV* plays. *The Famous Victories* is rather crudely and tersely written, combining into one play the materials that Shakespeare turned into three. Some scholars have speculated that it may be a memorial reconstruction of one or more earlier plays. *The Famous Victories* includes not only the Prince's misspent youth, coronation, and rejection of his followers, but his victory at Agincourt and marriage to the French princess, which Shakespeare dramatized in *Henry V*. The opening scene of *The Famous Victories* provided some of the inspiration for Shakespeare's Gadshill robbery. One of the Prince's companions, 'Jockey Oldcastle', is the original of Shakespeare's Falstaff, who was called Oldcastle in early performances. The rather coarse and intimidating manner of the Prince in this scene is worth noting; Shakespeare took pains to make his Prince appear more fair-minded, returning the stolen money:

Scene 1

[*Enter the young Prince, with Ned and Tom.*]

> PRINCE: Come away, Ned and Tom.
> NED and TOM: Here, my Lord.
> PRINCE: Come away, my lads.
>> Tell me sirs, how much gold have you got?
> NED: Faith, my Lord, I have got five hundred pound.
> PRINCE: But tell me, Tom, how much hast thou got?
> TOM: Faith, my Lord, some four hundred pound.
> PRINCE: Four hundred pounds, bravely spoken lads.
>> But tell me, sirs, think you not that it was a villainous part of
>> me to rob my father's receivers?
> NED: Why no, my Lord, it was but a trick of youth.
> PRINCE: Faith Ned thou sayest true.
>> But tell me sirs, whereabouts are we?
> TOM: My Lord, we are now about a mile off London.
> PRINCE: But sirs, I marvel that Sir John Oldcastle
>> Comes not away. Zounds, see where he comes.

[*Enter Jockey Oldcastle*]

> How now, Jockey, what news with thee?
> JOCKEY: Faith my Lord, such news as passeth,
>> For the town of Deptford is risen
>> With hue and cry after your man
>> Which parted from us the last night,

And has set upon and hath robbed a poor carrier.
PRINCE: Zounds, the villain that was wont to spy
    Out our booties?
JOCKEY: Aye, my Lord, even the very same.
PRINCE: Now base-minded rascal to rob a poor carrier.
    Well it skills not, I'll save the base villain's life:
    Aye, I may: but tell me Jockey, whereabout be the Receivers?
JOCKEY: Faith my Lord, they are hard by,
    But the best is, we are a horseback and they be a foot,
    So we may escape them.
PRINCE: Well, if the villains come, let me alone with them.
    But tell me Jockey, how much got'st thou from the knaves?
    For I am sure I got something, for one of the villains
    So belammed me about the shoulders,
    As I shall feel it this month.
JOCKEY: Faith, my Lord, I have got a hundred pound.
PRINCE: A hundred pound, now, bravely spoken, Jockey.
    But come, sirs, lay all your money before me.
    Now, by heaven, here is a brave show.
    But as I am true Gentleman, I will have the half
    Of this spent tonight. But sirs, take up your bags;
    Here comes the receivers. Let me alone. [*Enter two Receivers*]
1 RECEIVER: Alas good fellow, what shall we do?
    I dare never go home to the court, for I shall be hanged.
    But look, here is the young Prince, what shall we do?
PRINCE: How now you villains, what are you?
1 RECEIVER: Speak you to him.
2 RECEIVER: No I pray, speak you to him.
PRINCE: Why how now you rascals, why speak you not?
1 RECEIVER: Forsooth we be – pray speak you to him.
PRINCE: Zounds, villains, speak, or I'll cut off your heads.
2 RECEIVER: Forsooth, he can tell the tale better then I.
1 RECEIVER: Forsooth, we be your father's receivers.
PRINCE: Are you my father's receivers?
    Then I hope ye have brought me some money.
1 RECEIVER: Money? Alas sir, we be robbed.
PRINCE: Robbed? How many were there of them?
1 RECEIVER: Marry sir, there were four of them:
    And one of them had sir John Oldcastle's bay hobby,
    And your black nag.
PRINCE: Gogs wounds, how like you this, Jockey?
    Blood, you villains: my father robbed of his money abroad,

And we robbed in our stables!
But tell me, how many were of them?

1 RECEIVER: If it please you, there were four of them,
And there was one about the bigness of you,
But I am sure I so belammed him about the shoulders,
That he will feel it this month.

PRINCE: Gogs wounds you lammed them fairly –
So that they have carried away your money.
But come sirs, what shall we do with the villains?

BOTH RECEIVERS: I beseech your grace, be good to us.

NED: I pray you, my Lord, forgive them this once.

[PRINCE:] Well, stand up and get you gone,
And look that you speak not a word of it,
For if there be, Zounds, I'll hang you and all your kin. [*Exeunt Receivers.*]
Now sirs, how like you this?
Was not this bravely done?
For now the villains dare not speak a word of it,
I have so feared them with words.
Now whither shall we go?

ALL: Why, my Lord, you know our old hostess
At Feversham.

PRINCE: Our hostess at Feversham, blood what shall we do there?
We have a thousand pound about us,
And we shall go to a petty alehouse.
No, no: you know the old tavern in Eastcheap,
There is good wine: besides, there is a pretty wench
That can talk well – for I delight as much in their tongues,
As any part about them.

ALL: We are ready to wait upon your grace.

PRINCE: Gogs wounds, wait, we will go all together.
We are all fellows, I tell you sirs; and the King
My father were dead, we would be all kings,
Therefore come away.

NED: Gogs wounds, bravely spoken, Harry.

The next several scenes of the play follow the Prince's antics with his low-life companions. The Prince is committed to prison for inciting a violent brawl at the Tavern in Eastcheap. After the King secures his release, he gives the Lord Chief Justice a box on the ear. These events are alluded to in *2 Henry IV*, but the Prince is never shown in nearly as unflattering a light as he appears in The *Famous Victories*. Throughout the early scenes, he positively encourages the ambitions of his cronies, and earnestly wishes for the death of his father: 'My lads, if the old king my father were dead, we would all be kings.' He tells Ned, the model for Poins, 'So soon as I am King, the first thing I will do, shall be to put my Lord Chief Justice out of office, and thou shalt be my Lord Chief Justice of England.' He later says of his father, 'the breath shall be no sooner out of his mouth, but I will clap the crown on my head.'

In the event, the Prince is moved by his father's apparent death, though he does make off with the crown as in Holinshed and Daniel. The following extract also includes the new King's rejection of his followers; it provided a number of details to Shakespeare:

Scene 8

[*Enter the King with his Lords.*]

HENRY 4: Come, my Lords, I see it boots me not to take any
    physic, for all the Physicians in the world cannot cure me – no,
    not one. But good my Lords, remember my last will and
    testament concerning my son, for truly, my Lords, I do
    not think but he will prove as valiant and victorious a king
    as ever reigned in England.

BOTH: Let heaven and earth be witness between us, if
    we accomplish not thy will to the uttermost.

HENRY 4: I give you the most unfeigned thanks. Good my lords,
    Draw the curtains and depart my chamber awhile,
    And cause some music to rock me asleep. [*Exit Lords.*]

[*He sleepeth. Enter the Prince.*]

PRINCE: Ah, Harry, thrice unhappy, that hath neglect so
    long from visiting of thy sick father! I will go. Nay; but why
    do I not go to the Chamber of my sick father, to comfort the
    melancholy soul of his body? His soul, said I? Here is his
    body indeed, but his soul is whereas it needs no body. Now
    thrice-accursed Harry, that hath offended thy father so much!
    And could not I crave pardon for all? Oh, my dying father,
    curst be the day wherein I was borne, and accursed be the
    hour wherein I was begotten! But what shall I do? If weeping
    tears, which come too late, may suffice the negligence neglected
    too soon, I will weep day and night until the
    fountain be dry with weeping. [*Exit, with the crown.*]

[*Enter Lord of Exeter and Oxford.*]

EXETER: Come easily, my Lord, for waking of the King.

HENRY 4: Now, my Lords.

OXFORD: How doth your Grace feel your self?

HENRY 4: Somewhat better, after my sleep.
But good my Lords, take off my crown,
Remove my chair a little back, and set me right.

BOTH: And please your grace, the crown is taken away.

HENRY 4: The crown taken away?
Good my Lord of Oxford, go see who hath done this deed:
No doubt tis some vile traitor that hath done it
To deprive my son. They that would do it now
Would seek to scrape and scrawl for it after my death.

[*Enter Lord of Oxford with the Prince.*]

OXFORD: Here, and please your Grace,
Is my Lord the young Prince with the crown.

HENRY 4: Why, how now, my son?
I had thought the last time I had you in schooling,
I had given you a lesson for all,
And do you now begin again?
Why tell me, my son,
Dost thou think the time so long,
That thou would'st have it before the
Breath be out of my mouth?

PRINCE: Most sovereign Lord, and well-beloved father,
I came into your chamber to comfort the melancholy
Soul of your body, and finding you at that time
Past all recovery, and dead to my thinking,
God is my witness, and what should I do,
But with weeping tears lament the death of you my father,
And after that, seeing the crown, I took it.
And tell me my father, who might better take it then I,
After your death? but seeing you live,
I most humbly render it into your Majesty's hands,
And the happiest man alive, that my father live:
And live my Lord and Father, for ever.

HENRY 4: Stand up, my son.
Thine answer hath sounded well in mine ears,
For I must need confess that I was in a very sound sleep,
And altogether unmindful of thy coming:
But come near my son,
And let me put thee in possession whilst I live,
That none deprive thee of it after my death.

PRINCE: Well may I take it at your Majesty's hands,
But it shall never touch my head, so long as my father lives.

[*He taketh the Crown.*]

HENRY 4: God give thee joy my son.
    God bless thee and make thee his servant,
    And send thee a prosperous reign,
    For God knows my son, how hardly I came by it,
    And how hardly I have maintained it.
PRINCE: Howsoever you came by it, I know not,
    But now I have it from you, and from you I will keep it.
    And he that seeks to take the crown from my head,
    Let him look that his armor be thicker then mine,
    Or I will pierce him to the heart,
    Were it harder then brass or bullion.
HENRY 4: Nobly spoken, and like a King.
    Now trust me, my Lords, I fear not but my son
    Will be as warlike and victorious a Prince
    As ever reigned in England.
BOTH LORDS: His former life shows no less.
HENRY 4: Well, my lords, I know not whether it be for sleep,
    Or drawing near of drowsy summer of death,
    But I am very much given to sleep,
    Therefore good my Lords and my son,
    Draw the curtains, depart my chamber,
    And cause some Music to rock me asleep. [*Exit omnes. The King dieth.*]

Scene 9

[*Enter the Thief.*]

THIEF: Ah God, I am now much like to a bird
    Which hath escaped out of the cage,
    For so soon as my Lord Chief Justice heard
    That the old King was dead, he was glad to let me go,
    For fear of my lord the young Prince:
    But here comes some of his companions,
    I will see and I can get any thing of them,
    For old acquaintance.

[*Enter Knights ranging.*]

TOM: Gogs wounds, the King is dead.
JOCKEY: Dead, then gogs blood, we shall be all kings.
NED: Gogs wounds, I shall be Lord Chief Justice
    Of England.
TOM: Why how, are you broken out of prison?
NED: Gogs wounds, how the villain stinks.

JOCKEY: Why what will become of thee now?

    Fie upon him, how the rascal stinks.

THIEF: Marry I will go and serve my master again.

TOM: Gogs blood, dost think that he will have any such

    Scabbed knave as thou art? What man, he is a king now.

NED: Hold thee, here's a couple of angels for thee,

    And get thee gone, for the King will not be long

    Before he come this way:

    And hereafter I will tell the king of thee. [*Exit Thief.*]

JOCKEY: Oh how it did me good, to see the king

    When he was crowned:

    Me thought his seat was like the figure of heaven,

    And his person like unto a God.

NED: But who would have thought,

    That the king would have changed his countenance so?

JOCKEY: Did you not see with what grace

    He sent his embassage into France? To tell the French king

    That Harry of England hath sent for the crown,

    And Harry of England will have it.

TOM: But twas but a little to make the people believe,

    That he was sorry for his father's death. [*The Trumpet sounds.*]

NED: Gogs wounds, the King comes,

    Let's all stand aside. [*Enter the King with the Archbishop, and the Lord of Oxford.*]

JOCKEY: How do you do my Lord?

NED: How now Harry?

    Tut my Lord, put away these dumps,

    You are a king, and all the realm is yours:

    What man, do you not remember the old sayings?

    You know I must be Lord Chief Justice of England,

    Trust me, my lord, methinks you are very much changed,

    And tis but with a little sorrowing, to make folks believe

    The death of your father grieves you,

    And tis nothing so.

HENRY 5: I prithee Ned, mend thy manners,

    And be more modester in thy terms,

    For my unfeigned grief is not to be ruled by thy flattering

    And dissembling talk, thou sayest I am changed,

    So I am indeed, and so must thou be, and that quickly,

    Or else I must cause thee to be changed.

JOCKEY: Gogs wounds how like you this?

    Zounds, tis not so sweet as music.

TOM: I trust we have not offended your grace no way.

HENRY 5: Ah Tom, your former life grieves me,
        And makes me to abandon and abolish your company for ever
        And therefore not upon pain of death to approach my presence
        By ten miles space; then if I hear well of you,
        It may be I will do somewhat for you,
        Otherwise look for no more favour at my hands,
        Then at any other man's: And therefore be gone,
        We have other matters to talk on. [*Exeunt Knights*]

Cultural contexts

Shakespeare's plays on Henry IV, while they dealt with events two hundred years in the past, would have been recognized to have bearing on contemporary social concerns. In particular, the issues of rebellion, and the proper relation of monarch and subject, would have been of interest to Elizabethan audiences, as well as to state censors. Shakespeare had to exercise care in handling these topics, but he could also count on their being compelling to playgoers.

The topic of rebellion was particularly fraught. The Tudor state was at great pains to instill a horror of civil discord in its subjects, having a *Homily Against Disobedience and Willful Rebellion* read out regularly in churches from 1571 onward. This sermon presented the orthodox Elizabethan view of the natural order of the state and proclaimed 'what an abominable sin against God and man rebellion is, and how dreadfully the wrath of God is kindled and inflamed against all rebels.' For a playwright to depict rebellion on the stage was extremely problematic. When Shakespeare's colleagues included a civic uprising in their play *Sir Thomas More*, the Master of the Revels instructed them to 'Leave out the insurrection, wholly, and the cause thereof.' The eight passages missing from the Quarto of *Henry IV: Part II* all deal in some way with the topic of rebellion, and may have been removed for that reason. On the other hand, some defenders of the theatre argued for its ability to inculcate public virtue. In *An Apology for Actors*, Thomas Heywood stated that 'Plays are writ with this aim and carried with this method: to teach the subjects obedience to their king, to show the people the untimely ends of such as have moved tumults, commotions, and insurrections, to present them with the flourishing estate of such as live in obedience, exhorting them to allegiance, dehorting them from all traitorous and felonious stratagems.' Whether the *Henry IV* plays can be said to do this is open to debate, but it is certainly true that for much of their history they have been interpreted as endorsing orthodox Tudor notions of passive obedience.

One reason for the issuing of the *Homily Against Disobedience* in 1571 was the Northern Rebellion of 1569, one of the most serious challenges to Elizabeth's power. This episode bears some striking relations to the rebellions depicted in the plays. It was, in fact, carried out by the same family, the Percies of Northumberland, still a dominant influence in the North of England. They had the help of the Catholic Bishop of Ross, whose role in the rebellion may be compared to that of the Archbishop of York in Shakespeare's plays. The cause of the rebellion was religious as well as political: the Northern lords wanted to unseat Elizabeth in favour of her cousin, Mary Stuart, a Catholic, who had been temporarily driven out of Scotland. Her role corresponds roughly to that of Mortimer; during her imprisonment in England she became something of a pawn to those who wished to use her claim to advance their own interests. The rising illustrated the powerful force represented by the great aristocratic families of the countryside, a force that monarchs from Henry IV to Elizabeth had constantly to contend with.

Another problem for the English monarchy was the emergence of powerful and charismatic subjects. At the time the *Henry IV* plays were written, the Earl of Essex was a valiant military leader whose popularity made him a potential rival of the Queen. Many in Shakespeare's audience might have seen shades of Essex in the character of Hotspur. Like Hotspur, Essex was obsessed with honour and upheld medieval notions of chivalry. Like Hotspur, Essex had achieved military successes that were a mixed blessing to his sovereign, notably his sacking of Cadiz in 1596. Like Hotspur, Essex was hot-tempered, sensitive to affronts, and not afraid to defy the monarch openly. Essex even had connections to the Percy family; the ninth Earl of Northumberland was his brother-in-law. A few years after Shakespeare depicted Hotspur meeting his death at Shrewsbury, Essex went to the scaffold in 1601 after an ill-considered uprising. Essex's rebellion and execution were played out in the context of Shakespeare's Lancastrian history plays. As was mentioned in Chapter 1, his followers arranged a performance of a play about Richard II on the eve of the uprising and Queen Elizabeth later complained that, in popular opinion, 'I am Richard II, know ye not that?' The problems of rule, legitimacy, and popularity, discussed in *Part I*, III.ii in relation to Richard, Bolingbroke, Hal and Hotspur, would have been pertinent ones in the England of Elizabeth.

The question of succession was also a nagging public concern at the end of Elizabeth's reign. As an unmarried Queen with no direct descendents, Elizabeth had to choose an heir, and there was much political maneuvering over this question. The leading candidate, and eventual successor, was James VI of Scotland, son of Mary Stuart, whom Elizabeth had executed in 1587. Like Shakespeare's Prince Hal, James was a problematic heir, surrounded by disreputable favourites and addicted to hunting and gaming. He also showed signs of impatience to claim his new throne. The concerns of the King in *Part II* and Prince Hal's premature taking of the crown may have suggested, to an Elizabethan audience, the anxieties attendant upon the anticipated demise of the Queen.

Another contemporary concern that is explored in the play is the recruiting and treatment of soldiers. England had no standing army in the late sixteenth century, but the threat of the Spanish Armada and ongoing conflicts in France and the Low Countries meant that soldiers were continually being recruited during time Shakespeare was writing the play. Paul Jorgenson reports that between the years 1596 and 1599, when Shakespeare was engaged with the story of Henry IV, there was 'an almost total mobilization for defense' resulting in record numbers of conscriptions (p. 130). Whereas in 1594–5 the number of men levied from the counties had averaged just over 2000 men, the totals for the next four years were 8840, 4835, 9164 and 7300. The means by which Falstaff abuses 'the King's press' (the power of conscription) discussed in *Part I*, IV.ii and displayed in *Part II*, III.ii, were familiar features of Elizabethan military practice. A number of Elizabethan pamphlets detail the way corrupt commanders, chosen because of their influence at court, used the conscription process for private gain, assembling companies of poor and incompetent soldiers who, at the termination of their service, were reduced to poverty and begging. One captain, Barnaby Rich, complained that in many cases of recruitment 'the election is made of rogues, runagates, drunkards, and all sorts of vagabonds and disordered persons, such as are fitter to garnish a prison, than to furnish a camp' (Campbell, p. 247). Dudley Digges blamed the incompetent and unscrupulous captains, 'such decayed unthrifty gallants as to get a little money by the sale, spoil or slaughter of their companies make means to be favorably sent from the court to the camp, as commanders, before they know how to obey' (ibid.). When Falstaff speaks of his soldiers pilfering linen from hedges, he is echoing an observation made by Rich in 1574: 'as [soldiers] travel through the country, where they chance to lie all night, the goodwife hath sped well if she find her sheets in the morning' (Jorgensen, p. 252). Falstaff's unfortunate recruits – 'food for powder' as he describes them – are reduced to stealing their clothing, are led heedlessly 'where they are peppered', and if they survive, are 'for the town's end, to beg during life.' The depiction of the soldier's lot in the *Henry IV* plays reflects a serious social problem in Elizabeth's England. Falstaff's recruits are often comic, but their overall wretchedness draws attention to the fact that war, whether domestic or foreign, has grave consequences that extend far beyond the dangers of battle.

A final issue relevant to the plays is the condition of Elizabethan taverns, inns, and brothels – sometimes one and the same establishment. Taverns provided inexpensive food and drink and an atmosphere of social freedom, but they were also rough and dangerous places. In *King Lear*, Goneril, complaining of the disorderly behavior of her father's knights, says that 'this our court, infected with their manners,/ Shows like a riotous inn. Epicurism and lust/ Makes it more like a tavern or a brothel/ Than a grac'd palace' (I.iv.240–3). Mercutio gives a succinct picture of tavern violence in telling Benvolio, 'Thou art like one of those fellows that when he enters the confines of a tavern claps me his sword upon the table and says "God send me no need of thee!" and by the operation of the second cup draws him on the drawer, when indeed there is no need' (*Romeo and Juliet*, III.i.5–9). Overnight stay in inns was particularly dangerous, as Shakespeare demonstrates in his depiction of the unscrupulous chamberlain in *Part I*, II.i. William Harrison's account of inns in *The Description of England* matches well with Shakespeare's:

> …many an honest man is spoiled of his goods as he traveleth to and fro, in which feat also the counsel of the tapsters or drawers of drink and chamberlains is not seldom behind or wanting. Certes I believe that not a chapman or traveler in England is robbed by the way without

the knowledge of some of them; for when he cometh to the inn, and alighteth from his horse, the hostler forthwith is very busy to take down his budget or capcase in the yard from his saddle bow, which he peiseth slyly in his hand to feel the weight thereof.   (McDonald, p. 238)

Of course, the reputation of taverns and brothels as hotbeds of vice and crime was one they shared with another popular institution, also located in the 'Liberties' outside the city: the public theatre. As Barbara Hodgdon points out, 'most writers singled out brothels, theatres, and taverns or alehouses as the major locales of criminal activity. In crowding these venues into one space, *Henry IV: Part I*'s tavern is ideally suited to embodying the subversive behaviors associated with all three' (p. 208). In depicting the Eastcheap tavern on the stage of the Theatre, Shakespeare's company did not have to work hard to transport their audience imaginatively to a festive and dangerous world.

4 Key Productions and Performances

Shakespeare's *Henry IV* plays have been popular on the stage throughout English theatrical history, though *Part I* has been performed much more often than *Part II*. Pre-twentieth-century productions of either play were generally centred on star performances of Falstaff, or more rarely, Hotspur. Court records indicate performances of both parts during the season of 1612–3, celebrating the marriage of Princess Elizabeth to the Elector Palatine. *Part I* seems to have been referred to as 'The Hotspur', *Part II* as 'Sir John Falstaff', indicating the extent to which productions were already dominated by these starring roles.

Within a few years of Shakespeare's death, Sir Edward Dering conflated the two plays into a single one, given in a private performance in 1622–3. The Dering manuscript takes the better part of its text from *Part I*, cutting only the Carrier scene (II.i), the scene with the Archbishop and Sir Michael (IV.iv), and much of the scene with Glendower and the ladies in III.i – all cuts that have been reproduced in subsequent productions. It preserves much of the historical material from *Part II*, but jettisons many of the new comic characters, including Pistol and Doll, Shallow and Silence, and Fang and Snare. Dering seems to have been limited in the number of amateur actors he had available, as he even keeps out the Lord Chief Justice and reassigns various speeches in plausible ways to keep down the total number of players required.

After the Restoration, Thomas Betterton regularly performed *Part I*, graduating from Hotspur to Falstaff. James Quin, who also began as Hotspur, became the most successful Falstaff of the age. Both parts were regularly performed in the eighteenth century, though *Part I* was given about twice as frequently, and both were substantially adapted; oddly, Quin cut the 'play extempore' of *Part I*, 2.4. Colley Cibber was a famous Shallow; his son Theophilus a famous Pistol. In the nineteenth century, the penchant for antiquarianism resulted in rigorously researched medieval productions like the *Part I* of Charles Kemble in 1824. In 1864, Samuel Phelps returned to a more authentically Shakespearean text than had been used for centuries. The plays were given with some regularity at Stratford and the Old Vic in the early twentieth century, though they were still primarily star vehicles.

With the influence of Tillyard's cyclical view of the history plays in the second half of the twentieth century, it became more common to perform the two plays together, though individual productions of *Part I* remained popular. But after the war, in Britain especially, large-scale paired productions of the two parts became significant theatrical events, often key performances in the history of a particular company. This chapter will focus on this phenomenon and will therefore limit itself to productions originating – but not necessarily remaining – in Britain. Two-part large-scale productions of *Henry IV* have turned the play into a kind of national epic through which the British theatre periodically assesses the state of the nation. This chapter examines five key productions, each representing a particular producing organization: the Old Vic, the Shakespeare Memorial Theatre, the Royal Shakespeare Company, the English Shakespeare Company, and the National Theatre. These five productions have all bought into the notion of *Henry IV* as a unified artistic work, but they have expressed the meaning of that work and its reflection of national identity in very different ways.

Old Vic, 1945–6

The Old Vic productions of 1945–6, which played at the New Theatre and later on Broadway, were recognized at the time as unusual in playing the two parts together. Audrey Williamson noted that that it was 'rare to have Shakespearean histories played in such a way that the audience may follow the historical events and get thoroughly to know the historical characters' (p. 183) Citing Dover Wilson, Williamson argued that the two parts 'constitute one whole play rather than two separate ones' and that therefore this production was of 'special interest'. In practice, however, the production was one that very much looked back to the old tradition of actor managers and star performances. Critical and popular interest focused not on the plays' historical trajectory or political meaning but on the two star performances: of Ralph Richardson as Falstaff, and of Laurence Olivier as Hotspur and Shallow.

Richardson and Olivier were the leading classical actors of the century, working at the height of their powers. (John Gielgud was their only equal.) They were also, along with the director John Burrell, artistic directors of the Old Vic Company, which had been London's predominant home for Shakespeare in the first half of the century. At the end of World War II and in the years immediately following, the Old Vic had an unparalleled reputation and was seen by many as a *de facto* National Theatre. The *Henry IV* productions were an ambitious project designed to showcase the company's stars and cement its place in the British cultural world. Richardson and Olivier – rivals as well as partners within the company – sought to outdo each other in their star turns to the extent of comparing levels of applause at the curtain calls. (While Richardson's more prominent role could be expected to prevail in *Part II*, Olivier generally won out in *Part I*, and was reportedly furious when he didn't.)

Richardson's Falstaff received nearly unanimous praise and is often considered the greatest of the twentieth century. In the circumstances, it was quite a subtle performance, marked by intelligence, dignity and physical grace. Though Richardson's Falstaff was enormously fat, he moved quickly and lightly in ways that matched the deftness of his wit. Unlike most previous actors, who had worn heavy boots to disguise their legs, Richardson had specially padded tights made so that he could move with more agility. He played the role on the balls of his feet, occasionally 'capering about' in a manner Gordon Crosse found implausibly 'acrobatic', though he remained 'the most gentlemanly Falstaff' Crosse had seen (p. 128). His fat suit, made from toweling and horsehair, was built up in anatomical layers so that it moved naturally with Richardson's body. Kenneth Tynan praised the 'great finesse' with which he crossed the stage, using his arms like fins 'as if to paddle the body's bulk along'. For Tynan, this Falstaff's principal attribute was 'not his fatness but his knighthood. He was Sir John first, and Falstaff second ... Richardson never rollicked or slobbered or staggered: it was not a sweaty fat man, but a dry and dignified one' (Wells, p. 235).

Quickness of wit was the signature feature of Richardson's conception. When Olivier initially broached the project, Richardson weighed his qualities as an actor and considered what he might bring to the role: 'I thought about it. I have a certain alacrity of thinking that might help me with the part' (McMillin, p. 21). That quality – defined, perhaps unconsciously, in punning opposition to Falstaff's 'alacrity in sinking' in *The Merry Wives of Windsor* (III.v.12) – guided the characterization. In *Part I*, Falstaff's intelligence expressed itself in playful merriment: Alan Dent praised him for his 'appearance of perfect good nature, pleasantry, mellowness, and hilarity of mind' (McMillin, p. 25). He received special notice for the inspired inventiveness with which, on the spur of the moment, he formulated his excuse for his Gad's Hill cowardice. He moved upstage, then suddenly turned and cried 'By the lord, I knew ye as well as he that made ye,' with a delighted roar of laughter (Crosse, p. 128). In *Part II*, the keenness of Falstaff's mind was revealed in darker and richer shades according to Audrey Williamson:

> Ralph Richardson's Falstaff, a grand buffoon and rapscallion in *Part I*, proceeded in *Part II* to a still richer understanding which could catch the somber understanding of 'Do not bid me remember mine end,' and suggest, as Falstaffs do rarely, the attraction of the man for the Prince as well as the considerable brain behind the wit.

His scene with Doll drew particular praise; Christopher Fry said, 'There was all human mortality in it, moving out into the audience like a slow sea wave' (Miller, p. 98). In this scene Richardson was helped by Joyce Redman's performance as Doll; the paucity of female roles in the play meant that he had a major star to work with in this relatively small part. Gordon Crosse praised her 'rapid transitions between rage, maudlin affection and real grief', though he questioned her Irish brogue, as well as the decision to make her cognizant of the Prince and Poins and thus egg Falstaff on to incriminate himself.

The essential nobility of Richardson's Falstaff came through in the rejection scene. Many critics stressed what Williamson called this Falstaff's 'greatness of spirit' (p. 185); Tynan noted 'a charity … a magnanimity and a grief' that supported W. H. Auden's audacious identification of Falstaff with Christ (McMillin, p. 23). Williamson noted that the shock of the rejection 'has a spiritual as well as a material basis' (p. 186). Richardson faced upstage as the new King delivered his crushing speech; he then slowly turned to face the audience, struggling to control his tears, and spoke his line to Master Shallow with quiet dignity. The Prince Hal, Michael Warre, was himself moved to tears by Richardson in nearly every performance (Miller, p. 95).

Laurence Olivier, the other star performer, took a showier approach to his two roles, which afforded him the opportunity for a virtuoso contrast. His Hotspur was visually striking and possessed of a magnetic charisma. Olivier donned a ginger wig and beard – his make-up allegedly took him three hours to put on – wore a tight-fitting costume, and affected poses that flaunted his athleticism and physical allure (McMillin, 25–6). His scene with Margaret Leighton's Lady Percy – another star in a supporting part – was passionate and sexy, revealing a 'rough tenderness' in the character (Crosse, p. 128). His approach to the part was romantic rather than political – he stood apart from the other rebels, animated by his personal desire for honour rather than grievances against the King (McMillin, p. 24–5). He made the most of Hotspur's fiery verse speeches, according to Audrey Williamson: 'The rhetoric poured out like molten silver, and that anomaly that caused Shakespeare to give to this fire-eater and ballad-derider the brightest poetry in the play was drowned by the actor in a raging music' (p. 184).

The most famous feature of his characterization was the stammer he affected on the 'w' sound, inspired by Lady Percy's *Part II* reference to Hotspur 'speaking thick.' As Scott McMillin has pointed out, several previous Hotspurs had stammered: Matheson Lang in 1914, Baliol Holloway in 1923, Gyles Isham in 1931 (p. 27). But Olivier's choice had particular payoffs. It gave Hotspur some touching vulnerability and provided Hal an easy opportunity for mockery in his burlesque of Hotspur. ('Fie upon this quiet life, I w-w-want w-w-work.') It set up the *coup de théâtre* of Hotspur's death, one of Olivier's showcase effects. Stabbed in the neck, Olivier held his hand over the wound for some moments as the blood poured between his fingers, then collapsed, in full armour, down a flight of steps onto the stage. His last line produced an effect of heartrending pathos as he struggled to get out his final words – 'No, Percy, thou art dust, / and food for w-w-' – requiring

Hal to finish his line magnanimously with 'For worms, brave Percy.' It was the kind of show-stopping moment for which Olivier was famous, carefully set up throughout the play for maximum theatrical effect: the hallmark of the kind of star performance Olivier set out to give.

His choice of Shallow in *Part II* was a shrewd one, allowing him one of his trademark displays of his theatrical range. (Later that season he would play Sophocles's Oedipus and Sheridan's Mr. Puff on a double-bill.) Beverly Baxter described his performance as 'like something devised by Grimm in collaboration with Dickens ... fantastic yet as real as human vanity' (Cottrell, p. 124). He wore a tall pointed cap, stringy white hair, a long goatee, and a pointed nose – one of his most elaborate make-up jobs in a career full of them. He used a high, quavering voice and impulsive sudden movements. He was senile but lecherous, doddering yet quick-tempered, palsied yet spry; Gordon Crosse complained that he 'relied too much on tumbling and rolling about the stage' (p. 128). His most shameless scene-stealing occurred in III.ii, while Falstaff was trying to recruit soldiers. Olivier had decided that Shallow, as a rural justice and gentleman farmer, might well keep bees. Accordingly, he would frequently interrupt the scene to wave his hat violently at imaginary swarms of the stinging insects, to Richardson's great annoyance.

In spite of these gimmicks, Olivier managed to achieve subtlety and pathos in the role. Kenneth Tynan felt that the Gloucestershire scenes 'threw across the stage a golden autumnal veil, and made the idle sporadic chatter of the lines glow with the same kind of delight as Gray's *Elegy*' (Wells, p. 237). Tynan praised the 'sharp masculine kindness' and 'quick commiserating eyes' of Olivier's Shallow, and his genial concern for his guests; but he also noted the 'beady delectation that steals into his eyes at the mention of sex', his 'fatuous repetitions' and 'giggling embarrassment' (237–8). Tynan thought Shallow was the best performance Olivier had given in his two seasons leading the Old Vic and that he and Richardson between them had summed up English acting at its best.

While the two stars monopolized critical attention, the Old Vic company was a deep and seasoned one and many roles in both plays were strongly cast. Of female players, along with those already mentioned, the great Sybil Thorndike condescended to the role of

Mistress Quickly. Harcourt Williams, 'bristling with daemonic eloquence', was an unusually formidable Glendower; Miles Malleson made a strong doubling of Northumberland and Silence. As the King, Nicholas Hannen was benign and sympathetic, his usurpation downplayed. Williamson found him 'a king anxious indeed to preserve peace in his kingdom, but also a father saddened by the dissolute fecklessness of his heir and eldest son, trying with patience and an almost wistful disappointment to bridge the rift.' With the two *Henry IV* plays given together but without *Richard II* or *Henry V,* the political dimensions of the Lancaster family were subordinated to the personal ones. Usurpations and 'foreign quarrels' were left out of the picture: the final deathbed reconciliation played to the audience's desire for family harmony. The dying father was stressed at the expense of the Machiavellian politician.

The one great weak point of the production, by all accounts, was Michael Warre's Hal. He was criticized as a 'light-weight', a 'stripling', and 'in the junior school' and at best was damned with the faint praise of having come 'creditably through his ordeal' (Williamson, p. 186; McMillan, p. 29). This fate may have been inevitable for an inexperienced company member playing with some of the world's most famous Shakespearean actors. To a large extent, the productions were tailored to make Falstaff and Hotspur the leading characters, as they had been in Victorian and Edwardian productions. It may be that even though the Old Vic played the two parts of *Henry IV* together, the company was still thinking of them as basically star vehicles for Olivier and Richardson. The Old Vic productions lacked the interest in Hal and his father that was developing in critical circles in the wake of Tillyard. In any event, all of these tendencies would be countered in the next major production of the *Henry IV* plays, which made a star out of Richard Burton as part of an epic cycle focused on Hal.

Shakespeare Memorial Theatre, 1951

In commemoration of the Festival of Britain, the Shakespeare Memorial Theatre staged all four Lancastrian history plays as a cycle, the first such production in Britain. The production was influenced by current scholarship on the history plays and by the patriotic nature of the occasion. The Festival of Britain was an attempt to celebrate the national character and heritage during the years of post-war austerity. The cycle, for which Anthony Quayle was the overall artistic director, presented the histories as a parable of fortitude, growth and redemption, centred on the ideal King, Henry V. Robert Speaight summed up the project as having 'rich rewards for the playgoer, new light for the student, and ripe instruction for anyone concerned with the management of the common weal' (Wilson and Worsley, p. 90). The general tone was one of seriousness, nationalism, and high moral purpose.

John Dover Wilson wrote an essay accompanying the productions that emphasized value of considering the plays as a unity in order to arrive at proper responses to Hal and Falstaff:

> Two of Shakespeare's greatest characters are leading figures in a whole series of plays and may be seriously misunderstood when considered within the framework, or from the point of view, of one play alone. I have in mind of course Henry of Monmouth and Sir John Falstaff, the first of whom has been almost universally judged (and condemned) by critics on the strength of his soliloquy in Act I Scene 2 of *Henry IV Part I* and of his action at the end of *Part II*, with hardly any regard to the dramatist's presentation of him between these points, or as the victor of Agincourt in *Henry V*.   (Wilson and Worsley, pp. 3–4)

The productions downplayed such traditional showcase roles as Richard II, Hotspur, and Falstaff in favour of the dominant figures of Henry Bolingbroke, played by Harry Andrews, and Prince Hal, played by Richard Burton. The political education of the hero of Agincourt became the through-line of the whole series; the rejection of Falstaff was inevitable and necessary. Staging the four plays together corrected, in Wilson's view, a fundamental popular misconception of the Hal/Falstaff relationship. Wilson felt that 'no one who witnessed with proper understanding the four performances at Stratford will ever again be able to think of Falstaff and his royal partner, whether as Prince Hal or King Henry V, in the way Hazlitt and Swinburne, Bradley and Masefield, had taught us to think of them' (pp. 4–5). The production allowed no sentimentality over the fate of Falstaff and no criticism of Hal; to attribute 'mean and caddish actions' to the 'young and ardent knight' played by Burton would, in Wilson's words, 'have been stupid' (p. 5).

One of the distinguishing features of the cycle, in terms of staging, was the use of a semi-permanent quasi-Elizabethan set designed by Tanya Moiseiwitsch and adapted slightly for each production. The Shakespeare Memorial Theatre had been remodeled for the occasion, and the addition of side boxes and an apron stage gave a somewhat more Elizabethan configuration to the cavernous proscenium hall of the building. The set was a mostly symmetrical construction of bare oak timbers resembling in some respects an Elizabethan stage with a large front apron, a curtained 'inner stage', and a catwalk above that could serve for battlements and balconies. The stage could be adapted with draperies, furniture, and portable set pieces to a variety of specific locations, each with its own distinctive look. The throne, on a dais in the downstage right corner, anchored the set. Some critics found the unchanging unit setting rather austere, but the use of colorful curtains and banners and the rich medieval costuming provided visual spectacle and variety, especially as the cycle approached the pageantry of Henry V's coronation.

The mid-century scholarship that nourished the production, such as E. M. W. Tillyard's *Shakespeare's History Plays* and Wilson's *The Fortunes of Falstaff*, tended to emphasize the horrors of civil war; so one might have expected the emphasis to be on the curse laid on England by Bolingbroke's usurpation. In practice, however – perhaps in keeping with the sentiments of post-war Britain – the emphasis was on the nation's ability to rebound from adversity through the forthright perseverance of Henry IV and especially the visionary purpose of his son. After *Richard II*, in which Michael Redgrave's effeminate and poetic Richard was defeated by Harry Andrews's stern and manly Bolingbroke, the cycle moved quickly to redeem England from any lingering curse. The critic of *Truth* felt Andrews conveyed the sense of Bolingbroke as 'a fundamental patriot, not without remorse at his own ruthless advent to the throne, but resolved to be King who, at all costs, must rule' (Wilson and Worsley, p. 70). In *Vogue*, Siriol Hugh Jones described the King as 'the pivot point and corner stone of the whole edifice', praising Andrews's 'heroic, splendid portrait, finely spoken, noble to the eye and most movingly developed from powerful youth to haunted old age' (ibid.). While the vigour and virility of Andrews's performance could not quite excuse Henry's usurpation of the throne, his son's heroic destiny was to wipe away the stain.

Richard Burton's Prince Hal was, almost from the start, the noble hero of Agincourt rather than a tavern wastrel. Harold Hobson, reviewing the production in the *Sunday Times*, found that Burton's performance could hardly even be called good according to the traditional demands of the play, but in its emotional impact, and charting of a new course, it approached greatness. 'Mr. Burton looked like a man who had had a private vision of the Holy Grail ... Instead of a lighthearted rapscallion Mr. Burton offers a young knight keeping a long vigil in the cathedral of his own mind' (8 April 1951). Ivor Brown concurred that a dominant note of the productions was 'Prince Hal's sense of destiny' (*Observer*, 8 April 1951). Burton's steely, unsmiling demeanour quenched some of the tavern revelry, but offered several powerful premonitions of the hero to come. In his first scene with Falstaff and Poins, he was withdrawn and almost sullen, 'not an easy-hearted convivial boon companion' according to T. C. Worsley, but one who 'has to be lured into that role' and for whom the 'I know you all' soliloquy comes 'as no sort of surprise' (Wilson and Worsley, p. 49). For that moment, Hal looked after his departing companions and then turned to regard the audience over his shoulder, giving the speech 'with a curious simplicity and tonelessness, and yet with a suggestion of strong emotion held in check' (David, p. 136). In the play-within-the-play of *Part I*, II.iv, Burton's Hal became coldly serious as soon as he said, 'There is a devil haunts thee in the likeness of an old, fat man.' According to Worsley, 'The accusations come unsmiling from that dead-pan face, and, as they unwind, an uneasy feeling falls on the company and freezes their laughter' (p. 50). When Quayle's Falstaff tried to play the moment off as a joke with 'My lord, the man I know', Burton made Hal's reply, 'I know thou dost' into an accusation that caused 'a queer, horrid silence'.

The subsequent moment of 'I do, I will' was not, at least originally, specially marked. As Scott McMillin has discussed, this moment is one that modern productions often emphasize, but it used to be merely a part of the tavern high-jinks; in the 1945 Old Vic production, for instance, Michael Warre's Hal threw a cushion at Falstaff on this line. The Stratford promptbook calls for no special business other than a loud cheer from the crowd at 'Banish plump Jack, and banish all the world' together with bustling activity in response to the knocking at the door. But McMillin speculates that Burton introduced the note of seriousness at some point during rehearsals or the run: 'Burton seems to have been responsible for this interpretation, but exactly when he introduced it is difficult to say' (p. 48). This reading is certainly in keeping with Burton's approach to the role; and his friend and mentor Philip Burton has recalled suggesting the reading to him in 1951 (ibid.). A serious treatment of 'I do, I will' was noted in the next Old Vic production in 1955 (Brown, p. 154). Given Burton's gravity throughout this scene, it seems likely that he used it as well.

Burton's treatment of Prince Hal paired well with Anthony Quayle's Falstaff, who was designed, from the beginning, to be rejected. Quayle acknowledged openly that he wished to show 'the unsympathetic, even repellent aspect of the character'. While acknowledging that Shakespeare makes Falstaff 'irresistibly lovable', Quayle insisted that he is also 'frankly vicious' (Wilson and Worsley, p. viii). Quayle, who was not yet forty at the time, made himself up as a hideous old man, with bald pate, protruding nose, clown-like white hair projecting upward from the sides of his head, and an absurdly curled moustache and beard. He wore a short tunic that revealed his puffy padded legs but had huge hanging sleeves, ludicrous with scalloped edges and contrasting lining. His Falstaff was, as various critics reported, 'a tenor-voiced monster, with a nice turn of philosophy'; 'a sick man who brags, but not as though he believes his own bluster'; 'superbly funny, but openly contemptible' (Wilson and Worsley, p. 67, 68). In portraying this unlikable and mean-spirited Falstaff, Quayle was attempting to support the overall enterprise of which he was artistic director rather than create a crowd-pleasing characterization. 'Mr. Quayle is strictly loyal to the Festival's historical design', the *Times* critic noted. 'His makeup is grotesque rather than laughable; he speaks the jests with a metallic precision; and his smile when it appears is a painted smile' (Wilson and Worsley, p. 67). There was something cringing and desperate about this Falstaff. In making excuses to the Prince and Poins, 'he would stand between them like a cornered rat, head settled into hunched shoulders and his body pinched and withdrawn, while beneath bushy brows his eyes shifted from one to the other of his captors, measuring, calculating, seeking a way out' (David, p. 136). The explanations, when they came, were exuberant and confident, but did not quite eradicate the sense of bestial meanness about this grasping parasite.

Michael Redgrave, who played Richard II and Hotspur as well as directing *Part II*, also subordinated his star power to the overall design. As Hotspur he eschewed the romantic flair of Olivier in favour of a more flawed and human character who would not upstage the Prince. Instead of a showy stammer, he adopted a rough Northern dialect, which he allegedly spent many hours in Northumbrian pubs perfecting. His scenes with Lady Percy (Joyce Redman) were marked by a coarse, almost animalistic sexuality, 'a tone of violence', noted Worsley, 'which you would never find at the Court' (p. 46). Redgrave felt that the key to the character 'lay in the fact that he was a rough, down-to-earth countryman who was ignorant in the ways of the court and proud of it' (McMillin, p. 45). He was energetic and impetuous but fell short of real nobility; Worsley felt his character, 'for all its good points, sits just a little lower than Hal's – or at least what Hal's, we already feel, potentially may become' (p. 46).

One interesting feature of the production, given its attempt at a unifying British mythology, was the unusual respect it played to the Welsh. For the first time on the English stage, Glendower and his daughter were played by Welsh actors, and their conversation consisted not of mumbled gibberish ad libs but of eloquent and poetic Welsh dialogue. Hugh Griffith, who played Glendower, wrote the dialogue (for which a translation was provided in the promptbook) and a Welsh actress, Sybil Williams (Burton's wife), both spoke it and sang a moving Welsh song. Griffith gave unprecedented dignity and authority to Glendower, who until that time had been played largely for comedy. Having another Welshman, Burton, in the role of Prince Hal, whose Monmouth birth is much discussed in the plays, gave the production further pan-British appeal.

Part II was, of the four plays of the cycle, the one that stood to benefit the most from performance in the context of the other plays. W. A. Darlington noted that 'in its place in this sequence *Henry IV: Part II* becomes more important, because more comprehensible, than ever it can be when standing alone' (Wilson and Worsley, p. 73). What this meant in practice, notably, was that the character of Falstaff, who historically tended to dominate productions of *Part II*, was subordinated to the overall story of the King and Prince. 'It was the drama rather than the fooling that one best remembers,' remarked the critic of the *Birmingham Mail*. 'Harry Andrews, who has been proving so strong a fulcrum in this series, carried the aged, ailing King along his last troubled stretch with finely controlled dramatic power' (Wilson and Worsley, p. 73). T. C. Worsley concurred that 'the great scenes of Henry IV's death gain immeasurably from our having traced the relationship of father and son from its beginning' (p. 72). These scenes were cited by many critics as highlights, not only of the play, but of the entire series. The *Manchester Guardian*, noting that 'the real heroic link of the first three plays of this ambitious sequence' is the life and death of Henry IV, praised the 'unbroken power' of Andrews's performance in the death scenes (p. 74). The *Birmingham Post* felt that 'the dramatic scales were tipped heavily in favour of royalty chiefly by the playing of Harry Andrews as Henry' (p. 73). As the dying King, Andrews 'beautifully encompassed the tragedy of failing strength. Yet as the grasp loosened on the uneasy scepter, and the royal glance faded from the eyes, the leonine head was occasionally lifted in a hint of the old dominance' (p. 74).

The rejection of Falstaff, a long-anticipated moment in this sequence, was given surprisingly little notice by reviewers. However, some showed that they had bought into the production's strategies for endorsing the rejection. The *Evening Standard* critic 'got ready to blush' at what he considered a 'loathsome scene' of the new King 'publicly humiliating' his former friend, but then found that 'Richard Burton acted the scene with such youthful dignity and fine distaste for his duty as to lift it on to a higher plane altogether' (Hodgdon, p. 40). The rejection took place amid a spectacular coronation procession, with rose petals falling around the new Henry V. Burton gave the speech from a platform stage centre; Falstaff was in an unemphatic position stage right, and even Dover Wilson felt that he should have put up more of a fight for himself:

> Was that 'confident brow' ever browbeaten? Or could that 'throng of words, that came with such more than impudent sauciness' from him, be checked and put to silence by 'Father Antic the law?' The Devil they could! He should have been carried off by force, struggling with the officers and indignantly protesting 'My lord, my lord' until out of earshot.

But Quayle's Falstaff went meekly on his way, as attendants brought on the banner, shield, and helmet of Henry V, closing the play with an image of its heroic protagonist and a foreshadowing of his valiant acts in the final play of the cycle. These two productions demonstrated the effectiveness of a serial performance of Shakespeare's history plays and provided a compelling if conservative view of Hal's rise to greatness.

The next time the *Henry IV* plays were performed at Stratford, in 1964, it was as a kind of afterthought to the epic *Wars of the Roses* series of the previous season. Peter Hall and John Barton, who had founded the Royal Shakespeare Company in 1960, scored one of the company's early triumphs with a three-play cycle cobbled together from the *Henry VI* plays and *Richard III*, with quite a bit of pseudo-Shakespearean verse added by Barton to give it thematic unity. The *Wars* cycle bore the stylistic influence of Brecht in John Bury's designs and the potent interpretive influence of Jan Kott. The Polish critic's *Shakespeare Our Contemporary*, read by Hall in pre-publication typescript, governed the productions' view of politics as a cycle of totalitarian violence and corruption; at the end of *Richard III*, the ascension of Richmond represented not a redemption of England but only another phase in the bloody and interminable struggle for power. When the four Lancastrian histories were added to the cycle in 1964, they also fitted into this cynical mode. Since the bloody chaos that followed the death of Henry V was already being staged – and since the role of Hal was taken by Ian Holm, who also played Richard of Gloucester – it was unlikely that the *Henry IV* plays would come across as the development of a triumphant hero-king. Holm's Prince was another Machiavellian climber, who retained a degree of detachment while learning to manipulate those around him. His moments of triumph were tempered by an insistence on the brutality of the political arena he inhabited. To take only one example, he won at Shrewsbury by knifing Hotspur in the gut and tipping him into a pig trough. As Scott McMillin observes, 'one took no pleasure in knowing that a hero-King of England was emerging out of such violence' (p. 65).

Royal Shakespeare Company, 1975

Terry Hands directed the *Henry IV* plays as part of the Centenary season of the Royal Shakespeare Theatre, along with *Henry V* and

The Merry Wives of Windsor. The cycle opened with Hands's *Henry V*, a celebrated production that defined the company's style for the 1970s and made RSC fixtures of Alan Howard and the designer Abdel Farrah. The production emphasized the anti-illusionistic nature of Shakespeare's theatre and the nervous role-playing of the King. Howard's performance was acclaimed as a study of a young man growing into leadership in the face of ethical and emotional challenges. Accordingly, when the company went back to stage *Henry IV*, beginning with *Part I*, many critics found the exercise rather redundant: they had already seen the maturing of Prince Hal and didn't need to see it again.

The *Henry IV* plays took over many motifs from *Henry V*. Hands used a stripped-down company with no supernumeraries and much meaningful doubling. Farrah had designed a steeply-raked black stage platform intended 'to launch the actors into the audience ... like the deck of a great aircraft carrier' (Beauman, *Henry V*, p. 31). On this the actors were arranged in choreographed movements and meaningful groupings that eschewed naturalism in favour of overt theatricality. In *2 Henry IV*, for instance, Rumour was played by a group of actors who began speaking chorally, then moved about the stage into different groups, sharing the lines while they pantomimed movements suggestive of the true and false reports. In *1 Henry IV*, scenes often overlapped in significant ways with actors from one scene remaining onstage in some provocative juxtaposition with the following scene. At the end of the first scene, the King stayed to watch Hal and Falstaff at the tavern, as though visualizing the 'riot and dishonour' his preceding speeches had described. As the next scene ended with Hal's 'I know you all' soliloquy, he in turn remained to watch the King and the rebellious lords, reflecting on the political life he would soon confront. Further, many scenes shared symbolic furniture and properties. The chair that Falstaff sat in as a mock-throne in the tavern was in fact the same one that the King used at court. When the King tried to instill in Hal a sense of the threats the rebels posed to England, he pointed to the same map the rebels had been using to divide the country in the previous scene. When, in the stress of his interview with the King, Hal wanted to evade his father's bullying, he crossed to a barrel left from the tavern scene and grabbed a cup of sack (McMillin, p. 73). These juxtapositions tied the various plot-strands of the play together, and revealed the production's clear emphasis on the psychological nuances of the father-son relationship at its centre.

Where the 1964 *Wars of the Roses* cycle had focused on the politics of the plays, the 1975 Henries emphasized the personal, particularly with regard to Hal and Henry. Alan Howard had demonstrated a special aptitude for portraying psychological conflict, specializing in neurotic and high-strung characters. His Henry V was a leader on the verge of a nervous breakdown, barely holding himself together under the pressures of war. His Hal, when added to the mix, was a man struggling with a domineering and unpredictable father and an uncertain identity. Role-playing was a key motif in all the plays of the sequence, with Hal rehearsing for the part of player-king. The programme was filled with quotes from Erving Goffman and B. F. Skinner on the psychology of self-presentation and this theme was developed in Howard's performance from Eastcheap to Agincourt. Hal's tavern antics and battlefield bravery were both aspects of a search for self.

Hal's most important relationship was not with Falstaff but with his father, who was given a striking and unorthodox performance by Emrys James. In a marked contrast to the sturdy warrior played by Harry Andrews, James played the King as 'a manic little dictator', 'a mean and ranting neurotic, with a good line in emotional blackmail', 'a snarling, sardonic, guilt-laden autocrat' (*Punch*, 7 May 1975; *Telegraph, Times*, 25 April 1975). Small of stature, mercurial of disposition, and capable of sudden virtuoso shifts of vocal quality, James's Henry was a usurper convinced of his own inadequacy, who asserted his authority through shrill theatrical gestures. In refusing to redeem Mortimer, he shrieked with indignation and flung a coin down on the floor, retrieving it in 'a rapid shuffling return at the end of the scene'. He forced Northumberland and Hotspur to kneel before dismissing them; he subjected Hal to smothering embraces. As James saw the character, 'Here's a man who hasn't learned how to handle his emotions and his solution to the problem is to suppress them completely. Except in moments of extreme stress. Then they come out' (quoted in McMillin, p. 79).

By contrast, Brewster Mason's Falstaff was mellow and dignified, 'magnanimous, seignural and valiant', in Irving Wardle's phrase (*Times*, 25 June 1975). Mason was a large-framed, dignified actor of gravity and distinction: his roles with the RSC had included Kent,

Claudius, Julius Caesar and Cardinal Wolsey, but he lacked the coarseness and vitality for Falstaff. His muted gentlemanly performance was appealing but understated – some reviewers found him too much on one note – and he received much less attention than James's King, as Scott McMillin discusses:

> It was certainly clear why Hal preferred the companionship of this surrogate Eastcheap father to the tantrums of his real father at court. The trouble was that Mason had to underplay a part that teems with broad possibilities while James was ringing all the changes on a part that is supposed to be fairly predictable.   (McMillin, p. 80)

Accordingly, *Part I* disappointed some reviewers, who were intrigued but often irritated by James's King, had faint praise for Mason's Falstaff, and found Howard's performance redundant after *Henry V*. With *Part II*, however, Hands's vision emerged more strongly. His *Part II* would not concern itself with the rise of a new hero-king; he and Howard had already charted that out, as a separate journey. Instead, Hands showed the death of a whole way of life. His *Part II* was haunted with images of decay and decline. Suspended at the back of the stage were a tangle of 'gnarled, winter-withered branches', a constant reminder, in Michael Billington's phrase, that the play was 'haunted by death, sickness and decay' (Hodgdon, p. 72). A bare floor-cloth was scattered with leaves for the scenes in Shallow's orchard; ravens croaked ominously at significant moments. The poignancy of Hands' *Part II*, and its sense of anguish and loss, became a signature quality for the entire trilogy.

The Gloucestershire scenes were particularly memorable, with their bizarre collection of wasted and dying characters. A syphilitic and carbuncular Bardolph enjoyed an easy fellowship with the elderly justices; Mason's Falstaff seemed most at home here, reflecting on mortality in this elegiac setting. Richard Moore's Pistol was another grotesque, looking and sounding 'like the incarnation of something primitive discovered by Dr. Leakey at Olduvai' (*Financial Times*, 25 June 1975). Trevor Peacock's Silence was a particularly memorable figure, bent double with age, literally grown into a hoop like Sycorax, so that he had to be rocked back and forth in order to swallow his toasts. Harold Hobson found him 'an amazing creation…a figure of astonishing decrepitude' (*Sunday Times*, 29 June 1975). At the drunken party in Shallow's orchard, his sudden

merriment represented a momentary kindling of the human spirit
in the face of corruption and mortality:

> He perceives some joke that is hidden from the rest of humanity, and
> breaks into a raucous song that is happiness undiluted, joy incarnate. So
> astonishing is this that his companions ask him for an explanation, and
> he replies, 'I have been merry – twice' with such relish that you would
> think that to have enjoyed yourself actually on two occasions in a long
> life is a privilege few could hope to have.   (ibid.)

Within the grim world of Hands's *Henry IV* plays, such moments
of joy were rare: for Prince Hal especially, a character 'apparently
anguished by a wholly modern melancholy,' according to John
Barber (*Telegraph*, 25 June 1975). In the tavern scenes, Barber detected
'the grinding boredom of a man who has outgrown his old companions and is only too thankful to quit them'. Yet his taking of the
crown, and his eventual coronation, were moments of agony for
him, according to Robert Cushman:

> When Alan Howard as Prince Hal...tried on the English crown for
> the first time, I thought the weight would kill him. It is a strange kind
> of agony that possesses his face; it shifts to accommodate hope, joy,
> triumph, without ever ceasing to be pain....That agonized assump-
> tion of royalty is, in every sense, [the production's] crowning moment;
> and it nails, not just this play, but the triptych of which it is the centre.
> (*Observer*, 29 June 1975)

The rejection of Falstaff was a *coup de théâtre*, with Howard entering at the head of his coronation procession in golden armour, 'like
a robot, masked and glistening from head to foot in yellow metal'
(*Telegraph*, 25 June 1975). This awesome and inhuman figure pulled
off his mask just before the rejection speech, which seemed 'torn out
of him: the anguish near to tears' (ibid.); he 'cover[ed] his face in
agony with his hands ... it is clearly a wretched duty for him to turn
the old man away' (*Financial Times*, 25 June 1975). The blow to Falstaff
was plainly meant to be fatal, as the production's final image attested.
Rather than be herded off to prison with his comrades, Falstaff 'walked
slowly up the central aisle between the impassive figures of Prince
John and the Chief Justice. Pausing briefly, he stood under the bare
branches as a raven croaked out the last "speech" of this *2 Henry IV*,

turning Prince John's bird of rumoured war into a harbinger of Falstaff's future' (Hodgdon, p. 87). This grave final note summed up the somber quality of Hands's production, which was felt by some critics to be the strongest of his Lancastrian trilogy and the one most suited to the new style he was pioneering at the RSC in the mid-seventies: 'In amplitude of life this is the richest play of the three, and certainly the hardest to reduce to any prearranged scheme. As such, it brings the best out of Terry Hands' (*Times*, 25 June 1975). The RSC would return to the *Henry IV* plays about once per decade, often in productions by the company's reigning artistic director. Trevor Nunn used them to open the Barbican in 1982, in a production designed by John Napier that recalled the teeming urban world of his epic version of Dickens's *Nicholas Nickleby*. Adrian Noble's productions in 1991 were notable chiefly for the ruined Falstaff of Robert Stephens, whose offstage life matched the pathos of Shakespeare's Sir John. Further productions followed in 2000 and 2007 but to date no RSC *Henry IV* has demonstrated the enduring impact of the Hands productions of 1975.

English Shakespeare Company, 1986–9

The most important version of the *Henry IV* plays in the 1980s was part of a cycle directed by Michael Bogdanov as the inaugural production of the English Shakespeare Company. Bogdanov, together with actor Michael Pennington, created the company as a vehicle for contemporary populist Shakespeare. Their opening productions were of the two parts of *Henry IV* and *Henry V* and were designed as political statements commenting on the Thatcher government and the Falklands war. Bogdanov's avowed intention was to make Shakespeare (and his reading of Shakespeare) relevant and accessible to people beyond the typical London theatre-going public:

> The plays ... are vehicles for very heated debate, or should be, about things that are happening with our world ... and it's a question of how we can actually improve the things that we find around us and how we can make this a better world to live in and give our children and grandchildren a better life ... I think that Shakespeare was writing with

that in view and that we should be doing productions that make those same statements and challenge people in that way.   (Interview with the author, 19 April 1991)

Bogdanov's vision of the Lancastrian histories was influenced by the cynical political reading of Jan Kott in *Shakespeare Our Contemporary* and by urgent concerns in contemporary Britain: 'The Henrys as a whole were a microcosm in 1400 of in fact what is still the situation in the British Isles – a divided nation with the various factions fighting against each other and particularly against Westminster rule' (ibid.). Bogdanov was responding to a Britain bitterly divided and torn by violence: 'The parallels were plain. The Henrys were plays for today, the lessons of history unlearnt .... Nothing had changed in six hundred years, save the means' (Bogdanov and Pennington, p. 25). Bogdanov's sympathies were plainly with the rebels and outsiders; the court of Henry IV was represented as cold and oppressive and Michael Pennington's Hal was a Machiavellian antihero.

The productions, designed for touring, made the most of a stripped-down and eclectic theatrical style. Chris Dyer's set was primarily a bare stage, with sliding scrim panels at the rear which allowed strong entrances, silhouettes, and cyclorama lighting effects. Two large scaffolding towers could be wheeled on from the wings, and a catwalk could be lowered from the flies. Stephanie Howard's costumes drew from all periods. While Bogdanov had tended to use modern dress for Shakespeare, he decided that the Hal/Hotspur duel at the end of *1 Henry IV* required medieval costumes and weaponry; accordingly, he allowed the designer and actors to draw from a range of periods and styles, choosing based on character and situation rather than logical chronology. The court figures wore frock coats or scarlet uniforms suggesting the nineteenth century, while the denizens of the tavern were contemporary rockers and punks. Gadshill wore a tall Mohican hairstyle and tattoos; Pistol sported a leather jacket emblazoned 'Hal's Angels'. Doll Tearsheet had torn fishnet stockings and a mini-skirt. Prince Hal was casual in jeans and boots, while Falstaff wore the checked trousers and loud jacket of a mid-twentieth-century vaudeville comedian.

Many of the supporting characterizations were sharply defined. The rebels had distinctive regional accents, and supported the sense of a divided Britain. John Price's Hotspur was a rough Northern lad, with a warmly physical relationship with his Lady (Jennie Stoller). Andrew Jarvis's Douglas was a shaven-headed berserker, who fought at Shrewsbury in a kilt, stripped to the waist and wielding two broadswords in a fury of Scottish defiance.

1 Henry IV opened with the company assembled onstage amid a jumble of props and set pieces singing a rousing song written for the occasion, inviting the audience to learn 'Of a king who was mighty, but wild as a boy,/ And list to the ballad of Harry le Roy.' The song provided the back-story of the Lancastrian usurpation, and hinted at the trajectory of Hal's character through the three plays. It also provided a distinctive introduction for Michael Pennington's Prince Hal, who watched the other company members in an attitude of 'chilly detachment' (Weil and Weil, p. 58). A lean charismatic actor, whose high forehead and penetrating gaze denoted a searching and active intelligence, Pennington stood apart from the company casually dressed in jeans, waiting, listening, and plotting the future, a tightly-wound clock ready to strike.

Pennington's Hal was well-partnered by John Woodvine's magisterial Falstaff, a performance that managed to incorporate broad comedy, dexterous verbal wit, and psychological conviction. Woodvine played Falstaff as a slightly down-at-heel gentleman who has never abandoned his sense of aristocratic privilege. Like Hal, this Falstaff was a scheming opportunist but with enough heart to win the loyalty of both his followers and the audience. Michael Billington described him as 'alternately sly as a fox and warm as a coal-fire with a voice that aspires to the Silver Ring and a heart that belongs among the punters on the Downs' (*Guardian*, 23 March 1987). Woodvine's resonant bass-baritone voice handled the text with effortless finesse, notably in the soliloquies on honour, sack and Justice Shallow. He easily accommodated the sometimes coarse comic business that often marks Bogdanov's productions. Breakfasting with Bardolph in *Part I*, III.iii, he cracked six eggs into a tankard, topped it off with gin, sloshed the mixture around and drank it off in a gulp, while Bardolph played a maudlin air on the slide trombone; the audience burst into applause.

Pennington's otherwise chilly Hal treated Falstaff with some affection, and seemed to relish the exuberant tavern wordplay, but it was his relationship with his real father that consumed him. Their interviews were filled with Oedipal torment. In *Part I*, Hal's initial excuse was smirking and insincere, the rote response of a surly teen-ager forced to apologize for a prank. When compared to Hotspur, however, he exploded in a rage of jealous resentment. Bogdanov forestalled the reconciliation at the end of the scene, as Hal refused his father's embrace. 'How little Hal would give to this father was stunningly clear, as was the violence that would erupt in the king-dom from their refusal to understand each other,' wrote Scott McMillin (p. 116).

At the end of *Part I*, Bogdanov adapted a device from Orson Welles's film *Chimes at Midnight* to further estrange father and son. Hal triumphed over Hotspur at Shrewsbury through greater ruth-lessness. Bested and disarmed, Hal lay cowering on the stage floor; when Hotspur magnanimously slid his sword across the stage to him to ensure a fair fight, Hal promptly stabbed him in the back with it. His victory, and his potential redemption in his father's eyes, were compromised by a trick of Falstaff's. Bogdanov followed Welles in rearranging the text so that the King was present to hear Falstaff's claim that he was the one who killed Hotspur; and as in Welles, he evidently believed it, to Hal's mute fury. Their scene in *Part II*, after Hal's unpromisingly casual entrance and his gaffe in eagerly seizing the crown, finally brought father and son into accord, as Stanley Wells relates:

> Hal, entering to the dying King, looked ready for a game of tennis; but the subsequent reconciliation became the play's emotional centre, marked by a closeness of physical contact as well as emotional rapport that made Falstaff's rejection inevitable; when it came, the sense of pain was confined to Falstaff; police brutality in both the carting of Doll Tearsheet and the committal of Sir John to the Fleet suggested that Hal had become head of a police state.   (p. 299)

Indeed, the Lancastrian regime that Hal eventually comes to head was marked, especially in *Part II*, by particularly cold-blooded politi-cal violence. The Gaultree conference ended with the rebels being forced to kneel for onstage execution – pistol shots to the back of the head – while Handel's 'The King Shall Rejoice' provided a jubilantly mocking soundtrack. The play ended with a similar touch of musi-cal irony: the gloating lines of Prince John about the coming war with France gave way to the pop song 'You're in the Army Now' by Status Quo.

The ending pointed the way toward the third production of the trilogy, *Henry V*, which defined Henry's invasion of France in terms of the Falklands War, British nationalism, and football hooliganism. (The tavern crew famously unfurled a banner that said 'Fuck the Frogs' as they headed off to war to the strains of Parry's 'Jerusalem'.) In it, Hal grew into a war criminal who shouted speeches from the back of a tank and ordered the execution of French prisoners with brutal indifference. But the seeds of this interpretation were present in the cold-blooded but charismatic Prince who stood alone in the opening ballad of *Part I*.

Bogdanov's productions toured internationally for three years, playing in Britain, Europe and the US, along with Tokyo, Hong Kong and Australia. For the second season Bogdanov added a three-part *Wars of the Roses* cycle as well as *Richard II*. Bogdanov's exuberant populism won over audiences around the world, though his heavy-handed politics and occasional vulgarity repelled some critics. Nonetheless, his versions of the *Henry IV* plays were the most vital of the late decades of the twentieth century. They were filmed in Swansea at the end of their last tour in 1989 and despite many changes in casting and business over the years, the videotapes remain a valuable record of a highly original and provocative interpretation.

Royal National Theatre, 2005

From the time of its founding in 1963, Britain's National Theatre had never produced the two parts of *Henry IV* until Artistic Director Nicholas Hytner staged them together in 2005. They opened during the week of a general election and many critics commented on the plays' scope and relevance as an overall picture of the state of the nation. Hytner had begun his RNT directorship in 2003 with a modern-dress *Henry V* that commented harshly and directly on the ongoing American-British invasion of Iraq. His *Henry IV* was less overtly political, and eclectic rather than contemporary in design, but it still reflected a dark vision of an England haunted by strife, decay and betrayal. Performed in the National's largest auditorium – bearing the name of its founding director Lord Olivier – and featuring an all-star cast, the productions were necessarily seen as an epic event, the National's grave assessment of the country's character.

The plays were staged as part of a season sponsored by the Travelex corporation designed to attract new audiences by keeping most ticket prices to £10. There was therefore a limited budget for stage and costume design, though the productions employed a fairly large company of 28 actors (Merlin, p. 4). Mark Thompson's set used a relatively small portion of the vast Olivier stage. A raked structure of planking, resembling a road leading away from the audience in forced perspective, came through the dark circular space, broadening toward the front. On either side were bare ruined trees, and above and behind were projection screens that sometimes localized the action to castle, church or countryside; but for the most part the action was confined to the wooden platform, a bridge to nowhere surrounded by darkness. Lighting and sound choices reinforced the sense of a gloomy spectacle unfolding.

The opening moments of *Part I* set the tone. The King spoke his first speech not in a throne room but on a road in the middle of a battlefield, as wailing widows mourned corpses strewed beneath the twisted trees. Hytner drew these images of grief and suffering partly from the devastating tsunami of December 2004, but largely from the chaos in Iraq:

> The big, unavoidable thing about these plays is that they're set against the backdrop of a catastrophic civil war…I want to create a sense throughout the play of a country in chaos. Something that's very present at the moment is what a world feels like when it's torn apart by a disastrous war.   (Quoted in Merlin, p. 17)

The battlefield bodies, beset by mourners or scavengers, became a major motif of the productions. They were used to close *Part I* and open *Part II*. In the latter case, they provided illustrations for a chorically delivered Rumour prologue; in the former, they gave a damning final image of Falstaff furtively looting corpses at Shrewsbury.

The Falstaff of Sir Michael Gambon was one of the most anticipated aspects of the productions. While reactions were mixed, his was certainly a prominent characterization. He was a physical wreck, wearing slippers for his gout, gaudy red pants and a stained vest, and a Beckettian toque crowned with an absurd feather. His seediness reminded many critics of his recent performance as

Davies in *The Caretaker* and his cringing, wheedling passive aggression was very much in the manner of Pinter. His words were, too often, scarcely audible; the absence of Falstaff's verbal brilliance and command was the most crippling weakness in the performance, though Gambon was not the only actor to be defeated vocally by the cavernous spaces of the Olivier. The very human nastiness of this Falstaff was communicated in many telling details: in *Part I*, I.ii, 'too hung over to face breakfast, he wraps his full English fry-up in a newspaper to eat later', stealing the salt and pepper pots from the café to go with it (*Daily Telegraph*, 5 May 2005). If Gambon was not a very lovable Falstaff, he was a very loving one and his dog-like devotion to Prince Hal showed the character at his most vulnerable. He had a repeated, imploring gesture of reaching his hand up toward Hal's face, 'as if trying to touch it and losing his nerve ... like someone sketching in the air something that may not be real, eager to grasp something that may disappear,' according to Susannah Clapp (*Observer*, 8 May 2005). In Michael Billington's assessment, 'if anything is clear from Hytner's production, it is that the love between Falstaff and Hal is all one way', so that even after the warning of the play-within-the-play, 'Gambon follows him around the tavern with the watery eyes of a desperate spaniel' (*Guardian*, 5 May 2005). Tim Walker found a similarly bestial metaphor for Falstaff's longing: 'the edgy way his piggy eyes follow Hal around the stage when he suddenly realizes he is losing his hold over him is particularly affecting' (*Sunday Telegraph*, 8 May 2005). This sense of unreturned love on Falstaff's part made the rejection particularly harsh: 'the new king is furious with the pleading, silently sobbing knight, but quite unmoved' (*Evening Standard*, 6 May 2005). Gambon seemed to deflate as he bent double in misery, shrinking along with his hopes.

According to Billington, Matthew Macfadyen was a joyless sardonic Hal – 'a brooding solitary who hangs out in taverns as a way of gaining his father's attention'. Tall and physically imposing – Macfadyen based his character in part on the historical Henry's demonstrated prowess as a warrior – he remained aloof in the Eastcheap scenes. Wearing jeans under a medieval jerkin, in one of the productions' touches of contemporaneity, he sprawled with regal arrogance in a worn armchair, 'neurotic, calculating, and full of cold contempt for his tavern colleagues' (*Time Out*, 11 May 2005). He was more emotionally susceptible to his father, a haunted figure played by David Bradley, who looked 'like a brass rubbing of a medieval tomb' (*Sunday Times*, 8 May 2005). For their *Part I* interview Hal made a stumbling belated entrance into what was evidently his father's private chapel; the King threw a prayer-book at him later in the scene. Hal's mixture of battlefield confidence and private vulnerability were nicely brought out in a bit of business in the parley before Shrewsbury. After Hal offered to save blood on both sides through a single combat with Hotspur, the King disdainfully kicked his gauntlet away with his foot. In a rehearsal discussion with David Bradley, who noted that King Henry thinks Hal may be an agent of divine punishment for him, Macfadyen observed, 'That's a terrible thing to lay on your son' (p. 26). As in several of the more recent productions, the pained relation of father and son became a keynote of the plays.

Also noteworthy was the strong contrast between the two parts, with the 'hectic, propulsive, action-filled' *Part I* set off, in Billington's words, against the 'elegiac, death-haunted and autumnal' *Part II*. David Harewood's vivacious Hotspur gave the former play great energy with a larger-than-life, crowd-pleasing performance that looked back to an older bravura-acting tradition. 'Today's fashion is for a quieter tone, a more conversational delivery, a narrower range of gesture and movement, but audiences will always thrill to a player who bestrides his ground with so much panache and conviction', wrote Lloyd Evans. Certainly he was the only one of the principals who seemed wholly in command of the huge Olivier stage. Hytner's casting just hinted at the possibility of ethnic conflict in the Percy rebellion, in that both Hotspur and his father, Northumberland (Jeffrey Kissoon) were played by actors of African descent; but the production didn't highlight this, and none of the reviewers commented on it.

The second part seemed more in keeping with Hytner's somber tone and many critics preferred it. Gravel-voiced RSC veteran John Carlisle gave unusual authority to Archbishop Scroop, making the rebellion scenes pointed and powerful. Similarly high-powered casting put a preeminent Shakespearean, John Wood, in the part of Justice Shallow, described by various reviewers as 'benignly dotty and ramshackle', 'sappily drooling with nostalgia', 'at once vain, pathetic, and swaggering', and 'a transcendent study in florid, nervously energetic self-delusion'. It was the one universally praised performance and gave the Gloucestershire scenes an autumnal pathos that provided the most humane note in the two plays. Michael Billington used them to sum up the productions' importance:

> If I dwell on the Gloucestershire scenes, it is not only because they are a high point of the evening. They express the sense of deep England that runs through both these plays. And the virtue of Hytner's production … is that it never lets us forget that these plays are explorations of our national psyche and landscape that belong very fittingly in the National Theatre.   (*Guardian*, 5 May 2005)

It is interesting to note that, bleak and blasted as the England they depicted was, Hytner's *Henry IVs* were still praised as 'a great national epic' (Paul Taylor, *Independent*, 6 May 2005). While the intents of the production were very far from those of Quayle's 1951 Festival of Britain celebration, critics and audiences still found in the plays a recognizable mirror of the national life. In good times and bad, and with whatever form of cultural self-analysis is available at the time, the two parts of *Henry IV* have become, in Britain at least, a kind of index of national identity: a ritual repeated, on a large scale and at infrequent but regular intervals, whereby the Shakespearean theatre assesses 'the very age and body of the time' and finds it more or less wanting.

5   The Plays on Screen

Despite their long-standing appeal in the theatre, the *Henry IV* plays have been virtually ignored as material for adaptation to the screen. The only feature film of the plays is Orson Welles's *Chimes at Midnight* (1966), with Welles as Falstaff and Gielgud as the King. Fortunately, it is one of the greatest of all Shakespeare films; though it is not necessarily a fully satisfactory version of *Henry IV*. A television version more closely corresponding to Shakespeare's text is the BBC production of Cedric Messina and David Giles (1979), which I will treat first in this chapter. It is important, not only as the most comprehensive and widely-available video version, but because it reproduces Anthony Quayle's Falstaff, nearly thirty years after his performance in Stratford and in a different medium. Of other film and video versions, the English Shakespeare Company's merits mention for its record of Michael Bogdanov's directorial choices, though it lacks John Woodvine's Falstaff. Gus Van Sant's *My Own Private Idaho* (1991, with Keanu Reeves and River Phoenix) is of some interest as an homage to Welles's *Chimes at Midnight*, though it cannot really be considered a film version of *Henry IV*.

Henry IV: Part I (BBC, 1979)

The BBC television versions of *Henry IV: Parts I and II* are part of an ambitious series undertaken in the late 1970s and early 1980s. Producer Cedric Messina set out to film the entire Shakespeare canon with British actors for the BBC and Time-Life films; the programmes were shown in the US on the Public Broadcasting Service under the title 'The Shakespeare Plays'. David Giles directed both parts, along with *Richard II* and *Henry V*, using the same actors for continuing lead roles. *Part I* was first broadcast in the UK on

9 December 1979 and *Part II* followed one week later. The series has become widely available through videotapes and DVDs in university libraries, and it may be the first, or indeed the only, performed version of the *Henry IV* plays known to many students.

While the *Richard II-Henry V* series lacks the aesthetic boldness and conceptual unity of Jane Howell's 1983 production of the *Henry VI-Richard III* tetralogy, the plays benefit by being performed in sequence. *Part I* begins, for instance, with a clip from *Richard II* of the murder of the king (Derek Jacobi), followed by a dissolve to Jon Finch, who played Bolingbroke in the earlier programme and is now evidently reflecting on his guilt. Nothing in the text specifically indicates that Henry IV is thinking of Richard's murder when he is 'wan with care' in the opening speech, but the flashback makes it clear. Finch's obsessive rubbing of his gloved hands might also indicate blood-guilt. (Finch played *Macbeth* in Polanski's film a few years before.) In a later scene the hands are shown to be leprous, in accordance with some chroniclers' accounts.

Like most of the BBC Shakespeares, the *Henry IV* plays are shot on a soundstage. This treatment works well for the early interior scenes of *Part I*, less well for battles or the Gad's Hill robbery. The small-screen treatment allows for a very intimate and conversational style, which shrinks the scale of both rhetoric and character but allows for psychological insight. Prince Hal (David Gwillim) muses quietly to himself in close-up for 'I know you all', speaking aloud but unaware of the camera. He begins the speech as an amused rationalization for his behaviour, and then as he begins to develop the plan further and sees that it might work, he speaks with increasing earnestness and a kind of awe. The speech is truly a moment-by-moment discovery rather than the revelation of a cynical, predetermined plan; and it is the close placement of camera and microphone, and the intensity of focus, that enable this interpretation. The moment is characteristic of Gwillim's performance. He is a thoughtful Hal, capable of sardonic humour but always controlled, always conscious of his future role.

Tim Pigott-Smith's Hotspur is perhaps reined in somewhat by the small-scale medium but he also turns it to advantage. During his account in I.iii of the perfumed messenger who demanded his prisoners, Hotspur is sitting at a council table along with the King and a number of other lords. Rather than a bombastic rant, Hotspur's speech is an amusing anecdote that gets many of the council on his side and infuriates the King. The proximity of the microphone allows Pigott-Smith to make the most of Hotspur's 'speaking thick'. He delivers his lines at a breakneck pace and is able to make good comic capital out of Hotspur's abrupt self-interruptions. When alone with his father and uncle, he is allowed to range around the room, increasing the scale of his acting. His exasperation over his inability to remember the name of Berkeley Castle is a comic high point.

The tavern scenes are dark and somewhat melancholy with a low-key Prince and a shrewd, rather cerebral Falstaff. Anthony Quayle, who played the part at Stratford opposite Richard Burton in 1951, gives a sly, subtle, small-scale performance of an old man living by his wits. He does not seem particularly gross in his appetites; he is a connoisseur rather than a glutton, a wit rather than a buffoon. The proximity of the camera allows us to see his mind at work. Giles often organizes scenes so that the person in the foreground is reacting to dialogue spoken behind him; we witness the character's thoughts in a way that would be difficult to achieve on the stage. When Hal and Poins attempt to call him on his lies about the robbery, Quayle's Falstaff, in the extreme foreground, assesses the changed situation and reflects on his options, before arriving at the triumphant expedient of 'I knew ye as well as he that made ye.' Later, when Hal dismisses Falstaff's fears of Percy and Douglas, the audience knows, from his face in close-up, that the Prince has in fact been quite alarmed by the news of the growing rebellion. Finally, at the end of the 'play extempore', television close-ups reveal that both Hal and Falstaff – though not the rest of the tavern audience – recognize the seriousness of the moment well before 'I do, I will.' This whole sequence is given a lot of gravity. As Hal's attacks on Falstaff's character grow more serious, Falstaff recognizes that he is in danger; accordingly, he tries to get the crowd on his side during his speech of self-defence. The camera allows us to see Falstaff's desperate calculation during the 'Banish not him' speeches, even as he leads the crowd into untroubled roars of delight and approval. After 'banish all the world', the tavern bursts into applause. But Falstaff's attention is all on Hal, who waits for the noise to die down before making his somber promise. The succeeding conversation about Falstaff's danger from the law has a feeling of real threat until Hal breaks the tension with his instruction to hide behind the arras.

The Welsh scene III.i is given a warm and charming atmosphere, though the setting is a little too obviously the same as the royal court, dressed up with tapestries, firelight, and a large dog. Glendower is funny but far from absurd; Mortimer seems a capable and authoritative figure who is genuinely interested in being king. He is beguiled by his beautiful and sexy wife but is not especially uxorious; he laughs indulgently at her Welsh endearments. The scene with the ladies has more laughter than sorrow or bitterness, though Lady Percy changes the mood suddenly, and definitively, at her refusal to sing. The scene ends with a tearful moment between the two women.

The encounter between the royal father and son in III.ii is introduced by a shot of the King washing his diseased hands, and his guilt for Richard's murder is an unspoken theme throughout the scene. On the one hand, the King's frustration is animated by an awareness of the 'displeasing service' he did to win the crown for his ungrateful son; on the other, Hal's silent presence through much of the scene acts as a kind of rebuke to the King. When Henry talks of how he won applause 'Even in the presence of the crownèd King', Hal shoots him a pointed look that could be taken as a moral challenge. When Hal does speak, he is relatively unruffled, addressing his father calmly and rationally and with a kind of sardonic humour, as though he really is using Hotspur as part of his master plan. He is similarly upbeat in the succeeding scene with Falstaff, entering in a parodic march and enjoying the humour of Falstaff's 'charge of foot'. For Hal, at this point, war does seem to be part of a game – a game he is playing for his own benefit – and it is left to Falstaff to acknowledge the seriousness of the move from tavern to battlefield at the end of the scene.

Interestingly, Quayle's Falstaff is the only character allowed to address the camera directly, which he does regularly once the action leaves the Boar's Head and begins the move towards Shrewsbury. This technique has something of the effect of placing Falstaff on Robert Weimann's *platea*, communicating directly with the audience, while the rest of the play is frozen in the *locus* of history. These soliloquies are startlingly personal, making excellent use of the intimacy of the TV medium. Falstaff confides in us about his wretched soldiers, laughing and twinkling at the camera, making us complicit in his exploitative attitude. By the end of the speech he is leering at us over his shoulder as he relieves himself. By contrast, Quayle gives his catechism about honour almost in a whisper, his face filling the screen. His repeated 'no's are grave and subtle, played as realizations in the moment; he is not telling a pre-scripted joke but experiencing a kind of existential awakening.

The battlefield sequences are rather contrived with unconvincing soundstage settings, clumsy lighting choices and plenty of artificial smoke. Hal shows surprising anger after rescuing the King; his assertion that 'they did me too much injury/ That ever said I hearkened for your death' is an explosion of bitter resentment at his father's mistrust. The Hal/Hotspur fight is protracted, bloody and exhausting. Tim Pigott-Smith's mouth is filled with stage blood as he gasps through Hotspur's final speech. Hal quite tenderly wipes his very gory face. He is equally moved by Falstaff's apparent death. 'Poor Jack, farewell' is spoken tearfully and sincerely and the close-up camera catches the reaction on Falstaff's face as he takes in this unexpected tribute. When he is resurrected, Hal is genuinely happy to see him alive, and enthusiastically agrees to gild his lies about Hotspur. He is evidently far from his final rejection of Falstaff and far from fully reconciled with his father. After the King's final speeches, Hal gives him another enigmatic look, once again undermining his father's authority through a stance of skeptical reserve, watching and waiting.

Henry IV: Part II (BBC, 1979)

Part II in the BBC series is dominated by two diseased men, Anthony Quayle's Falstaff and Jon Finch's King Henry. The former's increasingly mean-spirited stratagems for survival and the latter's furious struggles with mortality establish the atmosphere of the production. David Gwillim's enigmatic Hal, waiting and brooding, makes less of an impression; the rebel scenes are quite perfunctory.

In the induction, Rumour is (perhaps appropriately) a disembodied voice, played over a montage of flashbacks from *Part I*. The opening scene is very flat. Northumberland's 'worm-eaten hold' turns out to be a very comfortable castle identical with many of the interiors from *Part I*. Bruce Purchase's hearty, hairy Northumberland shows no signs of sickness, and foregoes the nightcap and crutch indicated in the text; he doesn't seem especially bothered by Hotspur's death, and his curses are far from apocalyptic. The subsequent rebel scenes are similarly underpowered, and heavily cut: the rebellion never seems a significant threat to the kingdom in this production.

Quayle's Falstaff, initially, seems to be on top of his game in *Part II*. The Lord Chief Justice, made to look somewhat ridiculous in a green cap and gown, gets nothing on Falstaff in I.ii. Their encounter is set in a street among a crowd of people and Falstaff quickly woos and wins these to his side. At the end of the wit-combat, however, Falstaff is panting slightly, and seems to have a side-stitch; and the lines on his gout and pox convey that he is feeling his age more than he has let on. He speaks to the camera, as in *Part I*, and Quayle's insinuating manner again makes the audience half-unwilling confidantes of this charming but thoroughly reprehensible schemer. In the subsequent conflict with Brenda Bruce's indignant Mistress Quickly, Quayle uses his sly smile and patronizing manner to great effect. He speaks urbanely to the Chief Justice, warning him as one man of the world to another about the dangers posed by Quickly's loose tongue. Falstaff has his way with both of them in this scene, and though the Chief Justice gets the last word, he speaks in exasperation after Falstaff has made a triumphant getaway, marching and humming to himself.

The Prince and Poins, in II.ii, are discovered playing dice. They are still reasonably affectionate with each other, though Poins shows some bitterness about Hal's disdain for him as a friend. Hal's supercilious mockery of Poins is quite unattractive here: in his pointed jibes and Poins's wounded reactions, we see the Prince's skill at getting under someone's skin. A visible facial scar reminds the audience of Hal's service at Shrewsbury and the close-up camera catches his brooding concern for his future responsibilities. He speaks about his father's illness with a curious waggling of his head, a physical tic that seems to betray strong emotion at certain moments in the play. Gordon Gostelow's spectacularly carbuncular and ragged Bardolph – more broadly played than any other character in either part – enters with Falstaff's letter. Poins evidently has been plotting to marry the Prince to his sister, and when caught out he becomes defensive. He also seems to resent the appeal Falstaff still has for the Prince and ends the scene in a somewhat surly posture. For his part, Hal brightens at the prospect of playing a trick on Falstaff; though listless at the beginning of the scene, he shows some life by the end.

Lady Percy is strikingly transformed from *Part I*. Played by Michele Dotrice (daughter of a famous Hotspur, Roy Dotrice), she had been a sprightly, rather merry young woman in *Part I*, playful even in her more serious remonstrances to her husband. Here she is a pale nun-like figure, with a white wimpled headdress. Her bloodless moonlike face fills the screen as she mourns for Hotspur. Her powerful tearful speech is given in its entirety and stops the motion of the play for a moment with its poignant invocation of memory and grief. It consolidates the impression, strong in this production, that in *Part II* everyone lives either in the past or in the future: the present is only a place for idly killing time.

This impression is heightened by the long tavern scene, II.iv. The same Boar's Head setting is used as in *Part I*, but without the warm atmosphere of the previous scenes. Under washed-out daytime lighting (despite the play's lines about the lateness of the hour), the tavern feels empty and depressing. Doll, played by Frances Cuka, is a tatty old creature with absurdly-braided red hair and a scarlet dress too tight and youthful for her. She gives a fine and detailed characterization. In relating the story of Master Tisick's advice about swaggerers, Doll manages to make it clear that she has slept with Master Dumbe, the minister. When confronted by Pistol, she laboriously produces a knife from under her skirts. Bryan Pringle's Pistol is not especially belligerent; he woos and kisses Quickly, hinting at their future relations in *Henry V*. In this scene, Falstaff comes across as weary and melancholy. When, momentarily roused after the rather half-hearted combat with Pistol, he turns lustfully to Doll, she breaks the mood by urging him to 'patch up [his] old body for heaven'. Quayle plays this moment as one of genuine mental trauma – he is confronted by the thing he has sought most to avoid. Startled by his reaction, Doll mentions the Prince as a way of changing the subject, but Falstaff never quite recovers his equanimity.

The Prince and Poins, while costumed as drawers in leather aprons, actually take the role of the musicians called for in the scene. Their music makes an appropriate background to the very affecting scene between Falstaff and Doll, played in quiet close-up. The revelation of the Prince and Poins at last lifts Falstaff out of his gloom, as he has to make shift for an excuse. The visual arrangement of the scene deliberately recalls the analogous moment *Part I*, with the two young men framing Falstaff in mid-shot while he concocts his story of dispraising Hal 'before the wicked'. For a moment, the old days of tavern fellowship are recreated; but when news of the rebellion comes, Hal hastily strips off his apron in anger and guilt.

The King's first appearance in III.i shows how much the world has deteriorated since *Part I*. He sits on the floor next to his bed, sick and haggard, with graying hair and visible signs of leprosy on his face. His hands, bandaged in white linen, are futile, fin-like appendages. In his sleep soliloquy, he makes no acknowledgment of the camera – apparently only Falstaff can address us directly – but speaks longingly to an abstract personification of sleep, somewhere in the air above him. The King's worsening physical and mental condition evidently makes him something of a trial to his lords, who have to humour and reassure him.

The Gloucestershire scenes provide a welcome respite from the generally grim tone of this *Part II*, though elements of decay are evident here as well. Robert Eddison's Shallow is a generally sprightly chap, but Silence is ancient and dour. The scenes take on some bucolic atmosphere from pastoral sound effects (squawking geese, lowing cattle) and the backdrop of an ivied farmyard wall. The ragged peasants drafted for the muster are present from the beginning of the scene: they stare in astonishment as Shallow rattles on about his exploits with the 'bona robas'. The soldiers are not especially comic apart from a crazily laughing Wart. Falstaff comes across as mean and predatory in this scene, not only with regard to the soldiers but to his hosts. When he says 'I will fetch off these justices' in a closing soliloquy to the camera, the effect is decidedly sinister.

The Gaultree scenes pass quickly and not ineffectively; the forest setting is one of the more persuasive 'outdoor' locations and Rob Edwards is a strong presence as Prince John. The nastier side of Quayle's Falstaff emerges again after Coleville is sentenced to execution: Falstaff gives him a smirking, grinning shrug as he is led away. In a nice touch, the pike Falstaff is carrying is revealed to be a shooting-stick, which he unfolds and sits upon while making his 'sherris' speech, again addressing the camera directly. This speech allows Quayle to reveal the more winning aspects of Falstaff: he delivers the encomium on sack with great gusto, as a true believer, and is very charming and upbeat. With the scene's end, though, the production reverts permanently to a somber mood in the sequence leading to the King's death and the rejection.

Finch plays the King's deathbed scenes for their full dynamic range, rising to rhetorical heights and then collapsing under his illness. His work is showy but compelling: sometimes he seems rather crazed, as though manic or delirious. Much of the scene is filmed in long takes, often in mid-shot, so Finch is able to get some theatrical scope out of the performance. There are some telling details, as when the Prince has to remove the ostensibly dead King's hand from the crown in order to put it on. The father-son reconciliation is played intimately with the two sitting together on the floor at the foot of the King's bed.

Meanwhile, as the coronation looms, Quayle's Falstaff gets nastier and nastier. He is eager and mean in his soliloquies plotting to fleece Shallow. In V.iii, he seems bored and annoyed with the old justices, though he observes that Shallow has 'a goodly dwelling and a rich' with real rapaciousness. On learning of the King's death, he announces his command of the laws of England with almost psychotic power-hunger and vengefulness.

As much as director David Giles has prepared the audience for the rejection, it still comes as an emotional shock. The newly-crowned Hal is visually transformed, his shoulder length hair cut off so that he resembles the famous image of Henry V in the National Portrait Gallery. In place of his usual drab brown jerkin he is dressed in ermine, and lighting from above seems to isolate him from all around him. However, the rejection speech itself is not an Olympian pronouncement; it is initially quite conversational and personal. When he announces that he has turned away his former self, the new King turns away from Falstaff, no longer meeting his eyes, and declaring himself for the benefit of the crowd at large. On the lines actually banishing Falstaff, however, the King speaks directly to him, loud and strong, with crushing force. For the final lines offering a pension, Hal is tender again, but in turning Falstaff's case over to the Chief Justice he steels himself and never softens as he exits. Quayle's eyes are seen to be full of tears and his blustery excuses to Shallow are unconvincing. Prince John and the Chief Justice, weighed down with regal panoply and surrounded by armed soldiers, bring the play to a close with the coronation bells still ringing. Giles's ending is not heavy-handed and his Falstaff has clearly been destined for rejection, but the final image does confirm the generally dark and joyless tone of this version of the play. The BBC *Henry IV* programmes remain useful as intelligent, textually faithful, and fairly conservative versions of the plays. They seem less dated than some others in the series, and contain a number of solid performances, but they are principally distinguished by Quayle's detailed study of a shrewd and unscrupulous Falstaff.

English Shakespeare Company, 2000

These videotape versions, available in many university libraries, are records of the English Shakespeare Company productions discussed in Chapter 4. They capture the highly original interpretive choices of those productions, but they have some unavoidable drawbacks. As taped records of live stage performances – they were filmed in a theatre in Swansea at the end of the company's two-year tour – they have neither the intimacy of a television version nor the immediacy of a live theatre event. Moreover, the cast changed considerably over the course of the tour, so the version caught on tape has only one of the original leading performances, that of Michael Pennington's Hal. Pennington was a little old for the part at the beginning of the tour, but in the theatre he gave a compelling performance, particularly when he matured into a battle-hardened Henry V. However, after two years on the road, and in the close-up medium of television, he necessarily looks miscast. Nonetheless, Pennington's intelligence and subtlety make this a striking if unorthodox reading of the role, and bring out the political dimensions clearly.

The other leads turn in creditable performances but are pale shadows of the originals. Barry Stanton, as Falstaff, is neither as genial nor as steely as John Woodvine; he doesn't provide the carnivalesque counterweight to the Lancastrian political world that was so important in the earlier version. John Price, the original Hotspur and Pistol, died in 1987 before the productions closed; his warm, lanky presence is sadly missed. Andrew Jarvis, a fierce, shaven-headed actor who was a memorable Douglas in the original casting, gives an odd, almost parodic performance as Hotspur. Michael Cronin, as King Henry, has a suitable air of buttoned-up Victorian authority for the production's historical scheme, but he evokes limited sympathy. These productions do provide an important record of Michael Bogdanov's directorial interpretation, with its emphasis on a disaffected country, divided by class and region, beginning to chafe against the oppressive government in Westminster: a parable for the Thatcher era in which the production was conceived.

Chimes at Midnight (1996)

Chimes at Midnight, Orson Welles's film version of the *Henry IV* plays, is also known simply as *Falstaff*. Both names are appropriate for this rich but partial account, one of the greatest of Shakespeare films and one of Welles's major achievements after leaving Hollywood. The film is certainly centered on Falstaff, embodied by Welles as a figure of heroic self-indulgence, warmth and good fellowship. But 'We have heard the chimes at midnight', a phrase used to introduce the film and then repeated in the Gloucestershire scenes near the end, conjures up the sense of celebration, nostalgia, pathos and loss with which Welles imbues the 'Merrie England' that his Falstaff represents.

Welles's heavily-cut screenplay was influenced by an abbreviated version of Shakespeare's histories entitled *Five Kings* that Welles produced for the stage early in his career. Even then Welles's understanding of Falstaff was tragic:

> I will play him as a tragic figure. I hope, of course, he will be funny to the audience, just as he was funny to those around him. But his humor and his wit were aroused merely by the fact that he wanted to please the prince. Falstaff, however, had the potential of greatness in him.   (*Christian Science Monitor*, 17 February 1939, quoted France, p. 169)

Like that play, *Chimes* pulls together materials from several sources, cutting and rearranging to create a strong narrative and thematic shape focused on Falstaff. In this case, he includes texts not only from the *Henry IV* plays, but from *Richard II*, *Henry V*, *The Merry Wives of Windsor* and even Holinshed's *Chronicles*, which are read in voice-over by Ralph Richardson to frame the events depicted. The story Welles tells is, in his own words, of 'the betrayal of a friendship', which stands as a metaphor for the transformation of a warm-hearted medieval England into a cold totalitarian state. Welles intended *Chimes at Midnight* as 'a lament...for the death of Merrie England...the age of chivalry, of simplicity, of Maytime and all that.'

Like most of Welles's later projects, the film bears some hallmarks of its chaotic production process. Welles shot it in Spain on a shoestring budget and had many of his leading actors for only very limited periods. The picture and sound quality is highly variable; much of the sound was added in post-synchronization with Welles himself providing voices for some of his Spanish extras and stand-ins. Nevertheless, Welles turned most of his production challenges to advantages, making brilliant use of editing, camera positioning, music, and the remarkable locations he found in Castile. The basic contrast of tavern and court is conveyed visually. Falstaff's world is one of wooden balconies, narrow hallways, and bustling movement, filled with bright light, merry whores and skipping rogues. The King's castle is one of cavernous interiors cut by diagonal shafts of light, with figures viewed at dehumanizing distances or tracked in gliding, floor-level shots. It is obvious from the beginning that Falstaff will never belong in this world; in one sense the film is simply a long prologue to his rejection.

The film opens with a long shot of Falstaff and Shallow picking their way over a snowy and deserted landscape, sharing the reminiscences of *Part II*, III.ii. They enter a dark wooden interior and sit in front of a roaring fire, their faces filling the screen, lit by the warm glow. Their reflections on Jane Nightwork and the merry nights of the past are treated with nostalgia and respect; the two old men seem kindred spirits, but each is lost in his own memories. Falstaff's huge face registers melancholy, but also satisfaction as he contemplates the exploits of a long and over-full life. Welles plainly identified with Falstaff: both were men of enormous talents and appetites who found themselves rejected by those they had once entertained, who could no longer make their way in a world dominated by values alien to them. Welles's portrait of Falstaff doesn't wholly eliminate the character's corrupt and venial side, but emphasizes his great love for life, for pleasure, and for the prince who will break his heart. Welles padded his already corpulent body so that his fatness has a heroic scale to it; he is like a mountain, barely fitting in the frame.

His great head, thickly-bearded, round-cheeked and white-haired, is like a globe: when in II.iv he says, smiling, 'Banish plump Jack, and banish all the world', he seems to be speaking literally.

The film's titles play over a montage of military pageantry that ends with a tableaux of hanged men, recalling Jacques Callot's prints of the *Miseries of War*: a concise summary of the film's trajectory. All is accompanied by Francesco Lavagnino's stirring martial score. Ralph Richardson's dry narration leads into an abbreviated scene of the King's quarrel with the Percies. Fernando Rey is an urbane and smirking Worcester; his performance here anticipates his sophisticated international drug lord in *The French Connection*. John Gielgud is a formidable Henry IV, shot from low angles as he speaks from his throne in a cathedral-like chamber. His frigid demeanor matches the setting; his frosty breath is often visible against the dark stone walls of the castle.

Keith Baxter's Hal is very much the nimble-footed madcap in his first scene with Falstaff, which incorporates much of the pocket-picking sequence from III.iii. Margaret Rutherford, as a grand-motherly Mistress Quickly, contributes to the friendly hominess of the tavern environment. The scene ends, however, with 'I know you all' played not as a soliloquy but as a meditation overheard by Falstaff and in part directed at him. Hal stands just outside the tavern, facing the castle, with Falstaff in the gateway behind him. There is an element of sardonic humour in his speech; Falstaff laughs at it nervously, and Hal gives him a wink at 'I'll so offend to make offense a skill.' But as Hal starts across the snowy wastes to the castle, first walking, then running, and finally jumping up and kicking his heels as his figure dwindles in the distance, there can be little doubt as to where his real future lies. Samuel Crowl, in a perceptive article called 'The Long Goodbye', discusses how this is a first of a series of linked sequences that prefigure the rejection: the entire film is essentially a time-lapse image of Hal's journey away from Falstaff.

Norman Rodway's Hotspur can't compete with the Hal-Falstaff relationship as a point of narrative interest. Though he has a few moments of courage and nobility late in the film, he is basically made into a buffoon. He begins II.iii reading the letter in a bathtub; he struggles with his boots, impatiently knocks his servants to the ground, and rushes about the castle half-naked. When he declares

'That roan shall be my throne', his self-dramatizing flourish causes him to drop the towel he is wrapped in, exposing his bare backside. His wife is light-hearted and indulgent; their scenes have no hint of pathos or tension. The entire episode is intercut with shots of trumpeters on the walls of the castle, swinging their instruments about in a parody of chivalric posturing, their martial horn-blasts mocking Hotspur's pompous masculinity.

The Gad's Hill robbery is one of the film's most visually striking episodes. It is set in a forest of tall straight trees, carpeted with leaves and dappled with filtered sunlight (against the sense of the text, where the robbery seems to take place at night). The thieves approach the travelers disguised as a procession of praying monks in voluminous white cloaks; Hal and Poins don black Zorro-style capes and broad-brimmed hats. The double robbery is a breathless chase sequence, with the flowing-cloaked figures dashing among the maze of vertical tree-trunks, the camera tracking alongside them as they run. Accompanied by a merry piping score, it is a wonderfully high-spirited sequence that actually overshadows Falstaff's later fictionalized reenactment. The story of the buckram men is underplayed in favour of the 'play extempore,' which is another energetic set piece. Falstaff is bodily heaved up onto a table, where he sits in his 'throne' wearing a saucepan on his head; streams of light from tavern windows mimic the film's court setting. With an adoring audience of prostitutes gazing from the balconies that surround the tavern's central atrium, Falstaff and Hal engage in playful imitations of John Gielgud's King. The momentary chill of Hal's 'I do, I will,' is broken by an exuberant flight from the sheriff, with Hal leaping under the bedclothes with a laughing wench.

In conflating the two plays, Welles cut the second rebellion; accordingly, much material from *Part II* precedes the battle of Shrewsbury. Falstaff is accosted by the Lord Chief Justice while marching out of the city; he presents his ragged soldiers to Westmorland, then visits Shallow to recruit more. He speaks his honour catechism directly to Hal, whose silence confirms his growing estrangement. The battle itself is one of the most celebrated depictions of combat in cinema history, influencing decades of later films. Using grainy black-and-white images, variable film speeds, vertiginous camera movements and literally hundreds of edits, Welles creates a Bosch-like nightmare of brutality. Beginning with sweeping cavalry charges, the ten-minute sequence ends with mud-covered warriors jerking spasmodically on the ground in heaps, as the camera cranes up to survey the ruins of the field. Throughout the battle, the figure of Falstaff, surprisingly nimble in his absurdly rotund armour, is seen running about from one hiding place to another, a comic survivor in a storm of death. Welles makes two original choices that prevent the battle from seeming like a conclusion to the film, and extend the narrative interest. Falstaff's apparent death earns no eulogy from Hal, for the breath steaming out from his visor gives away his shamming. Later, Falstaff's claim of killing Hotspur is believed by the King, who looks disparagingly on Hal. Falstaff smirks and shrugs, as the reconciliation of father and son is forestalled to the end of the film. Falstaff speaks his sherris soliloquy aloud in front of his troops; Hal listens for awhile, but then leaves to follow the army, dropping his cup of sack as he goes.

After the battle, Welles includes the King's sleep soliloquy, the conversation between the weary Prince and Poins, and the episode in the Boar's Head with Falstaff and Jeanne Moreau's tigerish Doll Tearsheet. The rejection is again foreshadowed as Falstaff attempts to follow Hal out of the tavern only to be caught up in the roistering crowds. The tavern, filled with dancers, becomes a chaotic maze in which Falstaff becomes entangled as Hal slips away from him. Hal disappears on horseback, the crenellated walls of the castle behind him, as Falstaff goes off to visit Shallow.

Hal's taking of the crown, and the King's death scene, are intercut with Falstaff's sojourn in Gloucestershire. Falstaff sits in front of the fire, flanked by the justices as they discuss the price of bullocks and the death of Double. Silence is relatively young, but with a painful stammer that prevents him getting many lines out before Alan Webb's domineering Shallow interrupts him. The news of the King's death arrives in one of the film's most celebrated shots, one that recalls the masterful deep-focus photography of *Citizen Kane*. Falstaff is seated against the wall at the far end of a large farm building while Shallow and Silence caper in the foreground. The camera is at a low angle; the scene is filmed in a single take. As Pistol enters with his message, Falstaff moves forward until he is towering over the camera and entirely filling the frame. His hubris is given unmistakable visible representation.

The coronation procession – filmed in the cathedral of Cordova – employs a visual strategy used elsewhere in the film: a fencelike image of massed vertical elements. Like the trees of Gad's Hill and the spears of Shrewsbury, the regal pennants of the coronation create an imposing contrast to Falstaff's round body. In this case they represent an insuperable barrier. Falstaff pushes between them to call out to Hal, but is instantly silenced by the new King, who at first does not even turn to face him. The camera shoots the King from a low angle, an imposing figure, framed by the pennants and the lofty vaults of the cathedral. Falstaff kneels on the ground, seen from above. The extreme contrast of angles, the reverberant silence of the stone building, and the cutting edge of the King's voice make the rejection severe and unequivocal. The offer of a pension momentarily softens Hal's voice, and the speech concludes with an emotional exchange of looks. Falstaff's expression conveys anguish, but also grudging understanding, and perhaps even something like a bitter pride in how far his protégé has come, and the awesome figure he now cuts. Baxter's Hal shows regret in his dark eyes, but then turns suddenly and disappears down the cathedral nave.

After perfunctory excuses to Shallow, Falstaff hobbles away across a darkened plaza, his breath smoking in the night air. His final line is a whisper. His silhouetted body, shrunk by distance and perspective, disappears through a round arch, momentarily casting a huge shadow on the stone wall behind him. In this visually elegant, emotionally crushing shot, Welles represents both the scale of Falstaff's ambitions and the poverty to which they have been reduced. Across the square, a tiny figure watches him go: the grieving Page, played by Welles's own daughter Beatrice.

Welles's film carries the story into the early scenes of *Henry V*. As the new King embarks his troops for England, he asks for 'the man committed yesterday' to be released; it is made clear that it is Falstaff to whom he refers. In attributing his fault to 'excess of wine', Hal looks sad and guilty; he evidently acknowledges to himself that he has broken Falstaff's heart, though he will not admit it to others. The subsequent scene follows Poins into a courtyard that is dominated by a huge coffin on a cart. Mistress Quickly relates Falstaff's death, and his followers push the cart out through the gateway into the waste ground between the village and the castle wall. As the camera cranes up to record the final disappearance of

Falstaff, Ralph Richardson's narrative voice-over, laced with irony, gives an encomium on Henry V adapted from Holinshed: 'So humane withal, he left no offense unpunished nor friendship unrewarded ... a pattern in princehood, a lodestar in honour, and famous to the world alway.'

My Own Private Idaho (1991)

Gus Van Sant's third feature film is a quasi-Shakespearean curiosity: it combines an homage to *Chimes at Midnight* with the story of a gay prostitute in search of his mother. Van Sant combined two projects in making the film: the primary story of Mike, played by River Phoenix, and a modern-day Falstaff story that he originally planned to film independently under the title *Minions of the Moon*. Mike is a narcoleptic street hustler from Portland, Oregon, who is in love with Scott Favor (Keanu Reeves), the film's Prince Hal. Scott, the son of the Mayor, is going through a period of rebellion, what he calls a crusade, slumming with prostitutes and drug addicts. Mike, whose position in the film's Hal/Falstaff story corresponds roughly to that of Poins, goes on an odyssey that leads him to Italy in search of the mother who left him in childhood. In the end, Scott returns to Portland to claim his inheritance upon his father's death, rejecting his old companions.

While the broad outlines of the story correspond to the plot of *Henry IV*, about one-quarter of the film follows Shakespeare's text much more closely. Thirty minutes into the film, after the basic story has been established, a character named Bob Pigeon appears who is plainly modeled on Falstaff. At this point, the film switches into a close paraphrase of scenes from *Henry IV*, beginning with the Gad's Hill robbery and extending through the tavern scene to the interview of Hal and his father. After that, the Mike plot again becomes predominant, but the final rejection sequence is also drawn nearly word-for-word from Shakespeare.

The language in these sequences is updated to reflect characters' changes of name and status, and modernized to the extent of eliminating the pronoun 'thou'. It still comes across as strange and, in the mouths of these particular actors, rather stilted. Hal's opening lines, about the irrelevance of Falstaff's concern with the time of day, are adapted so that they refer, not to cups of sack, tongues of bawds, and 'a fair hot wench in flame-colored taffeta' but to lines of cocaine, gay bars, and leather-clad hustlers. Some of the contemporary touches work better than others. When Keanu Reeves speaks Shakespeare's lines about how Falstaff (Bob) fled the robbery roaring 'as ever I heard bull calf'(*Part I*, II.iv.258–9) he slips momentarily into a Southern hayseed accent that is both persuasive and amusing. But for the most part the pseudo-Shakespearean language is alienating, as Van Sant perhaps intended.

Van Sant's film not only references *Henry IV*, it references *Chimes at Midnight*, sometimes literally shot for shot; Van Sant undertook a similar project with Hitchcock's *Psycho* a few years later. The introduction of colour to black-and-white compositions is one of the more striking changes (as it was with *Psycho*). In the Gad's Hill robbery, for instance, the thieves pose not as monks, but in the pink robes of disciples of Bhagwan Shree Rajneesh, an Indian mystic with a large following in Oregon. The scene is shot at night but is lurid with light and colour; the energetic chase comes close to matching the vivacity of the original.

However, Bob Pigeon, as played by independent filmmaker William Richert, has none of the charm of Welles's Falstaff, and the tavern milieu, here represented by an abandoned hotel, is cold and grim. Reeves's rather wooden style doesn't serve him too badly as Scott Favor, but the Hal/Falstaff scenes never approach the intimacy of his scenes with River Phoenix elsewhere in the film. The 'I know you all' sequence matches Welles shot for shot in a trash-strewn forecourt of the hotel. Bob's relationship with Scott is depicted as homosexual, though Scott himself is represented as essentially straight. His father the mayor is represented sympathetically: confined to a wheelchair by illness, he asks after his 'unthrifty son' more in sorrow than in anger. When he dies, it does not seem difficult for Scott to step into his world of politics and business and reject Bob, which he does in an elegant restaurant in a scene again modeled on Welles's original. After a close paraphrase of Quickly's speech on Falstaff's death, the film concludes, effectively, with simultaneous funerals. Scott looks across from his father's graveside to his rowdy former friends as they give Bob a drunken, New Orleans-style send-off.

The film's *Henry IV* pastiche includes occasional interesting deviations, as when Scott, rather than Mike, suggests the plan of robbing the Gad's Hill robbers. The film has a degree of wit, realized in details like the 'Falstaff' beer the characters drink. And while it is a mixed success – the 'Shakespearean' scenes are really the least effective parts of the film – it is an interesting meditation on the Hal/Falstaff relationship by an imaginative filmmaker. For students of *Henry IV*, and especially of *Chimes at Midnight*, it is certainly worth a look.

6 Critical Assessments

Plays as complex and varied as the two parts of *Henry IV* are necessarily susceptible to a variety of critical approaches. Plainly they raise the same sorts of critical issues as the other history plays, investigating the problems of government, the conflicts of monarchy and feudalism, and the tension between the sacred office of kingship and the all-too-human figure who must fill it. The plays' hybrid generic status – 'mingling Kings and clowns', to borrow Sir Philip Sidney's phrase – invites considera- tion in terms of their relation to established categories such as com- edy, tragedy and epic, as well as the new, quintessentially Elizabethan genre of the history play. Their overt theatricality, with scenes of play-acting and a continual emphasis on the performance of kingship, prompts consideration of the plays as self-reflexive explorations of Shakespeare's medium. Their use of oppositional worlds and paired, balanced characters suggests symbolic or archetypal readings, as does their central story of prodigal prince and scapegoated Falstaff. The emphasis on fathers and sons (real or surrogate) and particularly the vexed Freudian conflict of the King and Prince indicates a move into psychoanalytic territory. The virtual absence of women from the plays as well as the passionate relations, personal and political, between men, invite consideration in terms of gender theory. All of these approaches have been tried and have proved productive with these plays. But two main strands of discussion have dominated the critical tradition over the centuries since the plays were written: one about character, centred on the indomitable figure of Falstaff, and one about politics, centring on the Prince's unorthodox path to power.

Falstaff

Falstaff dominates discussions of the *Henry IV* plays from the beginning. Of all of Shakespeare's characters, he is the one most often alluded to in the seventeenth century; G. E. Bentley finds 131 references to Falstaff, compared to only 55 for the nearest contender, Othello (Hunter, p. 16). Early criticism of the plays centres on Falstaff's character, the question of his cowardice and his rejection by Prince Hal. Falstaff's incongruous appeal also contributed to discussions about the plays' uncertain genre. In 1598 Francis Meres mentions 'Henry the 4' as an example of Shakespeare's excellence in tragedy; a few years later Falstaff appears on the frontispiece of a book called *The Wits* as a paradigmatic figure of comedy. Mixed genres and inconsistent characters were unpopular with neoclassical critics of the seventeenth and eighteenth centuries, yet the appeal of Falstaff led many to make an exception. Dryden praised Falstaff's variety and complexity in 'An Essay on Dramatic Poesie' (1668). While acknowledging the classical precedent for characters dominated by a particular humour or defining trait, Dryden perceived that Falstaff 'is not properly one humour, but a miscellany of humours'; he is 'old, fat, merry, cowardly, drunken, amorous, vain, and lying,' but 'that wherein he is singular is his wit ... his quick evasions when you imagine him surprised' (vol. XVII, pp. 59, 60). In 'The Grounds for Criticism in Tragedy', included in the preface to his *Troilus and Cressida* (1679), Dryden used Falstaff as the definitive exception to neoclassical 'rules' of character:

> A character, or that which distinguishes one man from all others, cannot be supposed to consist of one particular virtue, or vice, or passion only; but 'tis a composition of qualities which are not contrary to one another in the same person ... Falstaff is a liar, and a coward, and a glutton, and a buffoon, because all these qualities may agree in the same man.   (vol. XIII, p. 236)

Elizabeth Montagu also found the *Henry IV* plays to be an exception to Neoclassical rules. In her essay comparing Shakespeare with the Greek and French dramatic poets, she argues that *Henry IV* is a well-constructed 'tragicomedy' and deserves to be exempted from classical genre norms: 'if the pedantry of learning could ever recede from its dogmatical rules, I think this play instead of being condemned for being of that species, would obtain favour for the species itself' (McMullan, p. 221). Among *Henry IV*'s chief virtues is the character of Falstaff, which is 'perfectly sustained through every scene, in every play, in which it appears' (p. 223). For Montagu,

Falstaff's comic character helps to excuse Prince Hal's misbehaviours, which are a necessary part of the story but might offend audience sensibilities if they were not carried out with such an irresistibly witty companion. Not all early critics found Falstaff so attractive. The anti-theatrical Puritan Jeremy Collier approved the severity of Falstaff's rejection: 'The poet was not so partial as to let his humour compound for his lewdness ... [Falstaff] is thrown out of favour as being a rake, and dies like a rat behind the hangings' (quoted in Knowles, p. 15).

The most famous and influential essay on Falstaff's character, and one of the most celebrated pieces of early Shakespearean criticism, is Maurice Morgann's spirited defense of 1777, 'An Essay on the Dramatic Character of Sir John Falstaff'. Morgann contends that, all appearances to the contrary, Falstaff is not a coward. The essay depends on an ingenious distinction between two kinds of perception: that of the 'understanding' – a rationalistic viewpoint by which Falstaff stands condemned – and a more intuitive set of 'mental impressions', which can grasp the great worth and richness of Sir John's character (p. 5). Morgann brings in other sorts of evidence as well, pointing out that all of the 'vulgar' characters in the plays – Fang, Snare, Mistress Quickly, Pistol, Davy, and the like – respect and fear Falstaff as a formidable man of war. Morgann also cites Coleville's surrender and the apparent fact that Falstaff's story of killing Hotspur is believed. Morgann notes the respectful company in which Falstaff often appears, his frequent references to court affairs, and his presence at the parley between Worcester and the King at Shrewsbury. As for Falstaff's behaviour at Gadshill, Morgann excuses it as the prudent retreat of an outmanned soldier. Shakespeare's primary concern is not with Falstaff's cowardice but with the comic value of his extravagant lies for excusing it, the humour of which erases their dishonour. At Shrewsbury, Falstaff shows courage in his ability to jest in the midst of danger; and even his feigning death when threatened by Douglas is merely an example of the triumph of his wit:

> There was no match; nothing remained but death or stratagem; grinning honour, or laughing life .... Falstaff falls, Douglas is cheated, and the world laughs. But does he fall like a coward? No, like a buffoon only; the superior principle prevails, and Falstaff lives by a stratagem

growing out of his character, to prove himself no counterfeit, to jest, to be employed, and to fight again.   (pp. 102–3)

Morgann's position in the essay anticipates the Romantic tradition of character criticism, which undertook quasi-biographical studies of Shakespearean characters as though they were real people. But Morgann is perceptive in his analysis of the sophistication of Shakespeare's art and his ability to draw complex, layered, and inconsistent characters that create the appearance of life:

> [Falstaff] is a character made up by Shakespeare wholly of incongruities; – a man at once young and old, enterprising and fat, a dupe and a wit, harmless and wicked, weak in principle and resolute by constitution, cowardly in appearance and brave in reality; a knave without malice, a liar without deceit; and a knight, a gentleman, and a soldier, without either dignity, decency, nor honour.   (p. 146)

Morgann's account of Falstaff's incongruous but attractive character opened up a debate about the ethics of Falstaff's rejection that persists to the present day.

Not everyone was impressed by Morgann's arguments; Dr. Samuel Johnson, asked by Boswell his opinion of the essay, replied 'Why, Sir, we shall have the man come forth again; and as he has proved Falstaff to be no coward, he may prove Iago to be a very good character' (Hunter, p. 25). In his edition of *Shakespeare's Works* (1795), Johnson discusses Falstaff even-handedly as 'a compound of sense and vice; of sense which may be admired but not esteemed, of vice which may be despised, but hardly detested' (Hunter, p. 23). Falstaff is filled with the contemptible faults of a thief and a coward (though he is guilty of 'no enormous or sanguinary crimes'), but he wins favour by 'the most pleasing of all qualities, perpetual gaiety, by an unfailing power of exciting laughter'. Yet for Johnson this power does not excuse his viciousness, but indeed heightens it:

> The moral to be drawn from this representation is, that no man is more dangerous than he that with a will to corrupt, hath the power to please; and that neither wit nor honesty ought to think themselves safe with such a companion when they see Henry seduced by Falstaff.   (Hunter, p. 24)

On the whole, eighteenth-century critics regarded Falstaff as a rogue who earned tolerance and sympathy because of his wit. Nicholas Rowe, in his edition of 1709, felt that though Shakespeare has made Falstaff 'a thief, lying, cowardly, vainglorious, and in short every way vicious, yet he has given him so much wit as to make him almost too agreeable.' Rowe therefore viewed the rejection with regret, and something like indignation: '… and I don't know whether some people have not, in remembrance of the diversion he had formerly afforded 'em, been sorry to see his friend Hal use him so scurvily when he comes to the crown at the end of the *Second Part of Henry IV*' (Vickers, vol. II, p. 195).

Samuel Taylor Coleridge took a somewhat harsher view of Falstaff, regarding him as a character of 'complete moral depravity, but of first-rate wit and talents' comparable to Richard III and Iago. Coleridge saw Falstaff as an outstanding example of Shakespeare's skill, specifically in the delineation of an almost superhuman intelligence. For Coleridge, as he is recorded by J. P. Collier in *Seven Lectures*,

> Falstaff was no coward, but pretended to be one merely for the sake of trying experiments on the credulity of mankind: he was a liar with the same object, and not because he loved falsehood for itself. He was a man of such preeminent abilities, as to give him a profound contempt for all those by whom he was usually surrounded, and to lead to a determination on his part, in spite of their fancied superiority, to make them his tools and dupes. He knew, however low he descended, that his own talents would raise him and extricate him from any difficulty. While he was thought to be the greatest rogue, thief and liar, he still had that about him which could render him not only respectable, but absolutely necessary to his companions.   (Quoted in Mack, pp. 236–7)

Coleridge's fascinating reading, existing only in this tantalizingly fragmentary form, presents Falstaff as a kind of corrupt philosopher-king, cynically manipulating those around him for his own pleasure and edification, and protected from consequences by his own sovereignty of nature. Coleridge's reading has all of the shortcomings of Romantic Shakespeare criticism, treating Falstaff naturalistically as though he were a real person with full subjectivity; but he also provides an insightful and surprising corrective to more sentimental eighteenth-century readings. Coleridge makes Falstaff a more formidable and more intellectual figure than he had generally been considered. In discussing how Falstaff makes himself necessary to his companions, however, Coleridge neglects the final rejection. For Prince Hal, Falstaff's necessity is of a finite duration.

The question of Falstaff's fate and its ethical and aesthetic meaning was raised again strongly in 1902 in A. C. Bradley's lecture 'The Rejection of Falstaff', later collected in his *Oxford Lectures on Poetry*. Bradley argues that, for those who don't enjoy the Falstaff scenes, the rejection may seem just, but for those who do, the King's actions cause 'a good deal of pain and some resentment' (p. 251). For Bradley, the problem is not only Falstaff's disappointment, but Henry's high-handedness: 'He had a right to turn away his former self, and his old companions with it; but he had no right to talk all of a sudden like a clergyman' (pp. 253–4). Bradley recognizes that such feelings of resentment on the part of reader or audience member are misguided and point to a failure to appreciate Shakespeare's full design. We are wrong to be shocked at Henry's conduct because it was an inevitable consequence of the characters and actions Shakespeare drew. Hal's first soliloquy shows his willingness to use others for his own ends. The rejection of Falstaff is an inevitable step in Henry's political career. The problem is that Shakespeare made Falstaff too attractive for us to let go of easily.

Bradley argues that Shakespeare 'overshot his mark' with Falstaff: that he created a character of such vitality and wit 'that when he sought to dethrone him he could not' (p. 259). For Bradley, Falstaff's attractiveness lies in what he calls 'the bliss of freedom gained in humour' (p. 262). Bradley sees Falstaff as a kind of comic genius, invulnerable to mockery, but successful in mocking all of the serious things in life. He is not only no coward but no liar: his account of the Gadshill episode is not a serious falsehood, but merely the characteristic expression of his supreme inventiveness and good humour. 'It is preposterous to suppose that a man of Falstaff's intelligence would utter these gross, palpable, open lies with the serious intent to deceive', Bradley declares; 'he no more expected to be believed than when he claimed to have killed Hotspur' (p. 265). Bradley reads Falstaff as a very light and free character, a character of 'ease' and 'bliss'. Bradley does acknowledge that the character changes in *Part II* as Shakespeare attempts to prepare the audience for the rejection. The emphasis on Falstaff's age, disease, and corruption in *Part II*, combined with the isolation and seriousness of Hal, are intended to create the conditions for a necessary break. But for Bradley these devices fail, so that the rejection still seems unjust and painful. This creates a problem in the resolution of the play, but in no way diminishes Shakespeare's achievement:

> The achievement was Falstaff himself, and the conception of that freedom of soul, a freedom illusory only in part, and attainable only by a mind which had received from Shakespeare's own the inexplicable touch of infinity which he bestowed on Hamlet and Macbeth and Cleopatra, but denied to Henry the Fifth.   (p. 273)

Bradley's transcendent Falstaff was brought to earth by the criticism of E. E. Stoll, who set out to put the fat knight in his place as a conventional figure of theatrical history. Stoll objected to Bradley's criticism generally as overly psychological and unhistorical, and his works represent a severe corrective. In *Shakespeare Studies* (1927), Stoll sought to demystify Falstaff, insisting that the character was simply the typical cowardly braggart soldier of Elizabethan comedy, like Jonson's Bobadill or Shakespeare's own Parolles. For Stoll, Falstaff plays a predictable, almost structural role, inflating his own reputation, exposing his true nature in cowardly actions, and then lying to cover his shameful behaviour. Like the *miles gloriosus* of classical comedy and countless Renaissance parallels, Falstaff is simply a comic butt, 'an ancient stage figure' characterized by 'cowardice and unbridled bragging, gluttony and lechery, sycophancy and pride' (p. 429). Stoll attacks the claims of Morgann and Bradley that Falstaff is merely playing at being a coward for the sake of a joke. In his exhaustive survey of theatrical braggart soliders, Stoll turns up many that experience versions of the Gadshill episode, getting into scrapes and lying their way out of them, but not one that displays the witty self-knowledge and gamesmanship that Romantic criticism attributes to Falstaff. Stoll will allow Falstaff neither courage nor philosophy:

> Falstaff is neither rebel nor critic. As clown he could be supposed to have neither philosophy nor anti-philosophy, being a comic contrast and appendage to the heroes and the heroic point of view. His cavillings at honour are made utterly nugatory and frivolous, and his jokes are but tell-tale parries and feints.   (pp. 474–5)

Stoll's rather reductive approach begs the question of whether Shakespeare could not transcend dramatic stereotypes with a richer vein of characterization; but, at the same time, Stoll does provide usefully concrete evidence for Falstaff's dramatic pedigree.

The approaches of Bradley and Stoll were synthesized in what was probably the most influential work of Falstaff criticism of the twentieth century, John Dover Wilson's *The Fortunes of Falstaff* (1944). For Dover Wilson, Falstaff was more than the simple stage-butt defined by Stoll; but while he had the 'touch of infinity' described by Bradley, he was nonetheless circumscribed by an English cultural tradition. Dover Wilson saw Falstaff as derived from the moral and religious drama of the middle ages. For him Falstaff was a type character: 'that reverend vice, that grey iniquity', a figure of riot and misrule who threatens to lead the young prince off the true path. Shakespeare's audience would have understood the conventions of the morality play that was being performed for them under the guise of a chronicle history; they could enjoy Falstaff because they understood his role:

> But they knew, from the beginning, that the reign of this marvelous Lord of Misrule must have an end, that Falstaff must be rejected by the Prodigal Prince, when the time for reformation came. And they no more thought of questioning or disapproving of that finale, than their ancestors would have thought of protesting against the Vice being carried off to hell at the end of the interlude. (p. 22)

Dover Wilson's morality reading is not limited to Falstaff; he sees each of the two parts of *Henry IV* as devoted to a moral virtue (Chivalry and Justice, respectively, with Hotspur and the Lord Chief Justice as their emblematic representatives). Dover Wilson's approach shifts the focus from Falstaff himself to Prince Hal: 'the technical centre of the play is not the fat knight but the lean prince' (p. 17). Dover Wilson's change of emphasis probably marks the point in the critical tradition at which the centre of attention in the two plays went from Falstaff to the political education of the future Henry V.

Nonetheless, Dover Wilson's approach is less reductive than Stoll's and allows for a fuller picture of Falstaff, whom he acknowledges to be 'the most conspicuous ... [and] certainly the most fascinating character in *Henry IV*' (p. 17). Falstaff contains multitudes, and easily absorbs contradictions. He is both a dramatic archetype and a true denizen of Elizabethan London, who 'symbolizes, on the one hand, all the feasting and good cheer for which Eastcheap stood, and reflects, on the other, the shifts, subterfuges, and shady tricks that decayed gentlemen and soldiers were put to if they wished to keep afloat and gratify their appetites in the London underworld of the late sixteenth century' (p. 25). Falstaff's symbolic status as an emblem of Riot does not prevent him playing the opposite role of Repentence. Wilson details how Falstaff's frequent quoting of scripture, perhaps a holdover from his inception as the Lollard Oldcastle, helps flesh out the Prodigal Son story of Prince Hal.

Dover Wilson's Falstaff, rich and various as he is, must nonetheless be rejected. It is the expected ending of the morality tale and a necessary part of the development of the central figure of the Prince. Dover Wilson, indeed, becomes a little heated in his support for Hal, comparing his conduct favorably to that of the former King Edward VIII: 'As, for ourselves, how characteristically muddle-headed is it that a generation which has almost universally condemned a prince of its own for putting private inclinations before his public obligations, should condemn Hal as a cad and a prig for doing just the opposite' (p. 123). The rejection is 'both right and necessary'; but it does not, in Dover Wilson's view, result in the destruction of Falstaff. Wilson cautions that the abrupt demise of Falstaff in *Henry V* has no bearing on *Henry IV*, which ends with the promise of Sir John's return. Dover Wilson speculates that Shakespeare intended further comic adventures for Falstaff in *Henry V*, and changed his mind only after the departure of Will Kemp from the Chamberlain's Men. As a character in *Henry IV*, Falstaff leaves the stage in an attitude of 'stout intrepidity' and 'more than impudent sauciness,' and in possession of Shallow's thousand pounds (p. 126). Dover Wilson ends his study insisting that *Henry IV* celebrates a 'double coronation' of two figureheads of order and of liberty. While Henry V represents the claims of law, duty and public service, Falstaff maintains his status as well as one free of all social conventions, 'our English Bacchus who, with the sprig of rue in his garland, reigns for ever from his state in the Boar's Head' (p. 128).

In a dryly cynical riposte in 1953, William Empson took Dover Wilson's high-minded moralism to task. With his trademark emphasis on ambiguity, and a prescient anticipation of performance and reception theory, Empson insisted that Falstaff remained available to multiple interpretations even within a single performance. The conservative-minded in Shakespeare's audience might see Falstaff as an corrupting influence and Hal as a virtuous prince, but that didn't prevent the groundlings from taking a different view: 'The plays were an enormous hit, appealing to a great variety of people, not all of them very high-minded, one would think' (p. 39). The ambiguity Shakespeare employed, sometimes 'riding remarkably near the edge, a bit breathtaking it may have been', allows the plays to continue to generate new and compelling interpretations centuries later. If Falstaff were so easily solved a puzzle as Dover Wilson presents him, he would not remain the endlessly fascinating character that he is, according to Empson, invoking contemporary theatrical interpretations. 'The actor and producer have to work out their own "conception" of Falstaff, in each case, and are sometimes felt to have worked out an interesting or "original" one,' Empson writes. 'The dramatic ambiguity is the source of these new interpretations, the reason why you can go on finding new ones, the reason why the effect is so rich' (p. 38). Empson insists on the ambivalence of the Hal/Falstaff relationship, but he does advocate that Falstaff has been a good tutor for Hal: as a Machiavellian schemer. Empson's partiality to Falstaff comes through in his suggestion, first developed in *Some Versions of Pastoral* back in 1935, that the Falstaff /Hal relationship parallels that of Shakespeare and 'Mr. W. H.' of the sonnets; the devoted older man and the callow young man who rejects him.

W. H. Auden, in his essay 'The Prince's Dog' (1959), also viewed Falstaff sympathetically while acknowledging the political mastery of Prince Hal. For Auden Falstaff is 'a comic symbol for the supernatural order of Charity as contrasted with the temporal order of Justice symbolized by Henry of Monmouth' (Hunter, p. 202). Prince Hal is the epitome of the 'worldly man' who has the public good at heart, though his methods, in Auden's view, make him comparable to Iago (p. 209). Falstaff, in his childlike 'unworldliness', is even more strikingly compared to Jesus Christ. Until his inevitable rejection, Falstaff 'radiates happiness as Hal radiates power, and this happiness without apparent cause, this untiring devotion to making others laugh, becomes a comic image for a love which is absolutely self-giving' (p. 210).

Recent evaluations of Falstaff have moved away from the question of his moral character, which, as Empson noted, 'may be said to have started the whole snowball of modern Shakespearean criticism' with Morgann's essay (p. 38). In the second half of the twentieth century, many critics noted that Falstaff serves a variety of roles as a figure of transgression, one who challenges the basic value systems posited elsewhere in the play, of hierarchical government and patriarchal authority. Drawing on the Marxian critic Mikhail Bakhtin, author of the influential study *Rabelais and his World* (1965), critics such as Michael Bristol have argued that Falstaff is a 'Carnivalesque' figure, whose Rabelaisian appetites deny the Lenten imperatives of Lancastrian politics and social order. Another new dimension has been the approach to Falstaff from a feminist perspective. In 'Prince Hal's Falstaff: Positioning Psychoanalysis and the Female Reproductive Body', Valerie Traub argues for the fat knight as an outsider to the patriarchal order, who in many ways can be seen as gendered female. This influential essay, first published in *Shakespeare Quarterly* in 1989, is part of a movement by feminist scholars such as Traub, Phyllis Rackin and Jean Howard to excavate female concerns and voices from the predominantly masculine world of the history plays.

Traub uses Falstaff's body – enormous, unruly, protuberant, leaking – to make connections between the 'grotesque body' celebrated in Bakhtinian Carnival and the reproductive female body that is rejected during childhood development, according to the psychoanalytic theories of Freud and Lacan. According to Traub, 'Shakespearean drama and psychoanalytic theory share in a cultural estimation of the female reproductive body as a Bakhtinian "grotesque body," and consequently repress this figure in their narratives of psychic development' (pp. 456–7). Traub contends that Prince Hal's subjectivity is constituted against the maternal figure of Falstaff, who must be rejected, and subsequently against the French Princess Katherine in *Henry V*, who must be subjugated both to Hal's masculine sexuality and his language. The reading of Falstaff as gendered female is not original with Traub, as she notes – Auden and Coppelia Kahn both observed Falstaff's resemblance to a pregnant woman and Patricia Parker included Falstaff among the 'literary fat ladies' of her book of that title (p. 461). But Traub goes further in insisting on the primacy of his female attributes in the psychological role Falstaff plays with Hal and in his eventual rejection: as Falstaff himself declares, 'my womb, my womb, my womb undoes me' (*Part II*, IV.iii.22). While previous psychoanalytic studies of the

Henry IV plays focused on Hal's relationship with Henry IV and Falstaff as rival father figures, Traub makes Falstaff a nurturing, potentially engulfing, and grotesquely corporeal mother. According to Traub, 'Hal's development as a male subject depends not only on separation and differentiation from a state of physical dependency and a fantasized state of psychic symbiosis but also on the exorcism of the figure responsible for and associated with that state: mother, mater, matter' (p. 464). The public rejection of Falstaff is thus an assertion not only of Hal's new status as King, but as a mature masculine subject.

Such new readings of Falstaff, and the role he plays in Hal's personal and political trajectory, point to a general trend in Shakespeare studies away from self-contained and autonomous characters and toward intersecting discourses of power, language and subjectivity. Falstaff is rarely, any longer, the courageous and engaging figure of Morgann's essay, or the irresistible humourist of Bradley, insulated from the world by 'the bliss of freedom'. Falstaff is more often a compromised figure, caught up in the cold world of Lancastrian politics, at times transgressing hierarchies but finally, through his own destruction, serving to reaffirm them. His subversive energies are now usually subject to containment, or else implicated in the practices of war and exploitation. A final defense of Falstaff's transcendent genius was mounted by Harold Bloom, who, strongly identifying with Falstaff, made him a central figure in his *Shakespeare: The Invention of the Human*. For Bloom, Falstaff represents the triumph of human wit, and, along with Hamlet, the triumph of Shakespeare's ability to create the impression of living, changing, extraordinary individuals: 'Falstaff and Hamlet are the invention of the human, the inauguration of personality as we have come to recognize it' (p. 4). Bloom defends old-style character criticism and places himself deliberately in the tradition of Morgann, Johnson, and Bradley, both in praising Shakespeare's brilliant creation of theatrical personalities and in having a high regard for Falstaff. Bloom calls Falstaff 'mortal god of my imaginings' and defends his vitality and wit in contrast to the cold machinations of his nemesis, Prince Hal (p. xix).

Bloom's defense of Falstaff incorporates a critique of modern, and especially post-modern, Shakespeare criticism, which in Bloom's view diminishes the mighty achievements of Shakespeare to the joyless workings of history and discourse. Bloom presents himself, rather like his hero Falstaff, as one who has been left behind by a world of soulless functionaries, the Prince Johns of the academy, and a criticism that no longer responds to human warmth and greatness. He certainly represents the tail end of a tradition that, honouring Falstaff, has dominated studies of the two parts of *Henry IV* for much of their history. This tradition has been replaced, gradually and then suddenly, by another stream of criticism that views the plays as studies of political power and Renaissance statecraft, with the figure of Prince Hal at their centre.

Prince Hal and politics

One of the first critics to address seriously the political dimensions of the *Henry IV* plays was the German scholar Hermann Ulrici in an 1838 study that was published in English as *Shakespeare's Dramatic Art* in 1846. Ronald Knowles has argued that Ulrici was a century ahead of his time in his historicist reading of the plays as an exploration of the contradictions of feudal society (Knowles, p. 29). As a Hegelian, Ulrici was interested not in the questions of character that consumed Romantic critics and allowed Falstaff to dominate scholarly debate, but in 'the unity of *historical idea*, the motive of the historical movement, and thus in the unity of the character and the spirit of the age presented' (quoted in Knowles, p. 38). For him, the essence of the plays lay in the struggle between the power of the king and the great feudal barons, a struggle Bolingbroke/Henry IV had participated in on both sides. Falstaff is of interest chiefly as a parody of the main political action of the plays: 'These comic scenes evidently contain a deep satire upon the represented history, their *parodical* character cannot be mistaken; they were designed to parody the hollow pathos of political history, and to tear from it its state robes and parade, in order to exhibit it in its true shape' (Ulrici, p. 346). For Ulrici, as for many twentieth-century critics, the *Henry IV* plays constitute a serious analysis of medieval politics: 'the elucidation of the character of Henry the Fourth's reign, and its mere semblance and lack of real depth, was the conscious or unconscious design of the poet' (p. 375). Ulrici's work had little immediate influence in England, where the focus was still on character; but many critics began to look beyond Falstaff at the political dimensions of the plays.

George Bernard Shaw, who was never shy on the subject of Shakespeare, decried *Henry IV* as inferior work, with 'neither the romantic beauty of Shakespeare's earlier plays nor the tragic greatness of his later ones' (*Shaw on Shakespeare*, p. 101). One of the chief reasons for his dislike is the character of Prince Hal, which Shaw sees as central to the play: 'the combination of conventional propriety and brute masterfulness in his public capacity with a low-lived blackguardism in his private tastes is not a pleasant one' (p. 102). He sees Hal's experiences in the tavern world as self-serving and hypocritical, based on no real affection for Falstaff and his friends: 'he repeatedly makes it clear that he will turn on them later on, and that his self-indulgent good fellowship with them is consciously and deliberately treacherous.' In the introductory paragraphs of a review of Beerbohm Tree's 1896 production of *1 Henry IV*, Shaw discusses the play primarily in terms of political chicanery, focusing on the efforts of the King and Hal to maintain their ill-gotten power. Hotspur he dismisses as 'no better than his horse'; Falstaff, he concedes, is 'the most human person in the play, but none the less a besotted and disgusting old wretch.' Shaw reserves his most stringent criticism for Hal, the 'able young philistine,' whose humour 'is seasoned with sportsmanlike cruelty and the insolence of conscious mastery and contempt to the point of occasionally making one shudder.' With regard to the rejection of Falstaff, Shaw wrote in *The Quintessence of Ibsenism* that the new King 'might, one thinks, have the decency to wait until he has redeemed his own character before assuming the right to lecture his boon companion' (p. 106). Shaw, with his fascination for politics, recognized the Lancastrian succession as the backbone of the play; but he viewed it with real distaste. Others who similarly indicted Prince Hal as a political opportunist were W. B. Yeats and John Masefield. Masefield's attack is scathing: 'Prince Henry is not a hero, he is not a thinker, he is not even a friend; he is a common man whose incapacity for feeling enables him to change his habits whenever interest bids him' (p. 112). Yeats objected mainly to the bellicose Henry V, whom he called a 'ripened Fortinbras,' but his condemnation encapsulates Hal's early career as well: 'He has the gross vices, the coarse nerves, of one who is to rule among violent people, and he is so little "too friendly" to his friends that he bundles them out of doors when their time is over. He is as remorseless and undistinguished as some natural force' (p. 81).

The critic who had the greatest impact in altering approaches to *Henry IV*, not only in scholarship but even on the stage, was E. M. W. Tillyard. Although his *Shakespeare's History Plays* has relatively little to say on the subject of *Henry IV*, its basic approach to Shakespeare's histories has been extremely influential. Tillyard popularized the notions that the histories are a meaningfully linked series of plays, almost a single epic work; that they reflect the biases of their chronicle sources, particularly Edward Hall's history of the houses of Lancaster and York; and that they promulgate an essentially conservative 'Tudor myth.' This myth abominates civic disorder, supports the divine right of kings, and represents the Wars of the Roses as a curse on England for the deposing of Richard II. Most importantly, it endorses the Tudor dynasty as the final lifting of that curse, part of God's providential plan.

The Elizabethan ideology of order, which Tillyard identified in the state Homilies and many other sources, was a comforting one for many at the end of the Second World War, when *Shakespeare's History Plays* was published. And while subsequent critics have questioned whether such an ideology was universally held, Tillyard demonstrated that the plays deal seriously with questions of political philosophy. Tillyard changed the critical paradigm, forcing scholarship examine the history plays as serious engagements with history and politics, not character-studies or failed attempts at tragedy (or comedy). However, in dealing with the *Henry IV* plays, Tillyard does not focus so much on the curse brought by Bolingbroke's usurpation as, surprisingly, on the development of Prince Hal as an ideal ruler:

> far from being a mere dissolute lout awaiting a miraculous transformation he is from the first a very commanding character, deliberate in act and in judgment, versed in every phase of human nature. But he is more than that. When the drawers think him the 'king of courtesy' they know him better than his enemy Hotspur and even his own father do. And when Shakespeare put the phrase in their mouths he had in mind the abstract Renaissance conception of the perfect ruler.   (p. 314)

Tillyard's infatuation with the Prince is nearly total. He praises Dover Wilson's *The Fortunes of Falstaff*, discussed above, for 'having helped to redress the balance between the Prince and Falstaff,' but goes beyond him: his Hal is no morality-play Everyman but the ideal Renaissance prince (p. 306). Tillyard goes out of his way, for instance, to excuse Hal for teasing Francis, noting rather shockingly that 'the subhuman element in the population must have been considerable in Shakespeare's day; that it should be treated almost like beasts was taken for granted' (p. 314). Tillyard endorses the rejection of Falstaff as necessary and correct, and even chides those who have sentimentalized the old knight because of their own smugness, blaming their views on 'the sense of security created in nineteenth century England by the predominance of the British navy' (p. 330). World War II taught Tillyard to fear the threat of disorder: 'Schooled by recent events we should have no difficulty now in taking Falstaff as the Elizabethans took him.'

Interestingly, Tillyard takes the Hal of the *Henry IV* plays as his ideal type; he finds *Henry V* and its hero to be inferior and uninspired work. Yet he is in no doubt that this character is the central figure of the Lancastrian histories, just as he is in no doubt that 'Shakespeare conceived his second tetralogy as one great unit' (p. 267). And while subsequent criticism would contest these views, they dominated discussion of *Henry IV* for the remainder of the century. Dover Wilson's book has already been noted. Lily B. Campbell's *Shakespeare's Histories: Mirrors of Elizabethan Policy* also supports a Tudor-myth reading of the plays, detecting Shakespeare's partiality in his 'making Henry, the rebel, to be plagued by rebellion; showing Henry, the regicide, as hoping vainly to placate an avenging King of kings,' and so forth (p. 229). Campbell focuses on the political dimensions of the plays, dismissing Falstaff as 'historically an intruder' (p. 213). She relates the plays directly to specifically Elizabethan concerns, such as the dangerously powerful subject, whether Hotspur or Essex.

One of the first challenges to the Tillyard view of the history plays came from A. P. Rossiter. His essay 'Ambivalence: the Dialectic of the Histories', first published in 1954 and reprinted in 1961 in the collection *Angel with Horns*, insists that 'the Tudor myth system of Order, Degree, etc. was too rigid, too black-and-white, too doctrinaire and narrowly moral for Shakespeare's mind' (p. 59). In the *Henry IV* plays in particular, Shakespeare expressed his complex understanding of human affairs through juxtapositions of the comic and serious, the elevated and the travestied. Falstaff is essential to the design of the plays in that he parodies the pretensions of Hotspur and the King. Hal is a role-player whose shifting identity reflects Shakespeare's fundamental ambivalence about the possibilities of integrity in public life:

> In History Shakespeare felt that men were constrained to be much less than their full selves. He knew the burden of princehood ... All the Lancasters are less than full men. None is himself; only what he wills to be for the time only. By and by he will 'be more himself.' Hal says it: Father says it. None does it.   (p. 63)

Rossiter was particularly vexed with the reduction of Falstaff to a morality Vice by Dover Wilson and Tillyard, and the impact that view had on such productions as the 1951 cycle at the Shakespeare Memorial Theatre (see Chapter 4): 'Already semi-deflated Falstaffs are reaching the stage – Welfare state Falstaffs, shrunk in the moral wash, preconditioned for pricking before they have got so far afoot as Shrewsbury' (p. 46). Such an approach reduces the complexity of the *Henry IV* plays, which often employ 'comic parallelism of phrase or incident' – between the robbing of the thieves at Gadshill and Henry's demand for Hotspur's Scottish prisoners, for instance. The repeated use of this kind of 'travesty-by-parallel' shows Shakespeare engaging critically with the Tudor-myth ideology, and finding it wanting: 'Throughout the Histories it is in the implications of the Comic that shrewd, realistic thinking about men in politics – in office – in war – in plot – is exposed: realistic apprehension outrunning the medieval frame,' which Shakespeare's intuition told him 'was *morally* inadequate.' (p. 59). Thus, in Rossiter's view, Shakespeare transcends the Tudor myth through an ongoing comic critique of the main political action of the *Henry IV* plays.

Another influential essay that challenged the conservative political reading of Tillyard and others came from the Polish critic Jan Kott, in his influential *Shakespeare Our Contemporary*. In his chapter 'The Kings,' Kott read the histories as showing the operations of a 'Grand Mechanism' of politics, with power an irresistible if destructive goal achieved at any price and quickly lost: 'Feudal history is like a great staircase on which there treads a constant procession of kings. Every step upward is marked by murder, perfidy and treachery ... From the highest step there is only a leap into the abyss' (pp. 10–11). Kott dwells mostly on *Richard II* and *Richard III*, focusing on what he sees as an endless cycle of usurpation and new rebellion. He admits to disliking *Henry IV*, finding it a dishonest 'apologetic drama' because 'the young prince grows up into a wise and brave king,' a point of view some critics would dispute (p. 50). He does approvingly cite the scene of Falstaff's recruiting, which 'might have been put, as it stands, into a play by Brecht.' But he feels that the *Henry IV* plays differ from the other histories in their 'cheerful' tone. Nonetheless, his generally cynical view of Shakespearean politics had a considerable impact on performances of the *Henry IV* plays. Kott's nihilistic ideas influenced Peter Hall and John Barton's *Wars of the Roses* productions at Stratford-Upon-Avon in 1963, to which the *Henry IV* plays were added a year later (see Chapter 4).

Kott did not have much direct impact in the academy; Anglo-American Shakespeareans mounted their own, more scholarly attacks on Tillyard and the conservative political readings of the history plays. Derek Traversi, in *Shakespeare from Richard II to Henry V*, accepts the idea of a linked four-play sequence centred on the figure of Prince Hal, but argues that the Tillyardian frame reduces their complexity as individual works of art. In *Divine Providence and the England of Shakespeare's Histories*, Henry A. Kelly showed that there were a variety of political 'myths' – Lancastrian and Yorkist as well as Tudor: some endorsed Bolingbroke's usurpation as providential and their coexistence undermined any sense of a single Elizabethan World Picture. He notes that 'in neither of the plays named for Henry IV are the Lancastrians dramatized as being punished by God for their acquisition and continued possession of the throne' (p. 232). Kelly argues that while many characters within the plays invoke the notion of a providential God intervening in human affairs, they generally do so in an interested way, in support of their own political motives. Other qualifications to a monolithic Tillyardian position came in Robert Ornstein's *A Kingdom for a Stage: the Achievement of Shakespeare's History Plays*, which returns to a humanist examination of character, and Moody Prior's *The Drama of Power*, which focuses on the complex political dilemmas confronting the King.

In *The Meaning of Shakespeare* (1951), Harold C. Goddard reads *Henry IV* as 'a single drama in ten acts'. His reading focuses on the Prince and on what Goddard sees as his degradation as he becomes more and more like the political hypocrite, his father. Goddard alters Dover Wilson's morality play structure so that Hal is seen as standing between Falstaff and the King; his tragedy is that he follows the latter rather than the former. In a darkly psychological study of Hal that repeatedly references Dostoevsky, Goddard reads his assumption of his father's inheritance as a failure to be his true self, the self he had realized in the company of Falstaff. Comparing Hal to the sons of Karamazov, Goddard asserts that both Shakespeare and Dostoevsky realized that 'in proportion as the child fails to be himself he falls back in to the likeness of the racial [i.e. biological] father, while in proportion as he finds an imaginative father he rises, not into that father's image, but into his own soul's image, into himself' (vol. I, p. 214). In *Henry IV*, according to Goddard, Shakespeare shows the negative side of this proposition. Goddard's reading is colored by his intensely negative response to Henry V, whom he calls 'the perfect Machiavellian prince,' next to whom Richard III was 'a mere bungler' (vol. I, p. 267).

H. M. Richmond, in *Shakespeare's Political Plays* (1967), comes to a similar judgment about the Prince. His analysis of the two parts of *Henry IV* focuses on the difficulties the King has in maintaining his throne; for him Falstaff is an emblem of the lawlessness that is running rampant in England as a result of the King's own example. In consorting with Falstaff, Prince Hal may be educating himself but 'the major consequence of his escapades is that Hal is already bored by such lesser pleasures before he becomes king, and is excited by the prospect of the satisfactions of authority' (pp. 167–8). He is able to be more successful than his father because he is able to seize the initiative rather than having to be responsive to events. Morally, Hal is no better than Henry, and may be worse: 'By the end of *Henry IV*, all we can say is that he shows a manipulative quality equal to his father's, and even reminiscent of that subtle testing of his victims' personality into which Richard III had refined the role of Vice' (p. 171).

Other original readings of Prince Hal and his father focused on psychology and language. M. D. Faber's 1970 collection *The Design Within: Psychoanalytic Approaches to Shakespeare* incorporates several perspectives on the father-son relationships within the plays, notably Ernst Kris's discussion of Prince Hal's impulses toward parricide. He retreats to the tavern to avoid this temptation; his hostility toward his real father finds its expression in his destruction of his surrogate father Falstaff. In *Metadrama in Shakespeare's Henriad* (1979), James Calderwood reads the entire tetralogy in terms of what he calls 'the fall of speech'. Whereas under the divinely-sanctioned kingship of Richard II words had a direct, sacramental relationship to things, the reign of Henry IV marks 'the ascendance of the lie'. The King's words have no more authority than his counterfeits at Shrewsbury; in this world both Hal and Falstaff freely traffic in untruths. Language is only restored to authority when Hal becomes king, and 'the divinely guaranteed truths of Richard's reign and the ubiquitous lies of Henry's are succeeded by rhetoric, the language of conquest' (p. 7). Joseph Porter similarly approaches *Henry IV* through language in *The Drama of Speech Acts* (1979). Porter uses the myth of the Tower of Babel to characterize the polyglot world of the *Henry IV* plays. Hal's eventual success comes from his ability to accept the variety of language and wrestle with problems of translation: he takes office as 'a many-tongued monarch who, using a wide range of language purposefully and responsibly, initiates a reign of "high … parliament"' (p. 115).

One of the most important new considerations of the *Henry IV* plays came in Stephen Greenblatt's essay *Invisible Bullets*, first published in 1981 and later expanded into a chapter in *Shakespearean Negotiations* (1988). Greenblatt's work is anticipated by that of C. L. Barber, who in *Shakespeare's Festive Comedy* (1959) relates the Hal/Falstaff story to Elizabethan holidays and primitive scapegoat rituals in order to assert that 'the misrule works, through the whole dramatic rhythm, to consolidate rule' (p. 205). Greenblatt, one of the preeminent exponents of the 'New Historicism', reads the plays in relation to a variety of Elizabethan discourses; notably, pamphlets on 'cony-catching' in the London underworld and Thomas Harriot's *Brief and True Report of the New Found Land of Virginia*. Greenblatt's concern is the relation between authority and subversion: for Prince Hal, as for the Tudor state, the achievement of authority 'involves as its positive condition the constant production of its own radical subversion and the powerful containment of that subversion' (p. 41). Greenblatt notes Hal's appropriation of the language of tinkers and drawers, comparing it to the recording of Native American speech for purposes of exploitation. Hal plays at being a common man in order to rule common men more effectively. His 'I know you all' scheme represents an essentially theatrical approach to creating royal power. The temporary role of madcap prince creates the conditions for his success as reformed king. Greenblatt details, and indicts, the way Hal uses his tavern companions to consolidate his own position, comparing his action to his brother's double-crossing of the rebels at Gaultree:

> In this play … moral values – justice, order, civility – are secured through the apparent generation of their subversive contraries. Out of the squalid betrayals that preserve the state emerges the 'formal majesty' into which Hal at the close, through a final, definitive betrayal – the rejection of Falstaff – merges himself. (p. 53)

Within the *Henry IV* plays, as within the Tudor state, those in power allow, and even create, apparent subversion only to contain it ruthlessly and so maintain their power.

Leonard Tennenhouse similarly reads the *Henry IV* plays as using misrule to consolidate rule: 'It cannot be accidental that the *Henriad*, which produces Shakespeare's most accomplished Elizabethan monarch, should also produce his most memorable figure of misrule' (p. 83). Through his misspent youth, Hal takes on a populist energy, but that energy, in the end, helps him to legitimate his rule: 'the figures of carnival ultimately authorise the State as the State appears to take on the vigour of festival' (pp. 83–4). Richard Helgerson's *Forms of Nationhood* makes similar claims:

> The exposure of kingship in a narrative and dramatic medium that not only displayed power but revealed the sometimes brutal and duplicitous strategies by which power ostensibly maintained itself might be thought to subvert the structure of authority it ostensibly celebrated. But though the plays do bear a subversive potential, neither it nor their festive power of inversion have in fact made themselves felt in any historically disruptive way. (p. 244)

Helgerson relates the rejection of Falstaff to the departure of Kemp from the company, seeing in both a suppression of the plebeian forces of carnival in favour of the authorizing power of prince or playwright. For such critics, the disruptive energies released by the oppositional elements within the world of *Henry IV* are always contained by Lancastrian authority, through the unfolding of Prince Hal's Machiavellian master plan.

Not all historicist accounts of Hal read him negatively. In his essay 'Shakespeare's Walking Plays: Image and Form in *1* and *2 Henry IV*', John Rumrich reads the plays in terms of their concern with perambulation over the land of England, in particular the processional ritual of 'beating the bounds' of the parish at Rogationtide. Hal's personal journey takes special meaning in the context of the plays' imagery of walking, which Rumrich reads both metaphorically and historically:

> Walking ... would have had associations both with continuity, as a means of maintaining the possession of historical property and identity, and with change, in crossing borders or developing character. It is Hal's peculiar virtue in these plays to be able to balance the dialectic that walking implies, and he does so in part by carefully unfolding his own character.   (p. 123)

For Rumrich, the predominant back-and-forth motion of the plays helps Hal to expiate his father's crime by reenacting it, when he steals and then returns the crown in IV.v of *Part II*.

Like many recent critics, Graham Holderness reads the *Henry IV* plays in political terms, but argues that they are more concerned with medieval than Elizabethan politics. For Holderness, Shakespeare had a genuine historical sense, and understood the conflicts and contradictions of medieval feudalism as distinct from the political realities of his own day:

> If our argument is accepted, it becomes possible to discover in the plays a clear, historically informed apprehension of the political struggles of later mediaeval society; in particular the long struggle between monarchy and nobility which developed out of the contradictory nature of the feudal order, and was arrested by the accession of the Tudors.   (p. 19)

In *1 Henry IV*, Shakespeare dramatizes the conflict between aristocratic and monarchical power through the confrontation of Hotspur and the King. King Henry, in opposing Hotspur, must oppose the ideology of chivalric meritocracy that brought him to power: 'In terms of the *feudal* dimension of his ideology he acknowledges Percy as a legitimate contender, and dismisses his son's claims as negligible; in term of his *monarchical* aspirations he must seek to crush Percy and validate lawful inheritance as a structural principle of the state' (pp. 48–9). In giving dramatic form to this ideological conflict, Shakespeare reveals his grasp of the contradictions of late medieval society.

Another critic concerned with Shakespeare's historical understanding in the *Henry IV* plays is Paola Pugliatti. Her *Shakespeare the*

Historian emphasizes the ways in which Shakespeare expresses different historiographical perspectives within his history plays rather than relying on a single viewpoint such as Tudor providentialism. With regard to the *Henry IV* plays, she stresses the shift in focus between *Part I* and *Part II*. In a chapter on 'Time, Space and the Instability of History in the *Henry IV* sequence' she identifies three key 'axiologies' – rule, misrule and rebellion – which determine the conflicts within the plays. In the first part, they are kept discrete by time, though each is to some extent contaminated by the others. In the second part, the boundaries between rule, misrule and rebellion begin to disintegrate as each invades the others' physical spaces:

> While, in fact, the first play mainly establishes these axiologies and meanings and gives them a comparatively clear set of distinct prerogatives, in the second we see their progressive disfigurement and finally their utter corruption: trespassings and interferences, in fact, are comparatively ineffectual in the first play, where they figure merely as hints and suggestions of what may in the end happen and as partial and temporary distortion of the prerogatives of each of the spaces; while in the second they are responsible for the blurring and final collapse of the issues for which each of the spaces stands. (p. 108)

Correspondingly, the plays end without a singular understanding of the historical events they depict: rather, they represent the coexistence of multiple divergent histories.

The proliferation of new theoretically-informed readings of Shakespeare since the last decades of the twentieth century has encouraged many new approaches to the *Henry IV* plays. Jean E. Howard and Phyllis Rackin, in their feminist study of the history plays, *Engendering a Nation*, read *Henry IV* in terms of gender, politics and geography. While noting the paucity of female characters in the aggressively masculine world of the plays (especially compared to the *Henry VI-Richard III* tetralogy), they find evidence of a transgressive female presence in the plays' marginal spaces: particularly the tavern of Eastcheap and the mystical world of Wales. These manifestations are sometimes deeply threatening to the patriarchal ideology of the dominant world of the court – as in the alarming report, in the first scene of *Part I*, of the 'beastly shameless transformation/ By those Welshwomen done' on the genitals of dead English soldiers. Other manifestations are more seductive, like the exotic figure of

Glendower's daughter, speaking and singing in Welsh. The Eastcheap tavern, presided over by Mistress Quickly, Doll Tearsheet, and a gender-bending Falstaff, is a feminized theatrical space, antithetical to the masculine court but filled with vitality and transgressive pleasures. Behind these projections of a dangerous but alluring femininity, perhaps, lurk anxieties about a female monarch, but also an awareness of the importance of women and other marginal figures in the bustling and energetic world of contemporary mercantile London – including the theatre. Just as the epilogue to *Part II* acknowledges the presence of women in the audience, Howard and Rackin argue that the plays acknowledge the contradictions of the Elizabethan theatre, 'devoted to the pieties of dominant history and giving voice, simultaneously, to social forces which challenge that hegemony, among which we must include the entrepreneurial energies of the women in the tavern and the women in the theatre audience' (p. 185).

In exploring the worlds of socially marginalized characters – whether defined by gender, class, or nationality – Howard and Rackin call attention to the plays' richness and heterogeneity. Rather than limiting the plays to a dominant character like Falstaff, or a monolithic conception of kingship, recent criticism tends to open the plays up to multiple perspectives and plural, competing histories.

Further Reading

Texts and early performances

Editions

Part I

Arden, Second Series, ed. A. R. Humphreys (London: Methuen, 1960; Routledge, 1994).

Arden, Third Series, ed. David Scott Kastan (London: Routledge, 2002).

Bedford, *Texts and Contexts*, ed. Barbara Hodgdon (Boston: Bedford, 1987).

Cambridge, ed. Herbert Weil and Judith Weil (Cambridge: Cambridge University Press, 1997).

Norton, ed. Gordon McMullan (New York: W. W. Norton & Company, 2003).

Oxford, ed. David Bevington (Oxford: Oxford University Press, 1987).

Part II

Arden, Second Series, ed. A. R. Humphreys (London: Methuen, 1966; Routledge, 1989).

Cambridge, ed. Giorgio Melchiori (Cambridge University Press, 1989, 2007).

Oxford, ed. René Weis (Oxford: Oxford University Press, 1997).

Parts I and II

In *The Complete Works of Shakespeare*, updated fourth edition, ed. David Bevington (New York: Addison-Wesley, 1997). Used for line references and quotations in this handbook, though I have used British spelling for consistency.

Longman Critical Edition, ed. Ronald L. Levao (incorporating texts from the Bevington edition plus sources and criticism) (New York: Pearson, 2007).

On Shakespeare's theatre

Andrew Gurr, *The Shakespearean Stage, 1574–1642*, third edition (Cambridge: Cambridge University Press, 1992). A full account of Elizabethan staging conditions.

Robert Weimann, *Shakespeare and the Popular Tradition in the Theatre*, ed. Thomas Schwartz (Baltimore: Johns Hopkins, 1978), an influential study of the social dynamics of Elizabethan stagecraft.

Sources and cultural contexts

Geoffrey Bullough, ed., *Narrative and Dramatic Sources of Shakespeare*, vol. IV (London: Routledge and Kegan Paul; New York: Columbia University Press, 1962). Contains substantial passages from the sources for both parts, including Holinshed, Daniel and *The Famous Victories* as well as Hall, Stow and other historians, and possible dramatic sources for individual episodes.

Lily B. Campbell, *Shakespeare's Histories: Mirrors of Elizabethan Policy* (San Marino, CA.: Huntington Library, 1947). Though dated and contested, still a productive source for intersections of Elizabethan politics with the history plays.

Peter Corbin and Douglas Sedge, eds, *The Oldcastle Controversy: Sir John Oldcastle, Part I and The Famous Victories of Henry V* (Manchester: Manchester University Press, 1991). Contains the text of *The Famous Victories* as well as a pro-Oldcastle play that was included in the Third Folio of Shakespeare.

Samuel Daniel, *Complete Works*, vol. V (New York: Russell, 1963).

The Famous Victories of Henry V, Tudor Facsimile Texts (New York: AMS Press, 1970). Facsimile of the text in the Bodleian Library.

Russ McDonald, *The Bedford Companion to Shakespeare: An Introduction with Documents* (Boston: Bedford, 1996). An excellent source of contemporary documents, including the *Homily against Disobedience and Willful Rebellion*.

Paul A. Jorgenson, *Shakespeare's Military World* (Berkeley: University of California Press, 1956). A pioneering account of early modern soldiership.

Key productions and performances

Sally Beauman, *The Royal Shakespeare Company's Centenary Production of Henry V* (London: Pergamon press, 1976).

Sally Beauman, *The Royal Shakespeare Company: A History of Ten Decades* (Oxford: Oxford University Press, 1982). Covers Stratford productions up through Terry Hands's in 1975.

Michael Bogdanov and Michael Pennington, *The English Shakespeare Company: The Story of The Wars of the Roses', 1986–89* (London: Nick Hern, 1990). A discussion of the company's origin and its touring performances of seven history plays including the two parts of *Henry IV*.

John Russell Brown, *Shakespeare in Performance: An Introduction through Six Major Plays* (New York: HBJ, 1976). Includes discussions of several important productions as well as a model commentary on *Part I*.

John Cottrell, *Laurence Olivier.* (Englewood Cliffs, N.J.: Prentice-Hall, 1975).

Gordon Crosse, *Shakespearean Playgoing, 1890–1952.* (London: A. R. Mowbray, 1953).

Richard David, *Shakespeare in the Theatre* (Cambridge: Cambridge University Press, 1978). A collection that includes discussion of the 1951 and 1975 Stratford productions; the same author's essay 'Shakespeare's History Plays – Epic or Drama?' (*Shakespeare Survey* 6, 1953) contains valuable material on the 1951 cycle.

Barbara Hodgdon, *Henry IV, Part Two* (Manchester: Manchester University Press, 1993). Contains excellent discussions of productions by Michael Redgrave, Terry Hands, Trevor Nunn, and Michael Bogdanov as well as the BBC TV version.

Scott McMillin, *Henry IV, Part One* (Manchester: Manchester University Press, 1991). Contains detailed and thoughtful chapters on the British productions of 1945, 1951, 1964, 1975, and 1986 that are discussed in the present volume, along with *Chimes at Midnight* and the BBC TV version of 1979.

Bella Merlin, *With the Rogue's Company: Henry IV at the National Theatre* (London: Oberon Books, 2005). An account of rehearsals for Nicholas Hytner's 2005 production with Michael Gambon as Falstaff.

John Miller, *Ralph Richardson: The Authorized Biography* (London: Sidgwick & Jackson, 1995).

Stanley Wells, *Shakespeare in the Theatre: An Anthology of Criticism* (Oxford: Oxford University Press, 2000). Includes numerous references to *Henry IV* performances, from Colley Cibber as Justice Shallow to the Bogdanov *Henries* cycle.

Audrey Williamson, *Old Vic Drama* (London: Rockliff, 1948).

John Dover Wilson and T. C. Worsley, *Shakespeare's Histories at Stratford, 1951* (London: Max Reinhardt, 1951). An invaluable record of the 1951 cycle at the Shakespeare Memorial Theatre, directed by Anthony Quayle.

The play on screen

Versions discussed

Chimes at Midnight, directed by Orson Welles, 1966.

Henry IV, Parts I and II, The Shakespeare Plays, BBC/Time-Life, directed by David Giles, 1979.

The Wars of the Roses, English Shakespeare Company, directed by Michael Bogdanov, 1989.

My Own Private Idaho, New Line Cinema, directed by Gus Van Sant, 1991.

Further reading

Michael Anderegg, *Orson Welles, Shakespeare, and Popular Culture* (New York: Columbia University Press, 1999). An examination of Welles's engagement with Shakespeare throughout his career, with a chapter focusing on *Chimes at Midnight*.

Jim Bulman and H. R. Coursen, eds, *Shakespeare on Television* (Hanover, N. H.: University Press of New England, 1988). Contains several critical responses to the BBC Shakespeares.

Samuel Crowl, 'The Long Good-bye: Welles and Falstaff', in *Shakespeare Observed: Studies in Performance on Stage and Screen*

(Athens, Ohio: Ohio University Press, 1992). A seminal essay on *Chimes at Midnight*.

Charles Eckert, ed., *Focus on Shakespearean Films* (Englewood Cliffs, N. J.: Prentice-Hall, 1972). Contains some notes on *Chimes at Midnight* by Pierre Billard, made while the film was in production.

Richard France, *Orson Welles on Shakespeare: The W. P. A. and Mercury Theatre Playscripts* (London: Routledge, 2001). Contains Welles's original stage adaptation, *Five Kings*.

Jack Jorgens, *Shakespeare on Film* (Bloomington: Indiana UP, 1977). One of the first major studies of Shakespeare on film including *Chimes at Midnight*.

Bridget Gellert Lyons, ed., Chimes at Midnight: *Orson Welles, Director* (Rutgers: Rutgers University Press, 1989). Contains a continuity script for the film including the battle sequence, and interviews and other materials.

The McMillin and Hodgdon volumes cited above both refer to *Chimes at Midnight* and the David Giles BBC TV productions; the Bogdanov/Pennington book discusses the process of taping the English Shakespeare Company productions.

Critical assessment

Reference works, overviews, and collections

Catherine Geera and Adele Seef, eds, *Henry IV, Parts 1 and 2* (An Annotated Bibliography) (New York: Garland, 1994). Contains hundreds of references to critical works on the plays, mainly from 1940–85.

Graham Holderness, *Shakespeare's History Plays: Richard II to Henry V: Contemporary Critical Essays* (New Casebook Series) (London: Palgrave Macmillan, 1992). Contains several essays that challenge the Tillyard/Tudor Myth view of the histories from a variety of recent critical perspectives.

G. K. Hunter, ed., *Henry IV, Parts I and II: A Selection of Critical Essays* (Casebook Series) (London: Palgrave Macmillan, 1970). Contains essays by Johnson, Morgann, Bradley, Dover Wilson, Tillyard, Jenkins, Auden, and Barber among others.

Ronald Knowles, *Henry IV, Parts I & II, The Critics Debate* (London: Palgrave Macmillan, 1992). A concise but comprehensive discussion of critical responses to the *Henry IV* plays.

Emma Smith, *Shakespeare's Histories* (Blackwell Guides to Criticism) (Oxford: Blackwell, 2004). Along with several essays that address the *Henry IV* plays, this collection contains excellent discussions of the development of history play criticism in various theoretical categories such as genre, language, gender, and politics.

Hermann Ulrici, *Shakespeare's Dramatic Art* (London: Chapman Brothers, 1846).

Brian Vickers, *Shakespeare: The Critical Heritage*, 6 vols (London: Routledge, 1974–). Includes a wide range of responses to the plays from the seventeenth and eighteenth centuries.

Other works cited

C. L. Barber, *Shakespeare's Festive Comedy* (New York: Meridian, 1959).

A. C. Bradley, *Oxford Lectures on Poetry* (London: Palgrave Macmillan, 1909).

Michael Bristol, *Carnival and Theatre* (London: Methuen, 1985).

James Calderwood, *Metadrama in Shakespeare's Henriad* (Berkeley: University of California Press, 1979).

Samuel Taylor Coleridge, 'From *Seven Lectures*', in *Henry IV, Part I*, ed. Maynard Mack (New York: Signet, 1965).

John Dryden, *Works*, ed. Edward Niles Hooker, H. T. Swedenberg, Jr., and Vinton A. Dearing (Berkeley: University of California Press, 1956–2000).

William Empson, *Essays on Shakespeare* (Cambridge: Cambridge University Press, 1986).

M. D. Faber, ed., *The Design Within: Psychoanalytic Approaches to Shakespeare* (New York: Science House, 1970).

Harold C. Goddard, *The Meaning of Shakespeare* (Chicago: University of Chicago Press, 1951).

Stephen Greenblatt, *Shakespearean Negotiations* (Berkeley: University of California Press, 1988).

Richard Helgerson, *Forms of Nationhood* (Chicago: University of Chicago Press, 1992).

Graham Holderness, 'Theatres of History: Chronicle Plays', in Graham Holderness, Nick Potter and John Turner,eds, *Shakespeare: The Play of History* (Iowa City: University of Iowa Press, 1987).

Jean E. Howard and Phyllis Rackin, *Engendering a Nation: A Feminist Account of Shakespeare's English Histories* (London: Routledge, 1997).

Henry A. Kelly, *Divine Providence in the England of Shakespeare's Histories* (Cambridge, Mass.: Harvard University Press, 1970).

Jan Kott, *Shakespeare Our Contemporary*, trans. Boleslaw Taborski (London: Methuen, 1967).

John Masefield, *William Shakespeare* (London: Williams and Norgate, 1911).

Maurice Morgann, *An Essay on the Dramatic Character of Sir John Falstaff* (London: 1777; reprinted by AMS Press, New York, 1970).

Robert Ornstein, *A Kingdom for a Stage: The Achievement of Shakespeare's History Plays* (Cambridge, Mass.: Harvard University Press, 1972).

Moody Prior, *The Drama of Power: Studies in Shakespeare's History Plays* (Evanston, Ill.: Northwestern University Press, 1973).

Joseph Porter, *The Drama of Speech Acts: Shakespeare's Lancastrian Tetralogy* (Berkeley: University of California Press, 1979).

Paola Pugliatti, *Shakespeare the Historian* (London: Palgrave Macmillan, 1996).

Phyllis Rackin, *Stages of History: Shakespeare's English Chronicles* (New York: Routledge, 1991).

H. M. Richmond, *Shakespeare's Political Plays* (New York: Random House, 1967).

A. P. Rossiter, 'Ambivalence: The Dialectic of the Histories', from *Angel with Horns* (London: Longmans, 1961). Reprinted in R. J. Dorius, ed., *Discussions of Shakespeare's Histories* (Boston: Heath, 1964).

John P. Rumrich, 'Shakespeare's Walking Plays: Image and Form in *1* and *2 Henry IV*', in *Shakespeare's English Histories: A Quest for Form and Genre*, ed. John W. Velz (Binghamton, N. Y.: Medieval and Renaissance Texts & Studies, 1996).

George Bernard Shaw, *Shaw on Shakespeare*, ed. Edwin Wilson (New York: Dutton, 1961).

E. E. Stoll, *Shakespeare Studies, Historical and Comparative in Method* (New York: Palgrave Macmillan, 1927).

Leonard Tennenhouse, *Power on Display: The Politics of Shakespeare's Genres* (London: Methuen, 1986).

E. M. W. Tillyard, *Shakespeare's History Plays* (Edinburgh: T. & A. Constable, Ltd, 1944).

Derek Traversi, *Shakespeare from Richard II to Henry V* (Stanford: Stanford University Press, 1957).

John Dover Wilson, *The Fortunes of Falstaff* (New York: Palgrave Macmillan, 1944).

W. B. Yeats, *Collected Works, Volume IV: Early Essays*, ed. Richard J. Finneran and George Bornstein (New York: Scribner, 2007).

Index